The Case of the Unknown Woman

The Story of One of the Most Intriguing Murder Mysteries of the Nineteenth Century

by

F. Alexander Shipley

DORRANCE PUBLISHING CO., INC.
PITTSBURGH, PENNSYLVANIA 15222

All Rights Reserved
Copyright © 2010 by F. Alexander Shipley
No part of this book may be reproduced or transmitted
in any form or by any means, electronic or mechanical,
including photocopying, recording, or by any information
storage and retrieval system without permission in
writing from the publisher.

ISBN: 978-1-4349-0698-4
Printed in the United States of America

First Printing

For more information or to order additional books, please contact:
Dorrance Publishing Co., Inc.
701 Smithfield Street
Pittsburgh, Pennsylvania 15222
U.S.A.
1-800-788-7654
www.dorrancebookstore.com

To my wife, Robin, who encouraged my research and never doubted my quest to write this story

Acknowledgements

It is with grateful appreciation that I thank the following friends who helped this project become a reality. Tony Hall, Derron Palmer, and Bernice Young read early drafts and offered many valuable comments. When the manuscript was nearing the final drafts, I trusted the proofing to Janice Witheridge, Roberta Seaman, Branwen Cook, Joe and Georgia Harnett, Andy Roesch, Tom Brix, and Irwin Kreisberg. Each of these critical readers added suggestions that ultimately inhanced the entire work. I must also thank my daughter, Lauren Davis, and my son, Samuel, for the hours they spent sitting behind the computer lending their typing and technical skills.

Lastly a word of thanks to the newspaper reporters who covered the case. Their persistence and thoroughness in reporting and trying to solve the mystery forms the backdrop of this story.

Saturday, March 26, 1887

Sadie Van Ness stood on the top step of her porch and pulled her scarf more tightly around her neck. Even at 5:50 a.m., it was much colder than she thought it would be. Last night's walk home was damp, but the temperature the past few days was milder than it had been earlier in the month and it made her feel good to think the cold grip of winter was finally over. It was late March and she looked forward to the warmth of spring that would make her two-mile walk to work more pleasant.

But this morning, it was cold. Winter was not going away without one last icy reminder. The roadbed's soft mud had frozen over, and as she stepped onto it, she was careful in placing her feet between the hardened footprints and hoof marks left by yesterday's travelers.

When Sadie reached the corner of Maple and Jefferson, she stopped and waited. William Rubeck was on his way to work, and today, Sadie felt like company. Both worked at Bloodgood's Mill, a large manufacturer of felt goods in the next town. Bloodgood's employed Rahway people, and many who lived in this Milton section of the city worked at the mill.

Rubeck was not especially happy to see Sadie waiting for him. By nature, he was a nervous sort and she often liked to have fun at his expense. He looked upon her as a bit of a tease and being a newly married man, the younger girl's taunts made him uncomfortable. The pair didn't converse much as they walked along Jefferson Avenue and onto the brick bridge. To offer conversation he felt was safe, Rubeck noted how swiftly the current was running. But Sadie was in a mischievous mood, and began to coyly ask Rubeck if he knew anything about a party in the neighborhood the night before. Did he go? Was his wife with him? Did some of the girls have an eye for him? Did he make a play for any of them? These were all playful jabs, but to Rubeck they were sharp barbs. He could do nothing to combat her inquiries and her flirtatious manner unnerved him. He knew he had to end his discomfort and saw his chance to escape when they came to the first intersection. At Central Avenue, he abruptly turned right and headed east towards St. Georges. Sadie looked on amused, laughed to herself, and continued on her way to the mill.

Central Avenue was an avenue in name only. To either side of this stretch of road were open fields without even a single tree to grace the landscape. The roadway had been graded and curbed a few years back when there was anticipation that New Yorkers were interested in moving to the country. The migration had yet to start, leaving Central Avenue a lonely, desolate, rarely frequented thoroughfare. A fence that ran along the south side of the road had recently been repaired. Only two homes stood on Central, both close to St. Georges, the main roadway.

Rubeck had not gone down this rural path more than a hundred feet when he spied something lying next to the fence. Being a nervous man, he slowly and cautiously walked to within twenty feet of the thing. He could sense something was wrong. He pulled his neck down into his shoulders and gritted his teeth. He was quite sure he was looking at a woman, but didn't know if she was drunk or dead. Then he saw the blood. The breath that was in him was expelled. He didn't go any closer. He froze. Minutes went by; he didn't move. He looked, but he didn't look. He got the absurd idea that if he made any move at all, the thing would open its eyes and reach for him. He thought about turning quickly and running, but he was afraid his legs wouldn't respond. Minutes passed. Finally, as if out of a trance, Rubeck caught hold of himself, turned slowly, but then quickly retreated to Jefferson Avenue. He continued on to work. He didn't look back.

~~~~~

It was quarter after six and time for the Worth boys to leave for work. Seventeen-year-old Alfred was the first to bound out of the house into the sharp morning air. The four brothers all worked at Bloodgood's, but since Alfred, the youngest of the four, had just recently been employed, he didn't want to arrive late. Brothers Tom and Irving soon followed, and spotting young Alfred some fifty yards in front, shouted lighthearted epithets at him. Alfred, embarrassed by their needling, reached the corner of Central and decided to slow up.

Something caught his eye. Some one hundred feet from him, he saw what appeared to be a large bundle. Curiosity prompted an investigation, so he walked toward the "package." Seeing Alfred turn down Central, the brothers again began their harmless banter. Alfred no longer heard their voices. His entire being was focused on what he had discovered. It was the mutilated body of a young woman. Her face was covered with blood and mud. Her clothes were disarranged, muddy, and partly torn from her body. Her throat was cut from ear to ear.

Without realizing it, Alfred called for his brothers. Hearing the panic in his voice, they hurried to his side. Both stopped in their tracks. The three stood without a word. The scenario of the crime was etched before them in the muddy field. Tracks made in new fallen snow would not have created a clearer picture. The earth, made soft by the previous days' mild weather, had frozen over, capturing the frantic struggle that must have taken place. The ground around the body was chewed up and trampled with footprints. The girl was lying on her side. Her face was pressed into the ground as if the murderer's knee had held her head down as he cut her throat. The deep print of a man's heel close to her head was clearly preserved in the frozen mud. A fur cape, an umbrella, a woman's hat, and a small round willow basket were strewn around the area. Nine or ten eggs lay beside the basket, their whiteness creating a stark contrast in the brown mud. Distinct footprints of more than one person could be seen coming from Jefferson Avenue. Only one set of prints returned in that direction. Tracks of a wagon's wheels were visible on the road.

The silence was broken as Tom began directing his brothers. Alfred was told to hurry off and notify Chief Tooker. Irving was to go to the mill to tell the foreman what had transpired. Tom would remain at the site.

Alfred lingered only an instant and then bolted off toward the town. On the way, he met his fourth brother, Frank, and excitedly told him about the body. Frank's first impulse was to rush to Central to see the spectacle, but he realized it would be better to go along with Alfred, lest the police think this was a young rascal pulling a prank.

The brothers ran the entire one-mile distance and reached the Fulton Street residence of Chief William Tooker at approximately six forty-five. Alfred, out of breath and too excited to give a comprehensive account, had to take a moment to recover his composure. With his wits regained, he told the chief about a woman whose throat was cut lying on Central Avenue in Milton. The chief was sure the boy was not telling a tale. He could see it on his face. Something terrible had happened.

Tooker wasted no time and was soon on his way to the crime scene. Crossing St. Georges Avenue, he noticed people hurrying from several directions to the very place where he was headed. A few dozen people were already at the dreadful spot. Word was spreading quickly.

Tooker did not need to be an officer of the law to recognize that he had a murder on his hands. In the seven years that he had served as police chief, he had never been confronted with such a brutal crime. Not only had her throat been cut, but her bruised face and body gave indication that she had been savagely beaten. The ground surrounding the body added to the terror of the scene and gave testimony to the horrific struggle. If it were in his power, he would clear the area of the curious spectators and take the body of the poor girl to the morgue. He was, however, aware of the law and knew the County Coroner was the only one who had the authority to remove the remains of a victim. He had to contact the County officials, and fast.

Looking around he saw Lewis Marsh, a special policeman, and ordered him to guard the body and keep the crowds from coming too near. Tooker hurried downtown to the Exchange Building to telephone the County Physician and County Coroner, both located in Elizabeth, the county seat.

With this done, the chief returned to the crime scene and was amazed at the size of the crowd that had gathered. News of the murder had spread rapidly to all parts of the city and hundreds of people were at the site. Teams of horses pulling wagonloads of people were making their way to Central Avenue. Men, women, and children were flocking to the awful scene. Many were grouped about the body gazing at the horribly disfigured face and many others were milling around the fields kicking at the scrub grass searching for pieces of evidence. It was obvious that it had been impossible for the officer left in charge to control the crowd and now all hope of obtaining potential clues from footprints was lost, as the entire area had been trampled by the mob.

In this sea of faces, Chief Tooker noticed George Conger and George Wright walking toward him. Wright was carrying a black satchel. He was glad to see both, as Conger was his sergeant and Wright was the former police chief. Together, they could begin to try to restore order. However, Wright had news that couldn't wait. The black satchel he carried had just been pulled from the river beyond the

Jefferson Avenue Bridge. The three moved off, away from the crowd to examine the contents.

Finding a quiet spot some thirty yards away on the other side of the road, Tooker tried to open the bag. It was locked. Taking a knife from his pocket, he easily broke the simple lock with a quick twist. As he pulled out each item, he handed it to Sergeant Conger to hold. There were articles of women's clothing, a pair of shoes, a section of the *New York Herald* dated March 23, 1887, a comb and brush, one pair of scissors, and half of a pair of suspenders. Then, at the bottom of the sack, Tooker pulled out two items that aroused more interest. The first was a handkerchief with the name K. M. Noory, or Noorz, embroidered on it. It was difficult to decipher if the last letter was a *Y* or a *Z*. The second was a rubber stamp bearing the name Timothy Byrne.

Wright was about to draw something from his pocket when a number of citizens approached the lawmen. In front of the group was Benjamin Metzger, who walked up to Tooker and held out a bloody, white-handled knife. Metzger said he found it in the grass about twenty yards from the body. He handed it to the chief. Tooker looked it over, gave it to Sergeant Conger, and told him to put it in his pocket. The chief asked Metzger to show him the place where he found the knife and they walked back into the crowd.

When Tooker entered the multitude, he became aware of a curious conversation that was on the lips of the hundreds who were now on the site. Of the many people who had viewed the bloody face, no one knew who she was. He himself had not been too troubled that he didn't know the girl, and it would not be unusual if people from a particular section of town didn't know her, but it was uncanny that no one from anywhere around knew her. Not a single person recognized the girl. This was indeed strange, but he had little doubt that her identity would be revealed before long.

~~~~~

It was near ten o'clock when the officials from Elizabeth arrived. James S. Green, County Physician and brother of the Governor, immediately took charge of the proceedings and ordered that the body not be removed until it had been photographed and a map made of the area. Local photographer James Stacy was notified to report at once to take photos of the woman from all sides. William E. Clark, a respected local civil engineer, was called on to take measurements for a map of the place. Green next placed the criminal investigation in the hands of

County Coroner Dr. Thomas Terrill. Dr. Terrill was a man experienced in homicide cases, but he appeared genuinely appalled as he viewed the remains. Bystanders overheard him say that this was not a human act and that he had never beheld such a sight. From this point on, Terrill, with the assistance of County District Attorney William Wilson, would be in charge of solving the case. The investigation was set in motion.

The first order of business was to direct County Constable Charles Wright to summon "twelve good and lawful men" to serve as jurors in an inquest, which would be forthcoming. There was no problem finding people to serve, as the fields were filled with a good cross section of Rahway residents. Constable Wright summoned William Clark, the surveyor, to serve and act as foreman. Wright walked around and made his other selections, which included a night watchman, a hatter, a liveryman, a carriage factory foreman, the Clerk of the Freeholder Board, a ship's captain, a dry goods salesman, and four laborers. By ten-thirty, the twelve men had signed the coroner's certificate and the jury was intact. A hearing was scheduled for the next Wednesday, March 30.

The general bustle and the hubbub of so many conversations ceased when the ambulance from Ryno's Morgue was seen making its way up Central Avenue. As if pulled by some mysterious force, crowds from all ends of the field made their way toward the fence where the body still lay. All craned their necks and watched in silence, as the men from Ryno's gently lifted the girl, and placed her in the rear of the coach. The corpse would be taken to the morgue and prepared for an autopsy.

Even before the coach had rolled slowly away with its sad cargo, the same questions were being deliberated. Who killed the girl? What was the brutal assassin's motive? What was a young woman doing on this lonely stretch of road in the middle of the night? Nevertheless, of all the questions raised, the one that had everyone perplexed pertained to the identity of the victim. Who was she?

The rumors started to mount the moment the first two people had made their way to the site, but now the body was gone, and the crowd, which numbered close to a thousand, could focus their attention on solving these mysteries. In addition, by this time, beat reporters from the Elizabeth, Newark, and New York papers had arrived and were milking the crowd for potential leads. Most everyone was willing to give them a story. Two young men and several girls informed a reporter that yesterday they had seen a strange young woman carrying a satchel on the outskirts of town, but could not be certain if she and the dead woman were one and the same. Reports were issued that several tramps were seen hanging around just outside Rahway the past several days. Police Justice Jeremiah Tunison claimed he had seen the girl on Main Street on Thursday and again on Friday. Mrs. Jacob Moore, a respected colored woman, said she was walking home with a friend on Friday night around ten o'clock and heard screams. By tomorrow, the rumor mill would become unrestrained as reporters from as far off as Boston, Philadelphia, and Washington would be in town to try to break the story.

The first rumor that excited action came from a farmer who lived near the murder scene. He thought the girl was Katie Meyer, a German girl who worked on Dr. Meeker's farm. He had seen her working on Meeker's property five months ago. Officers rushed to the farm only to find the large farmhouse locked and empty. Neighbors informed the officers that Dr. Meeker and his family had been in Florida since early December. The inquiry ended when another young man came forward and said he knew Katie Meyer, he had seen the body, and it wasn't her.

Speculation had also started regarding the fiend who committed the murder. At first, it was believed the murderer was a resident of the town. The Milton section was racially mixed and viewed by those who considered themselves the more genteel citizens of Rahway to be a rough area filled with any number of unsavory characters, so it was quite possible the deed was done by a neighborhood tough. One Rahway native told Sergeant Conger as they were standing in the field, that he believed if he had a rifle he could hit the murderer from that very spot. A few hundred yards from where the two were standing was the home of Clinton Froat and William Keech, both of whom were already becoming prime suspects.

Clinton Froat was a newcomer to Milton having moved there from Elizabeth about five months earlier. Even in this unpleasant district, Froat's reputation was not good. It was said he was tough and lazy, and he was never seen doing a day's work. Although married, he always had women around his place and liked to have parties that ran long into the night.

William Keech, a relative of Froat, was looked upon with even greater disdain. He was an illiterate brute of a man who was often seen walking around carrying a club. His appearance alone made people shudder, for he only had one eye. There were stories circulating that he was a petty thief and that his wife was serving time in a prison for women.

All afternoon and into the evening, the only topics of conversation in the public houses, on the street corners, at the railroad depot, and in every home throughout the city, dealt with the murder and the victim. Who was the girl? Was the madman who killed her still close by? Would we be safe in our homes tonight? However, as night fell on the anxious city, there were no definite answers, and the whole affair was shrouded in so deep a mystery that everyone, including public officials and police, were completely baffled.

Sunday, March 27, 1887

It was Sunday, but Mayor Dr. John J. Daly was at his City Hall desk at an early hour. He was waiting for the city clerk to arrive so the two could discuss calling a special meeting of the Common Council for later in the evening. Sunday was not a day for meetings, but these were unusual circumstances. A murder in one's town was trouble enough, but to have the criminal still at large and the victim unknown caused extra anxieties. Newspapers were already referring to the case as one of the most horrible murder mysteries to occur in New Jersey.

In front of him was the initial autopsy report done on the slain girl. It showed she was 5'2" tall with light brown hair and blue eyes. Her age was estimated to be about twenty-five. The girl had not been ravaged (sexually assaulted) and she was never pregnant, although she was probably not a virgin. It disclosed the fact that death resulted from the knife wound to the throat, which was probably made after the girl had been rendered unconscious from the blows on the forehead by some blunt instrument. She had a roundish scar on the left side of the neck. Her nationality could only be guessed at, but Scandinavian, Irish, and German features were all noted.

When the city clerk, Franklin Marsh, entered the mayor's chambers, he brought news that crowds were gathered at the police station and were asking all manner of questions. Several were in a hostile mood and there was talk there would be a lynching if they got their hands on the perpetrator. The mayor knew he had to put a speedy end to this enigma and was willing to do everything in his power to help expedite a conclusion. Yesterday he had telegraphed Governor Green with a request that the state offer a reward for the apprehension of the killer.

Tonight, he would ask the Common Council to offer rewards for the arrest of the murderer and the identification of the girl.

Daly was a popular mayor with the citizenry, but with an election coming up in less than three weeks, an issue as disturbing as this could do harm to his re-election bid. Formerly a Democrat, Daly was in his second term, having won re-election as an Independent. In the coming April election, he was on the Republican ballot. His inclination to do what was best for his constituents made him a well-liked and respected mayor, but put him at odds with the Democratic bosses. Daly had crossed the party leaders so often in his first term that they removed him from their ticket in the next election. With this mystery hanging over him, his political foes would be scrutinizing his every move, ready to castigate him if any wrong decision was made.

~~~~~

Sergeant Conger had his hands full trying to deal with the crowd filing into the station house. He knew most of the men in line, but this event had made them uneasy and their reason and rationale was lost. Each came before him demanding to know of any developments and offering rumors and clues of vague import. They also came to see the possessions of the murdered girl that were spread on a table and suspended from lines in the rear room directly behind where Conger was standing. The articles were not ready to be shown to the public, but everyone wanted at least to get a glimpse of the bloodstained apparel.

As Conger fielded questions and made notes of reasonable clues, he could hear Chief Tooker going over the articles of clothing and other pieces of evidence found by the body with Detective John Keron who had arrived on a morning train. Keron was the former police chief of Elizabeth and was currently a member of the New Jersey Detectives' Association. State officials thought it wise to bring Keron aboard to work with the local police.

Detective Keron was intrigued by each of the items. As he fingered the rubber stamp, he knew, whoever and wherever Timothy Byrne was, he had to be found. The white handkerchief with the name K. M. Noory (or Noorz) could be an important clue. The girl's clothes and shoes might be helpful. But of all the items, Keron considered the basket that carried the eggs to be most valuable. It was a simple willow basket with a cover, in the shape of half an egg. It was well worn with use and the cover showed signs of being repaired with three dozen or so stitches of common white twine. A few small pieces of red onion peelings and several grains of oats were found clinging to the inside. Someone had to be able to recognize the basket or might remember selling eggs to someone that day. These were all possible leads, and Detective Keron was ready to search for answers.

~~~~~

Two blocks from police headquarters, on the corner of Irving and Hamilton, stood the undertaking establishment of Daniel K. Ryno. No sooner had the sun risen than crowds began to gather outside the building. People came from all parts of town and from all the surrounding towns. Morning trains brought in hundreds from all the cities on the rail. By eleven o'clock, a long line was stretching down Irving Street. Most who came to view the remains were simply curious; however, many came with hopes (or fears) of identifying the woman. Ryno had announced he would open the doors at eleven-thirty and as soon as the clock struck that half hour, the crowd rushed through the portal and scrambled up the stairs leading to the second floor where the girl was laid out.

The body, dressed in white, lay in a simple coffin with only the face and shoulders showing through a plate of glass. Even though the girl's face had been carefully washed and her hair combed, the bruises on her face were as prominent as ever. A piece of white linen concealed the ugly gash on her throat. Two policemen stood by the coffin to note any strange behavior or outward show of emotion that might be exhibited. Much sobbing was heard coming from those whose sympathies were touched as they gazed at the lifeless form. Also heard were gentle sighs of relief as those who came looking for a lost relative or friend found this girl was a stranger to them.

For the first hour, the line proceeded without incident. Just after the noon church bells tolled, a man approached the box, looked in, and stood transfixed as if in a trance. When the police tried to move him aside, he mumbled incomprehensible words and ran screaming down the back stairs and into the street. The officers followed, grabbed him, and asked for his name. The stranger gave no answer, pulled himself away, and ran down Irving Street.

The odd behavior raised suspicion and when word reached headquarters, Chief Tooker, Detective Keron, and Sergeant Conger went to find him. They had no trouble learning from eyewitnesses that he had gone to Mrs. Summerdyke's boarding house on Main Street. When they got to the large rooming house, they were surprised to find eager reporters had beaten them to the scene and were waiting on the front porch. Mrs. Summerdyke, relieved to see the police, led them into the parlor where they found the strange man sitting by the fire, his head buried in his hands, muttering to himself. As the officers tried to question him, he flatly refused to say anything about himself or the murder. Try as they might, neither Tooker nor Keron could get a word out of the man. The state detective suggested giving leave to the reporters with the hope that perhaps one might work an angle and get him to speak. The reporters were let in, but after besieging him with a barrage of questions from all sides, he uttered no response.

Finally, Chief Tooker came up with a clever ploy in an attempt to discover the man's name. Mrs. Summerdyke was instructed to have him sign the register book so that in the event the house was burned down with him in it, his relations could claim his remains. The subterfuge worked and the man wrote in the book, George Washington Gregory.

Knowing his name, the chief was able to persuade him to accompany them to the station house. Once there, Gregory acted like a madman. No longer silent, he said things that were vague and without sense. When asked where he lived, he responded, "Anywhere I happen to be at night." When asked what he was doing in this part of the state, he said he was sightseeing. Detective Keron thought it strange that he was wearing a new pair of trousers and asked if he had destroyed a pair that was bloodstained. Gregory gave a sarcastic laugh. In answer to a reporter who asked directly if he had murdered the girl, Gregory replied with a wave of his hand, "If I murdered the girl, and you can prove it, all right."

Tooker was becoming tired of his bizarre antics and wanted to know if he was carrying any papers or if he had any money. Gregory refused to answer. He was asked if they could search him. Gregory became indignant and told them absolutely not. With this, the police took it upon themselves to relieve him of his possessions. Keron and Conger pinioned his arms while Tooker went through his pockets. A watch was dropped onto the table, then a revolver, $17, a knife, a guide to the National Capital, and a personal letter. The letter was addressed from Warwick, New York, with a message regarding the resolving of a problem with some woman. Gregory, very upset with the liberties that were taken with him, refused to explain any of the items. At this point, it was decided that no more time should be wasted on this odd character and that he should be arrested and put in jail for the night.

~~~~~

The Case of the Unknown Woman

With a suspect locked away in one of the two, small, backroom cells, and Tooker and Keron out investigating leads, Sergeant Conger was left to man the office. It was not quite four o'clock. The crowd that earlier had been at the station had all but dispersed soon after the officers were called away on the Gregory matter. The only visitors of interest were a reporter from the *Elizabeth Daily Journal* and Dr. P. N. Burdge. The newspaperman told Conger that while he was at the crime scene, he found what he thought were bloodstains on the Jefferson Avenue Bridge. Dr. Burdge, who happened to also be at the site, was asked to examine the stains to ascertain if they were human blood. It was the doctor's opinion that it was indeed human blood. The reporter theorized that the murderer ran down Jefferson, stopped at the bridge, and threw the black satchel into the river. As he threw the bag, he put his bloody hands on the bridge. Conger wrote the information down and promised to pass it on to Chief Tooker.

A short time later, as he was sifting through notations he had made this day, William Brunt entered the office, pushing before him a young boy. Conger didn't know Brunt very well except that he lived up at Milton and he was the brother of the man who discovered the black bag. He also knew Brunt was one of the twelve men who yesterday were chosen to make up the jury panel. As Brunt came toward him, the sergeant could tell he was excited. There were tears in his eyes. He was ready to burst with news.

According to Brunt, he knew the identity of the killer and the girl. The boy he had with him was his fifteen-year-old son, Willie. The boy claimed to have seen a girl hanging clothes in the yard of Clinton Froat on Friday morning, the day of the murder. Her hair was braided and tied around in a knot on the top of her head, the same way as the murdered girl's. He was positive it was the same girl. He added that this morning, he saw the Froats get in a wagon and drive out of town going in the direction of Westfield. To him, it appeared they were fleeing the town. Conger had a gut feeling this could be the information needed to end the mystery. Everything fit the stories he had been hearing about the Froats.

Word was immediately sent out to Tooker and Keron that they were needed at the station. After a quick briefing, they headed for Milton and the home of Clinton Froat. Following close behind were a bevy of reporters who were becoming constant shadows of the police.

Froat's house was a run down structure near the corner of Maple and Jefferson. Young Willie Brunt's home was the next house on the block, separated by no more than forty yards. Brunt's General Store, which backed to the river, was directly across the road from Froat's. When the official body reached the home, Tooker alone stepped onto the small stoop and knocked. He waited for what seemed like several minutes. Finally, the door opened. Peeking from the dark hall was a frail old woman who was obviously frightened by the assembly outside the house. Tooker asked if Clinton Froat was there, but the answer didn't come from the woman. Standing behind her was a young boy, a husky lad who looked older than his probable age, who said that his father was away visiting in Westfield. The boy then came around the old woman and took her place as she dissolved into the background. He appeared to be an intelligent boy and when asked questions, he responded with no hint of hesitation. He told the chief his name was Willie Froat and he was Clinton Froat's stepson. Only he and Mrs. Henderschott were presently at home. His grandmother lived in Westfield, and his stepfather, mother, uncle, and Nancy left this morning to visit. He didn't think they would be back until after dark. The chief knew the uncle he mentioned was William Keech, but he wanted to know more about Nancy. Will said Nancy was a new girl from Ireland and he didn't know her hardly at all. The officers decided this was a story that needed to be checked out, so Tooker and Keron rode out to Westfield to find the Froat family and Nancy.

Throughout the day, the names of Froat and Keech kept coming up and Keron wanted to know everything about both men. The ride gave ample opportunity for Tooker to describe what little he knew. He had to admit that he really didn't know either, but he heard most of the stories associated with them and they weren't good. As far as he was concerned, their poor reputations and their proximity to the crime scene were enough to make them suspects.

It was becoming dark and they had not yet reached their destination when a wagon came into view coming from Westfield. In the darkness, it was difficult to make out forms much less faces, but the two officers had a feeling they were about to meet the Froats. When the carriage and the wagon met, they pulled alongside of one another and stopped. The large man driving the wagon must be Froat and the larger man next to him, a man with hard features and one eye, was definitely Keech. Behind them sat two women. One was an older woman, likely Mrs. Froat, and the other, a younger girl, with braided hair styled on the top of her head in a bun. From where he sat, Tooker could see how this girl could be mistaken for the dead girl. He didn't say anything.

Froat recognized the chief of police and asked him what brought him out this way. Tooker replied succinctly, "Official business," and turned his carriage around realizing there was nothing to Willie Brunt's story and his journey had been for naught.

~~~~~

The meeting of the Common Council was called to order at eight o'clock for the purpose of discussing the advisability of offering a reward for the arrest and conviction of the murderer of the unknown girl. Councilman John Farrell moved that an amount not exceeding one hundred dollars be offered for the identification of the dead person and that not over five hundred dollars be the reward for the arrest and conviction of the murderer. Councilman William McManus requested that council not act on the motion until after nine o'clock and moved for a recess. He explained the mayor was expected back from his meeting with the governor and would have information regarding a reward from the state. He reasoned that if the state offered a monetary reward it would save the City some money. A recess was voted on and approved.

Mayor Daly entered the chambers before the recess had elapsed with news from Governor Green. The session reconvened and the mayor reported that the state would offer a reward in the amount of around six hundred dollars. With this knowledge, the councilmen passed a resolution that a total of five hundred dollars be offered, two hundred for the identification of the woman and three hundred for the capture and conviction of the killer. The frugal council had saved the City a hundred dollars.

The meeting over, Mayor Daly went to his apartment located on the second floor of the Union County Bank Building. He went up the dark stairway, into his room and sat on his bed. He was too tired to light the gas lamp on the bed stand and welcomed the quiet of the night. It had been a long day. He wanted to be kept informed on all fronts and as a result, he was worn out. The whole affair was puzzling. Ryno, the undertaker, had come by his office late in the day and said that almost two thousand passed through the morgue and no one gave a credible identification. Chief Tooker had stopped by the council meeting after returning from his trip to Westfield and told the mayor there was little progress. Sitting in the dark, Daly was troubled that after two days they were no nearer to a solution than they had been from the start.

Monday, March 28, 1887

The murder was big news and because the girl and the culprit were still unknown and the latter still on the lam, it was even bigger news. The Rahway murder had become a bonanza for space writers for the daily papers. Monday found the town overrun with reporters from all the nearby cities. The major New York papers, including the *Times*, all sent reporters to cover the ongoing story. *The Washington Post* sent reporters as did the Associated Press. These newspapermen acted the part of amateur detectives, ferreting out information from all manner of sources, seeking to impress their readers with the belief that they were close to solving the crime. In reality, they would only confuse matters, as much energy would be wasted on false alarms.

Having had two days to cull through the "evidence," several papers published their theories concerning the crime and the possible motives. A number of papers believed that ravage was the primary motive. They purported that a girl came to the area by mistake in search of a residence in the vicinity. She reaches the lonely spot just as the egg thief (there was a belief that the basket of eggs was carried by the killer, not the girl) was coming to the same place. She asks directions. They converse. He tells her he will take her to her destination. He leads her to the open field and makes overtures, which she repels. He then attempts his assault. The girl runs. He chases her down and overtakes her. They struggle and he drags her to the fence. Her strength prevents him from accomplishing his purpose. He grabs something from the ground, perhaps a fence post, and strikes her once, twice. She falls unconscious. The villain, fearing she might recover and later recognize him, pulls out his knife and slashes hurriedly at her throat. He hurls the knife into the field. He then searches the pocket of the girl, grabs the bag, and runs off, forgetting the eggs. When he reaches the bridge, he tries to open the bag, but it's locked, so he throws it into the river and hurries off.

Those publications that felt robbery was a motive, constructed a slightly different tale. They suggested the girl came to Rahway by rail to seek employment (Pages 1, 2, 11, and 12 of the *New York Herald* found in the black bag contained "Help Wanted" advertisements). She carried the black satchel, a pocketbook, an umbrella, and a basket of eggs. Not knowing the area, she wanders a few blocks from the station where a man meets her and says he will show her to the address. He instead takes her to the isolated spot, robs, and kills her. They cite the fact that neither a pocketbook nor money was found makes this scenario credible. In addition, she more than likely had a pocketbook and the key to unlock the black bag was probably in it.

There were other papers proposing the motive had to do with a man who resorted to killing the woman to be rid of her. In this theory, both girl and killer come from New York. The killer had carefully planned his deliberate murder. He lured the victim to the very place he knew would be deserted, killed her, and made his escape.

A few of the more sensational rag sheets painted a lurid picture of a horrific slashing done by a crazed madman. They felt the brutality of the crime indicated a human demon was responsible.

The problem facing professional and amateur detectives alike was none of these theories could be discounted. All rumors, all identifications, all possible clues had to be addressed. Based on the possible motives, employment agencies in New York, Newark, and Elizabeth were contacted for names of women who might have been sent to Rahway for work. Reporters planted themselves at the railroad depot hoping to discover anyone who was around the station on Friday night. Newsmen and police traveled to New York to hunt for Timothy Byrne and many made their way to the tip of Manhattan to look through the records at Castle Garden.

Castle Garden was originally a fort built between 1808 and 1811 to protect New York from enemy ships coming into the harbor. Although fully armed, it saw no action during the War of 1812. In the ensuing years, the fort was changed into a restaurant and an opera house, but in 1855, it was converted to serve as an immigrant-processing depot. Here, a new arrival would be registered, have their money exchanged for U. S. currency, get information on boarding house accommodations and rail schedules, and receive help in securing employment. By 1887, nearly eight million people had entered the

United States through this facility. These were overwhelming numbers and it was difficult, if not impossible, to keep accurate records or to be able to trace a person's whereabouts once they left. Moreover, there was danger outside the gates of the center. Thieves and undesirables waited for the newcomers, ready to take advantage of them. These thugs would entice the unsuspecting immigrant with a promise of a job or a place to stay, or if their prey had a particular destination, they would offer to assist them in their journey. Many ferried across the Hudson and got on trains heading west to Newark, Elizabeth, and Rahway.

~~~~~

John Wingate, night watchman at the Rahway Train Depot, was ready to leave the platform, cross the tracks and head for home, but he had to pause and stop as a westbound train pulled in and blocked his way. It took longer than usual for the passengers to unload as the number of people coming to Rahway had increased. Soon, however, the "All Aboard" was shouted, the bell clanged, and the train lurched forward. Before Wingate had a chance to cross, a man who had just disembarked called out for him to wait. It turned out the man had been at the station on Friday night and recognized Wingate. He said he had met a tall mysterious stranger that night and now needed to report his story to the police. The night watchman's memory took him back to Friday night and he was beginning to remember the man. Rather than to just give directions, Wingate decided to accompany him.

The two reached headquarters where the railroad man introduced his companion. The man, who was from Linden, sat down and began his interesting account. He said he was at the station late on Friday night, March 25, when he noticed a tall man carrying an overcoat hurriedly crossing the tracks from Milton Avenue. The man came up to him and nervously asked the time of the next train to New York. When told it was not due for half an hour, the man seemed frightened and began to pace, stopping from time to time to stare down the westbound tracks into the darkness. After a while, the stranger came back to him and asked if he would join him for a drink. The Linden man obliged, and they crossed the tracks to the Park House Hotel. At the bar, he noticed something unusual about the tall man. All the time they were there, he kept his overcoat clutched tight to his right side. When paying for the drinks, he reached with his left hand to his right vest pocket. When they returned to the railroad station and the man bought his ticket he again reached with his left hand into his right pocket. The overcoat was never taken from his right arm. After purchasing his ticket, the man walked to the end of the platform beyond the lights. When the train arrived they both got in the same car but the tall man walked to the last seat and sat with his back to the light. The narrator concluded by saying he got off at the Linden Station and the tall man continued on. On Sunday, he read about the murder, thought of the tall man, and felt he had better report this to the police.

Tooker thanked the man for the information and sent him on his way. As Wingate was leaving, the chief reminded him to keep his ears open and to be sure to let him know if he heard anything.

The Linden man's story was of particular interest. Yesterday, while out on the streets, Tooker had heard two stories that when fitted to this one could prove to be of major importance. The first was given by a young man who said on the night of the murder he was returning home from a friend's house when he was met by a tall man who was coming from the direction of Central Avenue. The man asked the way to the railroad station. Since the young man was going in that direction, they walked together. The tall man didn't talk, but was breathing heavily and seemed to have difficulty swallowing. The route they took was four blocks south of and parallel to Central Avenue, rather secluded, and not lighted by electric lights. The young man thought it was odd that someone not familiar with the area would choose to travel on such a dark road instead of a more lighted one, which he would have passed before their meeting. When they got near the station, they parted company.

The second story relayed to Tooker came from Constable G. R. Harris who said his wife's sister saw a man on Jefferson Avenue near the murder site as she was coming home from work on Friday evening. She said he was tall and wore a derby hat and an overcoat.

~~~~~

A night in jail had made George Washington Gregory more amenable. Perhaps he finally realized he could be in serious trouble if he didn't cooperate, or perhaps it was the temperament of this strange man that he was susceptible to mood swings. Whatever the reason, Gregory was more willing to talk and even presented the police with an alibi. He told them he had been staying at the farm of E. B. Adams at Six Roads and was there all Friday night. It was Mr. Adams who gave him a new pair of trousers because the pair he had been wearing was so worn and shabby. He said he had never seen the dead girl before and it was her haunting appearance in the coffin that had set him off.

With this new information, officers were sent to the Adams's Farm. When given Gregory's story, both the farmer and his wife verified each detail. Adams stated firmly that Gregory had slept in his house the entire night and it was not possible for him to have left to commit the crime without their knowing it. He then produced the old pair of trousers, which were badly worn, but not torn or stained in a way to cause suspicion. Adams finished by saying he thought Gregory was a "trusty" man.

Now realizing Gregory was little more than a crank seeking notoriety, they released him. Upon hearing of his freedom, Gregory broke into a wild rage. He claimed the police grabbed a one hundred dollar promissory note when they searched him and demanded its return. He also promised he would "make it hot" for the state for connecting him to the crime. At this point, two officers lifted him off the floor and deposited him in the street. Once outside, he continued to cause a spectacle and before he reached the railroad crossing, he shouted back at the station, "I'll be back to kill all the reporters and police I can find!"

~~~~~

Out on the Clark border, another rumor was percolating, which had reporters and police hurrying off to a chicken farm named Bennett's Hennery. A machinist at Bloodgood's Mill set the story in motion. He claimed to have seen on Thursday last, a man and two women who asked directions to Bennett's. As the trio walked to the farm, they were seen by several others who remarked how the man was rough with one of the women. At the hennery, Mrs. Bennett asked the man his name and, noting his accent, where he was from. He said his name was Byrne and he was presently staying in Elizabeth, but his home was in Virginia. It was his wish to raise chickens after he returned south and it would please him, if he could inspect her farm. Mrs. Bennett replied she was not in the habit of letting strangers on her property, especially since her husband wasn't present, but she called her servant and directed him to show them around. Byrne went through the chicken house and carefully took measurements while the women occupied themselves by looking through the greenhouse. His business over, he abruptly left with his two female companions. They were last seen going down the road to Cranford. Mrs. Bennett told reporters the girls were more ladies than he was a gentleman, and she felt uncomfortable with his rudeness toward the younger girl.

Detective Keron considered this to be the lead that would bring the killer to justice and unveil the identity of the woman. The name Byrne, the chicken farm, and harsh treatment toward one of the women were all significant clues. At Cranford, he checked the railroad depot and learned that three tickets to Elizabeth were sold to a man and two women fitting the description. Keron also discovered that they had been seen in the Cranford Hotel and patrons believed they had boarded the 5:45 train. The detective went back to the depot and checked the schedule. He would be spending this night at home, in Elizabeth.

~~~~~

In a small saloon near the north end of Central Park, a *New York Sun* reporter was certain he was closing in on his man. He had spent much of his day trying to track down Timothy Byrne and found a person of that name matched an address at 218 East One Hundred and Eighth Street. The reporter hunted around the neighborhood and after paying a couple of hoods for information, he saw Byrne sitting alone in a dingy tavern. He walked in and went to the bar. The bartender, lazy from a lack of customers, slowly moved to where he stood, and took his order. While his beer glass was filling, he eyed Byrne as he sat slouched in his chair. The reporter took a sip of his beer, drew a deep breath, and went over to the table and sat down. Byrne was not drunk, however, it was apparent that liquor had dulled his senses. After a few benign questions, the reporter hit on the topic of the Rahway murder. At this, Byrne became agitated and began relating details that had nothing to do with this crime. He went on and on in a discourse of utter nonsense, becoming more and more emotional to a point of weeping. When he regained his composure, he boldly announced he knew the murdered girl and gave her name as Mollie Thomas. Hearing himself say the name seemed to sober Byrne. He looked at the reporter as if for the first time and loudly accused him of being a detective and told him he wasn't going to say another thing and to get out. The outburst must have startled the bartender who called out, "Malloy, you're a rascal. You've had your fun, now let the man alone." The reporter got up and left. The imposter wasn't Timothy Byrne, but a facetious drunk who was playing an insipid joke on an unwary newsman. The interview had been a waste of time and his breaking story a bust.

Tuesday, March 29, 1887

Mayor Daly opened the drapes of his office windows and looked down Main Street. It was raining and the street was quiet. From his second floor vantage point, he could see the police station where today, only a small crowd was gathered. He was certain as the day wore on and the weather improved, more would converge on the station to continue to press for information.

The mayor woke this day concerned that newspapers were beginning to criticize the way the investigation was being conducted. It was the opinion of one New York daily that the murderer was more than likely a local resident who happened upon the lone woman and committed an unpremeditated crime. They contended that the girl's throat was not slashed with a sophisticated weapon, but rather a simple pocketknife, the kind carried by many. The man was carrying a basket of eggs, proof that he was unprepared for the encounter. If he lived nearby, he could easily have gone home, changed out of his bloody clothes, and had time to destroy any evidence. A person living away from the city could not have gone any distance without being detected. The paper could not understand why all the homes in the vicinity were not searched, and that doing so at this time would be too late. The article was also critical that photographs had not been sent off to towns throughout the state and to the New York City Police. Lastly, the paper suggested that the new policy of screening persons before they could see the body and not allowing the general public to view the remains was unproductive.

An Elizabeth paper felt the Rahway and County officials should have called on police forces from neighboring towns to join in a coordinated effort. Instead, they kept all pieces of evidence under wraps so, in the paper's opinion, they alone could initiate and control the investigation. Even reporters had been denied access to the woman's effects, the knife, and the basket. They also commented, with a touch of amazement, that a city of slightly under seven thousand citizens would have a police force consisting of only two paid men.

Daly was bothered by these articles, but he also knew there was merit to their criticisms. His city had never experienced a crime of this magnitude and a small force had always been adequate. No one could expect them to now cover the many leads and rumors that were surfacing. His chief needed assistance, and today the mayor planned to deputize twelve men. It made him uncomfortable to think the murderer might be a local resident and he didn't like the idea of a house-to-house search, but he realized it might be necessary. He'd discuss the matter with Tooker and Keron. Coordinating the investigation was not as easy as it sounded. Each level of government, each department, each individual policeman wanted to direct the operation and above all, wanted to be the one to solve the mystery. Sharing evidence was not going to be done willingly. The mayor felt it was unseemly to allow citizens to satisfy their morbid curiosity by viewing the poor girl. Two thousand went through the morgue on Sunday with no concrete results. It was his opinion that if someone wanted to see the body, they must offer information to warrant the inspection.

Daly's train of thought was broken by the sound of someone coming up the stairs. There was a sharp knock and the door opened. It was Chief Tooker. Before Daly could ask him to sit down and give news of any progress, Tooker announced, "The Jersey City Police think they've got our man!" He handed the mayor a telegram. It contained a brief message that the police of that city had arrested a man on Sunday whose clothes were covered with blood and they have suspicions he is involved with the Rahway murder. Daly didn't have to tell his chief to catch the next train to Jersey City, for Tooker was already out the door and on his way.

~~~~~

Detective Keron stood in front of a stately row of townhouses on the north side of Elizabeth. It was not the neighborhood one would expect to harbor a wanted criminal. The unit occupying his attention was at the end of the row of six. Three brick steps led to a front door adorned with a heavy brass knocker. To the right of the doorway were two lace-curtained windows. Having tracked his prey to this address, he was beginning to question his detective instincts and worried that he was once more following a bogus lead.

The sound emanating from the knocker was louder than the detective had anticipated, but he was satisfied when he heard someone stirring within. A prim, finely dressed woman opened the door only wide enough to get a view of her visitor. Keron gave his name and stated that he was working on the Rahway murder case and there was suspicion that a companion of hers might be involved. The woman blanched, and after a pause, stepped back and fully opened the door.

The detective entered a room that was well furnished and accented with feminine details. The woman said her name was Julia Wagner and that she lived in this house with her sister. Keron guessed her to be about thirty-five and must be the older woman his sources had described. When he asked if her sister was at home, the woman went to the next room and called, "Jennie!" Almost immediately, a young woman came into their presence, drying her hands on a starched apron. When she saw there was company, she straightened her dress and stood more erect. In the course of his questions, the detective learned that the two had been living in Elizabeth since they were young girls. With the passing of their parents some years back, they had continued to live in the same house. As Keron sat and studied Jennie's features, he couldn't imagine how anyone could mistake her for the murdered woman.

The detective had yet to inquire about Timothy Byrne and was about to broach the subject, when a neatly dressed, strikingly handsome man came into the room. Keron rose and introduced himself. The man said his name was Tyler Barnum, a cousin of the two women, up from Virginia. When asked to give an account of his activities in the Clark area on Thursday, March 24, he explained he spent the large part of the day inspecting poultry farms in Clark and Cranford. He had plans to get in the business when he returned home and wanted to become familiar with all aspects of the operation. The detective asked if he used the name Timothy Byrne when he met Mrs. Bennett. The Virginian replied he never heard the name and he was positive he gave his proper name when he introduced himself to the property owner. The two women concurred with their cousin's statements.

After apologizing for the inconvenience he caused, Keron left the family assured that the young sister was not the one murdered and convinced the man from Virginia was completely innocent. As he walked to the depot, he was fearful that a new dynamic was taking place in this case. Thousands of people were reading newspaper articles and were drawing on their imaginations to shape their thinking. A plethora of faulty leads were bound to break out, which would not help to bring about a solution, but would instead cause the investigation to go further and further away from finding the truth.

~~~~~

The search for Timothy Byrne was not bearing fruit for any of the reporters or detectives trying to hunt him down. The New York City Directory contained only one Timothy Byrne who was listed at the same 108th Street address found by the *Sun* reporter.

A woman who lived in the same apartment building told reporters Byrne had lived there with a wife and two children, but had moved away. Some neighbors thought Byrne was a carpenter, but after questioning work crews in the area, nothing came of the tip. Shopkeepers were asked about him and his family, but most said they didn't know them. Byrne's uptown address was proving to be a dead end.

Another lead being hotly pursued was the company that made the rubber stamp. After some preliminary detective work, it was found that the Scotsford Manufacturing Company on Cortlandt Street in the Bowery had made the item. Representatives from Scotsford recognized the article as one of theirs and produced records of the order. The files revealed the stamp was ordered almost a year previous, on May 24, 1886, through an agent nicknamed "Liverpool." This particular broker, who hailed from Liverpool, England, was an independent agent who solicited work for a number of stamp and die companies. The Scotsford officials wanted it to be clear that although they made the stamp, they never had contact with Byrne himself. They added that "Liverpool" was still around and shouldn't be too difficult to find.

The Scotsford men were correct. It didn't take long for one thorough reporter to locate the Brit. "Liverpool" was cautious at first meeting; however, after having his palm greased, he became quite candid. He described Byrne as a solidly built man, about six feet tall, with light brown hair and a mustache. He remembered him being well dressed, yet at the same time exhibiting a coarse appearance. He had a gruff voice and on the two occasions they had met, he smelled of alcohol. The agent had not seen Byrne since the order was filled, but believed if he were still around, he could probably be found in one of the local gin mills.

If Byrne were a drinker, the reporters were faced with a daunting task. There were bars on every corner and down every side street in the Bowery, any one of which might be Byrne's hangout. All were unsavory places, hosting a clientele that was less than reputable. Many of these corner saloons had little back rooms specially set apart for the entertainment of young women. In surroundings such as these, it was very possible that Byrne became acquainted with a particular "fallen angel" and committed the murder to be rid of her or to rid her of her money. An unfortunate girl of this profession, especially if an immigrant, would most likely not be missed.

While checking one bar, a reporter met a grizzled customer who looked to be a regular denizen of the seedy establishment. He sat with a folded copy of *The World* and a bottle of cheap whiskey and when approached, seemed eager to talk about the murder. It was mid-afternoon, so the sot still had his wits about him, having only begun his daily sojourn. The rummy had never known a man named Byrne and the description did not single out anyone in his mind. As for the girl, he could not think of any of the regular girls who were missing. From his reading, he was of the opinion the crime was done to rob the girl, and for that reason, he'd "bet his watch against a nickel," that the murdered girl was not a Bowery gal. "First off," he maintained, "no Bowery girl had enough money to make her worth robbing, and secondly, the girls here were too streetwise to be led off to Jersey to be killed."

The story was the same for all the investigations. Bartenders knew all their customers and all their girls and were not missing any. None of them recognized the name Timothy Byrne. After much careful inquiry, done by many, no trace of the man was uncovered.

~~~~~

Another clue, which was bringing no results, was the white handkerchief with the embroidered name, K. M. Noory (z). Believing the girl might be a newly arrived immigrant, investigators poured through records at Castle Garden hoping to find any name with a resemblance. They found no person who registered with such a name. Employment office managers in New York City and in cities along the rail line were questioned. Perhaps they would remember securing a position for this woman in the Rahway area. Again, nothing was discovered.

~~~~~

Undertaker Ryno stepped back and viewed the unknown woman with a feeling of professional satisfaction. As she sat before him with folded hands, clad in the clothes she wore when found, she actually looked quite natural. The embalming fluid he used to preserve the body had begun to produce a more life-like countenance. Her hair, now combed, arranged, and topped by her hat and veil, gave her the appearance of a timid country girl and he thought she looked more like a Swede or a Scandinavian than Irish or German. However, it was the bluish-gray eyes, now pinned open, which created a striking expression and entirely changed the features of her face. He kept the white linen collar around her neck to hide the ugly wound. As he studied the ghastly figure, he wondered if she looked at all as she did when alive, and if not, would anyone ever be able to identify her.

Outfitting and positioning the woman in this manner was done at the request of Coroner Terrill. County officials, also aware of criticism in the newspapers, decided to take new photographs and distribute them throughout the state and the adjoining states. James Stacy was again called in to take the photos, which would include both frontal views and profiles. It was also suggested that he take photographs of the retina of her eye with the possibility that the face of the murderer might be reflected therein. Three days into the investigation, the officials of Union County realized they had to become more aggressive, even if their methods bordered on the unusual or the macabre.

~~~~~

Chief Tooker arrived in Jersey City and went directly to the station house on the corner of Wayne and Henderson. After formal introductions, Chief Murphy briefed him on information gathered to date regarding the murder suspect. The arrest was made on Saturday night, as the man was about to board a ferry to New York. A patrolman at the pier noticed his bloody clothes and confronted him. The man, who did not speak English well, gave his name as Anthony Knoll. He said he had just walked from New Brunswick and was trying to get to New York. When questioned about the blood, he said he had a nose bleed a few days ago and blood got on his clothes. The beat officer, suspicious of the weak story, arrested him and brought him in for further interrogation. Once at the station, Knoll was searched. In one pocket was found a small advertisement from a saloon in Newark announcing that boiled eggs would be given away on Sunday. Another pocket held a bloodstained knife. The man seemed somewhat surprised, but had no explanation for the bloody weapon. He didn't say anything more that made sense, so he was locked up. With no headway made over the next day, Murphy thought it time to notify the Rahway Police.

The background information having been given, Anthony Knoll was brought before the two chiefs. He sat in a chair with his head down, quivering with fear. Tooker was appalled to see the man had not been cleaned up since his arrest. He still had bloodstains on his shirt and coat and dried drops of red clung to his arm and ear. His feet were swollen, but Tooker's keen eye noted they were a smaller size than the footprints he had seen when he first arrived at the murder scene. When Murphy questioned him about the blood, the frightened man said he was attacked and beaten by four men at the Jersey City pier. Pressed to elaborate, he changed the story and said he had fallen down a flight of stairs. Tooker next asked him to give an account of his movements over the weekend. In his broken English, the man said he was from Texas and was currently without a place to call home. The explanation of his walk from New Brunswick to Jersey City was a confused tale of encounters with all manner of people, unsuccessful searches for employment, and stealthy attempts at hopping freight cars. Knoll was not familiar with Rahway, so he couldn't be sure if he crossed through the place or not. As he was about to continue his story, he suddenly grabbed his mouth and nose, covering both with his right hand. Thin rivulets of blood started to seep through the spaces between his fingers, dripping down his chin and onto his shirt. The poor wretch was hemorrhaging from the nose. Tooker sighed and shook his head. Anthony Knoll was nothing more than a pitiful tramp.

Wednesday, March 30, 1887

With each train that made a stop at the Rahway Depot, reporters stirred in anticipation, watchful for anyone who might get off carrying important news. No sooner did the cars come to a complete halt, than the scribes would position themselves in front of the exit doors ready to pounce on any newsworthy prospect. When the doors of the 8:40 local opened on this morning, a powerfully-built man holding a cigar tightly between his lips stepped out. He was followed by a shorter, heavyset man. A number of New York reporters recognized the bigger man and rushed toward him. Those not familiar with this new arrival trailed closely behind sensing an air of importance. Now surrounded, the man pulled the Havana from his mouth and addressed them with a wink, "Listen here, boys. I'm here on private business to look over property my relatives own in this town. So, if you'll just shut your eyes and not look where we're going, I'd appreciate it." He asked where he could hire a buggy and was directed to Eden Laing's livery stable just beyond the station on the corner of Milton and Broad. None of the reporters followed as the two men left the platform, but opened their notepads and began to scribble excitedly. Inspector Thomas Byrnes, Chief Detective of the New York Bureau had arrived and with him, his right-hand man, Detective Sergeant Frincke. At present, no one knew if the Rahway authorities had sent for the famous investigator or if he had come on his own accord. Those who knew Byrnes believed he came on his own, with designs to put another feather in his cap by showing Jersey detectives how to clear up their murder mystery.

~~~~~

The gossip started early this day with the posting of the reward monies being offered by the state and local governments. As expected, Governor Green sent word that the state would reward six hundred dollars for the apprehension of the person or persons who committed the crime. Rahway's council agreed on rewarding three hundred for the arrest and conviction of the criminal and two hundred for the identification of the woman for a total sum of five hundred dollars. Added to these figures, was a reward of five hundred dollars promised by the officials of Union County.

The list met with differing reactions. Many felt the civic leaders on all levels were being too parsimonious, and if they really wanted to get results, more would have to be added to the ante. The Honorable William P. Esterbrook, a wealthy resident and a leader in the Republican Party, was embarrassed by the amount and pledged a private reward of one hundred dollars, while imploring others to do likewise. Regardless of the total, most citizens agreed a reward would aid in bringing the murderer to justice and solving the riddle of the woman's identity.

One person no longer quite so sure, was Mayor Daly. Initially, the mayor thought a reward would bring a speedy end to the case, but he now had his doubts. A reward of seventeen hundred dollars was a handsome sum, and he had concerns that opportunists would flock to the city with fabricated stories for the sole purpose of securing the bounty. Such false claims would create more problems. Stories, which sounded the least bit plausible, would have to be investigated, thus keeping the police from working on legitimate clues. As it was, the police had already been deluged with tips, hints, leads, and rumors, which only resulted in scattering the efforts of the investigators. The mayor worried the reward would prove more of a hindrance than a help.

~~~~~

The courtroom used for police business was an area on the second floor of the two-room police station. When Coroner Terrill reached the top of the steps, he was caught off guard by the throng packed into the small room. Curious citizens along with reporters had gathered long before the doors opened waiting to observe the proceedings of the first inquest hearing. A loud din of voices filled the room as men, standing shoulder to shoulder, crammed into the space. Last Saturday, when Terrill scheduled the meeting for this location, he had no idea the case would become the focus of everyone's attention. Larger quarters would be needed for future sessions. Upon reaching the desk behind which he would stand and the jury would be seated, Terrill called for order. The hubbub continued and stopped only after a county police officer pounded his billy club on the large desk. Finally, there was silence and the first meeting of the inquest was called to order at ten-thirty.

City Clerk Stuart Marsh called the juror's roll and was answered by eleven of the twelve men. William Brunt was not present to respond. Since the hearings could not proceed without a full complement of jurors, the coroner instructed his officer to go out and find the delinquent juror. Terrill, embarrassed and offended by the delay, took this time to explain to the jury the seriousness of their position. He spoke of the weighty responsibility set before them and how he expected them to adhere to their duties in a sober manner. For the others in the room, the coroner's speech gave no entertainment, and their restlessness was becoming audible. Fortunately, just as the decorum of the meeting was about to be lost, William Brunt entered, led by the officer. As the two wedged their way through the crowd, catcalls and derisive comments were hurled at the tardy juror.

Terrill, who by this time had worked himself into an angry humor, laced into Brunt, holding back nothing save the expletives. Through the tirade, Brunt seemed surprisingly nonplused. When asked where he had been, he said he was out working on a clue and advised the coroner he could end everything right now if he arrested Clinton Froat and William Keech. Terrill could hear murmurs of agreement coming from persons in the room and shouted at the juror, "You're out of order! Take your seat with the others and keep your mouth shut!" Caught off guard by the coroner's caustic tone, Brunt walked meekly to the one unoccupied chair and sat down.

As soon as the commotion died down and Terrill regained his composure, he approached the jurors and announced, "Gentlemen of the jury, I had hopes to begin the official investigation of this case today, but after a consultation with Prosecutor Wilson, I have decided to adjourn this inquest until such a time as the jury deems suitable." The jury deliberated several minutes and decided to meet on Friday morning at ten o'clock in the council chambers at City Hall.

Having come to the hearing with expectations of a story with some import and getting none, reporters cornered the coroner seeking any thread of information. Although Terrill carefully veiled his comments, it was easy to understand the reason for the postponement. Not only was the prosecution without a single witness, they had no definite list of whom they would be calling to testify.

William Brunt also found himself the object of attention. Reporters were familiar with the names of Froat and Keech and were interested if there was anything new in Brunt's accusations. The juror reiterated his son's story of the girl in Froat's yard and all the other rumors about the two men, but added nothing they hadn't heard. He was quite sure they were guilty and left promising "to raise a disturbance at the inquest if action is not taken against them."

~~~~~

After the past Sunday, the mayor had closed the morgue to the general public and required anyone who wanted to see the body to report to police headquarters or the morgue to provide a valid reason. Upon receiving permission, the potential identifier would be escorted to the casket. Emil Mattis, a German brewer from New York, had fears the murdered woman was his lady friend, Louisa Welcher. Mattis had given her a gold ring on Wednesday as a sign of his affection after which she disappeared. He told his story to the police, but was so fearful his lover might be the victim, he refused to view the body. He did, however, agree to look over the murdered woman's clothes. As he started going through each article he became very grave until he noticed the black stockings. An expression of relief came over the German and he exclaimed, "Thank God, it can't be Louisa. She would have been wearing red!" Oscar Kleyh, an Elizabeth fireman, thought the girl was Frances Lerowitch, a young German girl who worked for Theodore Glaser near Linden. Glaser was located and brought in to view the body, and didn't think it was his domestic.

Working off a tip from a man who said he knew the girl, a reporter went to Ryno's with an unusual clue. According to the source, the girl could be identified by a peculiar physical imperfection. Ryno was asked to check if the victim had an underdeveloped right breast. The undertaker was dumbstruck and sent the reporter off, suggesting he do a better job of choosing his sources. The dead woman was well developed on both sides. Herman Zappf, a man who lived close to the murder scene, thought the girl was Maggie Collins. His claim was crushed when he described the earrings Maggie liked to wear. The murdered woman's ears were not pierced.

Not all the identifications were resolved in the space of a few questions or a few hours. Some stories were so plausible and the persons making the claims so definite, follow-up investigation was necessary. Such was the case with Mary Maltby, Mary Creney, and Kate Neary.

John Harrison, Superintendent of the Newark City Home for Women, told police the girl was Mary Maltby, a former inmate at the institution. According to Harrison, the young lady was raised by her grandmother until she reached her early twenties and could no longer be controlled. Mary became so incorrigible; the grandmother was resigned to place her in the Home where she was confined for four years. Sadly, upon her release, she fell back into her evil ways and ended up working in a saloon. A woman she boarded with said she had kept company with a man named Byrne who lived in New York or Brooklyn, but later broke off the relationship. Having seen two photographs of the dead woman and later seeing the body itself, Harrison was satisfied it really was Mary. He would return tomorrow with more proof.

C. H. Eldridge, President of the Hudson River and Maine Ice Company out of New York City, visited Rahway with the belief the victim was Mary Creney of Monroe County, New York. Mary had been a servant for his family since early January, but became so homesick she decided to return home. She left his employ last Wednesday. He didn't think she was murdered by a lover because he never saw her with a male friend. He believed she was carrying a fair amount of money. When asked if his former employee had any marks or scars, Eldridge said she had a scar on her right wrist and also a second identifying oddity. The middle finger on Mary's right hand was shorter than the index finger. When the body was examined, no deformity was observed on the hand of the corpse. Even so, Eldridge stated, "You need go no further, I'll swear the girl is Mary." Those around him were critical and admonished him for making the claim in order to get the reward. Eldridge, a solid-looking businessman, gave an offended reply, "I am in good circumstances, and will not take a cent if my identification proves to be conclusive." He vowed to return with another gentleman who would also identify the body.

It was 8:00 p.m. when John T. Neary walked into Ryno's and said he was looking for his sister Kate who had left New York for Elizabeth on Thursday. He was especially worried because she was carrying one hundred and twenty-five dollars in her purse. Ryno was immediately struck by the appearance of Neary who had a remarkable resemblance to the murdered woman. The name Neary was very similar to the name stitched on the white handkerchief. After giving minute descriptions of the carpetbag, the umbrella, and the green dress, Ryno brought Neary to the casket, now excited the mystery might be over. The man looked in the box, nodded, and said softly, "It's Kate." Ryno urged him to report to the police, but he said he had to return home and he would be back in the morning. Ryno watched him leave and disappear down the dark street.

Thursday, March 31 – Saturday, April 2, 1887

Since last Saturday, when news of the Rahway murder broke, the local police concentrated all their energies on the one case. Each day was spent chasing after leads and interviewing those who believed they could unlock the secret of the unknown woman's identity. Even though the authorities limited who could view the body, persons still came to the station with accounts of missing servants, sisters, daughters, and lovers. For every outlandish story, there were those that were intriguing enough to warrant further investigation.

Henry Ande, a baker from Elizabeth, had been searching for his daughter, Mary, since she mysteriously disappeared on the ninth of March. On that Wednesday, Mary told her parents she was going to spend the day seeking employment in one of the neighborhood factories. Evening came, but the daughter did not return home. Ande and his wife made inquiries among their friends and relatives, but no one had any idea where she might be. After reading about the girl killed at Rahway, the anxious parents asked to see photographs of the dead woman. When the photos were brought to them, both father and mother remarked how much they looked like their "Mamie."

On Friday, Mary's brother came to see the body and declared the girl was not his sister. He said there was some resemblance, but the color of the eyes was the proof it was not Mary. The brother also let on his sister had been receiving attention from a young worker employed at Watson's carriage factory in Elizabeth and he thought Mary might have run off with the man to be married.

Mrs. Sadie Mann of Camden read the descriptions in the papers, saw the photographs, and believed they matched the features of her sister Vinnie. Mrs. Mann came to see Chief Tooker and proceeded to present an interesting story complete with a captivating motive. Some weeks ago, Vinnie stormed out of the house, very angry and upset over a family matter, saying she was leaving for New York. It was Mrs. Mann's belief that Vinnie was enticed from Camden and killed at Rahway so someone else would be in line to inherit her share of an estate valued at approximately twenty thousand dollars. The Camden woman shocked Tooker when she accused their own father, Captain Rodger, of being the killer. Vinnie had been married, but was now separated and had no children. Mrs. Mann theorized that with Vinnie gone, the father, who she portrayed as an evil man, would inherit her sister's share.

Tooker half-heartedly sent off a deputy to try to locate the captain to ascertain his whereabouts the night of the murder. It was the chief's feeling that the suspicions of Mrs. Mann were premature, if not fantastic.

These were not the only false identifications during the latter part of the first week. The Maltby, Creney, and Neary leads, which sounded so possible on Wednesday, all turned out to be erroneous.

Mary Maltby walked into the Newark Police Station on Thursday as hot as a hornet. She was in a rage over the articles in the Wednesday papers describing her scurrilous behavior and was greatly aggrieved by the assaults made on her character. The girl said she was presently earning an honest living by working as a domestic in the home of a respectable family. She couldn't understand why Mr. Harrison would say such vile things and feared the negative reports would jeopardize her position. When Harrison learned Mary was alive, he sheepishly commented, "I didn't tell anybody I positively identified the photographs or the body. I only said they showed some slight similarities." Mary's brother later showed up at Ryno's and refuted Harrison's entire story.

Mary Creney was also found alive and well. A dispatch was received at the Western Union Office from Syracuse, New York, reporting that Mary was in the city amazed by the reports of her demise. Mr. Eldridge arrived in Rahway on Thursday with a gentleman friend who was brought in to support his identification. When they were informed of the telegram, they made no comment, but turned away and left town, trying to be as inconspicuous as possible.

There was great anticipation at police headquarters when Undertaker Ryno introduced John Neary to Chief Tooker and

The Case of the Unknown Woman

Detective Keron. Neary removed his hat, placed it crown down on a chair and shook hands. Ryno opened the conversation by pointing out the resemblance between Neary and the dead woman, after which Neary himself began presenting his narrative. While he was imparting his story, Keron looked into Neary's hat and spied the initials J. R. D. The detective, sensing something was amiss, interrupted Neary and asked him to explain the letters. For whatever reason, Neary decided to come clean. He told his audience his real name was John R. Douglas and he was an amateur detective from Boston. The red-faced officers roughly grabbed Douglas, pinned him down, and went through his pockets. The man, realizing he had gone too far with his deception, offered no resistance. The chief pulled out a badge and paperwork identifying him as a private detective. Angered by his charade, Tooker arrested Douglas on the charge of being a suspicious character. Again, the man put up no resistance. He was discharged the next day and was last seen boarding a train for New York.

~~~~~

As the mystery of the unnamed woman was becoming more profound, every person who was in town on the Friday of the murder tried to jog their memories to recall noticing any person who might be of interest. It is human nature to want to become part of a story that's on everyone's lips, so any remote encounter could be expected to grow into something significant in one's imagination. A young woman stopping by a Main Street shop to look at a pair of shoes, a girl with a foreign accent asking for directions, a nervous stranger waiting on the station platform, all became a potential piece to the strange puzzle. William Gee and Richard Feist, two railroad men, each contacted Chief Tooker on Thursday with information they hoped would be useful.

William Gee was the conductor on the 9:00 p.m. train from New York City on Friday night, March 25. Sitting in one car was a female passenger holding a ticket for Rahway. Gee couldn't help but notice the girl's peculiar behavior. She sat with her back to the center of the car and when he came to get her ticket, she handed it over her shoulder without turning around. When the conductor announced they were at Station Rahway, the girl asked if the train made another stop in the city, to which Gee replied, "It stops at the junction." The girl answered cryptically, "Well, that will do for me." Reaching the junction, which was no more than a mile down the line, the girl got off and started walking toward St. Georges Avenue. Gee believes the girl went north from there and ended up at Central Avenue where she was killed.

Richard Feist, freight agent for the Pennsylvania Railroad, was working at the Rahway Station on that Friday night and saw a young woman get off the 9:30 p.m. train from New York. She seemed anxious and disoriented, and paced along the platform giving the appearance she was waiting for someone. After about ten minutes, she left the station area and headed toward Elm Avenue. Elm runs parallel to Central, the next block over.

The freight agent's story, like most of the others, quickly made the rounds through town. When Axel Ostberg heard it, he thought the girl might be his sister Lovis. Ostberg, who worked for a family on Elm Avenue, claimed his sister was planning to visit him that weekend and was scheduled to arrive on Friday evening. He was worried she might have walked toward Elm, got confused, and ended up on Central.

Feist viewed the body on Sunday and could not be one hundred per cent sure if it was the same woman he saw at the depot. The lighting at the station was not too bright to begin with, but as he looked at the girl's face in the coffin, he admitted it was so bruised, he wondered if anyone would ever be able to give a positive identification.

~~~~~

City and County officials decided on Thursday afternoon that the public would be allowed to view the body one final time. Nothing concrete had developed over the week, and the press was calling for a public viewing with hopes that someone from somewhere would recognize the girl. Newspaper editors were chiding the civic leaders for not taking advantage of every measure possible to identify the woman of mystery. They wanted as many people as possible, from as far off as possible, to make the trip to Rahway. Also, editors were extremely indignant of late after discovering two important clues had been withheld from them. News leaked that the girl was wearing three finger rings, and a large brown button, which looked like the type worn on a man's overcoat, had been found by the body. They demanded these items be put on display. Under this pressure and with no solution in sight, the authorities capitulated. On Sunday, April 3, the public would have one last chance to identify the body. The papers were notified so articles would appear in their Friday and Saturday issues. In towns with weekly publications, notification of the event would be in the hands of the town crier.

Elijah Pippenger worked for Lewis Hyer's newspaper *The Union Democrat*. In his younger years, Pippenger's job on the *Democrat* was providing the manpower that worked the printing press. Around the time of the Civil War, however, editor Hyer purchased a steam powered press, negating the need to manually "turn the handle." The modern machine could have put Pippenger out of a job, but Hyer held "Ole Pip" in high esteem and assigned him the task of verbally announcing important news occurring between issues. Gregarious by nature, he was perfect for the job and became one of the best-known and popular personalities in town. For over twenty years, Pippenger, now in his seventies, walked the streets, ringing his bell and calling out news of auctions, lost children, public meetings, and important news "extras." The news on this day, fresh out of City Hall was big, and the crier knew he would be busy most of the weekend. "Last chance to see the murdered woman! Sunday at Ryno's Morgue! Doors open at 8:00 a.m.! Last chance to see the murdered woman!"

~~~~~

On Friday morning, April 1, Coroner Terrill called his jury together in the council chambers of City Hall. It was no surprise to anyone that shortly after calling the meeting to order, he adjourned the hearing until the next Friday, April 8. He was frank with all who were assembled and admitted the authorities had no evidence whatsoever and were not yet certain who they would call to testify besides the doctors who performed the autopsy and the brothers who found the body. They were hopeful some discovery would be made by next week to shed light on the case.

As juror Clark was leaving City Hall, word was passed to him that William Keech had committed suicide in Milton Lake. The news caused a stir and Clark, followed by reporters and detectives, rushed to the west end of town to search for a body. Once there, teams of men commandeered the few rowboats they found moored at the docks and rowed out to survey the lake. Others carefully went over the lake-edge and surrounding grounds looking for any signs of a drowning. The men hunted for more than an hour, but found no body or any trace of foul play. Clark was just about ready to call an end to the search when word came from an unidentified source that the report of the suicide was actually a tasteless April Fools joke.

There were still ongoing suspicions against Keech, but no one was more active in seeking his arrest than juror William Brunt. Brunt had approached the Rahway magistrate after Wednesday's adjourned meeting to issue a warrant, but was refused on the grounds there was no evidence. Undaunted, Brunt left for New Brunswick with a detective from that city to obtain one. Both were adamant it was Keech who committed the murder and felt he should be arrested even without a warrant.

Keech himself had remained in his house the past few days, available to anyone who wanted to interview him. Aware of the rumors circulating about his involvement, he maintained his innocence and didn't act at all like a man who committed a murder. To those who came to question him, he showed none of the signs of nervousness or remorse that would make one suspicious. He told one reporter, "I am innocent and know nothing more of the murder than the man in the moon. If I am to be arrested, why don't they take me? I'm right here." Some were starting to suspect he had nothing to do with the crime.

~~~~~

Detective Keron did not look forward to the spectacle scheduled for tomorrow. There had already been enough bungling stories to seriously retard his investigative work, and with the great number of people expected to come to the city on Sunday, matters would only get worse. The Maltby, Creney, and Neary leads were especially counterproductive because the bogus stories not only created faulty trails, but in some cases, they also suspended investigation efforts. Newspaper accounts had written the three stories up as though the identifications were accurate and the mystery solved. When the articles reached authorities in other parts of the state and in surrounding states, they telegraphed back asking if they should stop looking for clues. Keron knew that more people would mean more stories.

As it was, he received two more "reasonable" leads on Saturday. Mr. R. J. Jorgensen, a Brooklyn tailor, came to the morgue and identified the body as Wilhelmina Johnson, a twenty-two-year-old Danish girl who arrived in the country four months ago. Wilhelmina was employed by a family in Jorgensen's neighborhood and because he spoke her language, he was asked to serve as her interpreter. It was not long before she confided in him and told him she had left Copenhagen to search for her husband who had deserted her after seven months of marriage. Before her husband left, she told him she would follow after him wherever he went. In reply, he warned her, if she came to the United States looking for him, he would kill her. Jorgensen lost track of the girl two weeks ago and had fears she located her estranged husband who killed her as promised. When Jorgensen was taken to see the body, he was quite sure it was Wilhelmina. He didn't recognize any of the clothing, but stated it was because he had only seen her while working and she was always wearing housedresses. He pointed out the name on the handkerchief was a Danish name and could have been carried by a woman from that country. After the visit, he returned to Brooklyn promising to find additional proof. Keron and the others who were in on the interview had strong feelings the man was mistaken in his identification and his theory.

John W. Ross brought in an even better story. Ross, a fish dealer who ran a market on Broad Street in Elizabeth, was on the road peddling his fish and stopped at Gus Klien's tavern between Roselle and Cranford. While at the tavern, an old colored [sic] woman came in for a drink. The woman seemed pleased to be among company and began to speak to no one in particular. "Twas a long winter, but I ought to thank the Lord I got through it so comfortable. My house was always warm and cozy an' I warn't sick but only three days. Can't say everybody was lucky like me. That po' white gal that stopped by my house last Thursday was sure 'nough down and out. She seemed scared o' somethin', but was so pitiful, I let her stay the night. The little girl didn't say much o' anythin' and I couldn't make out much o' her foreign talk anyway. I thought best just to let her go to bed. Next mornin', she was gone 'for I had breakfast made." At that point in the woman's anecdote, Ross left the tavern and came to Rahway to find a policeman.

Klien's Tavern wasn't too far off, so Detective Keron decided to ride out to Roselle with Ross to check out the bar and the woman. By the time they arrived, the woman had already left. When questioned about her conversation, the bartender said he wasn't paying attention to the old woman and didn't hear a word of her story. He said she comes in every once in a while and likes to ramble on just to hear herself talk. The bartender did tell Keron her name was Sarah Ann Jackson and gave him directions to her house on Galloping Hill Road.

It was mid-afternoon when Keron and Ross reached the drab, colorless cottage that was the home of Miss Jackson. She must have seen them pull in front and stop because before they got down off the carriage, she was standing on the front porch. The old woman didn't receive many visitors and was curious to find out what the two men wanted. She smiled as they came to the foot of the steps. Keron gave a brief, "Afternoon Ma'am," and got right to the point. He asked her to retell her story of the white girl who spent the night with her last

Thursday. The smile on the woman's face faded, replaced by a tight-lipped stare. She took a few moments to look at Keron and then Ross and said curtly, "I ain't never had no white girl stay with me. I mind my own business and don't take in no strangers. I don't know who tol' you such a tale." When Ross responded that he himself had heard her talking at Klien's, the old woman said he probably drank too much and was hearing things. Keron started to question her further, but she cut him short saying, "I got no more to say and no more time fo' you. I think you best be goin'." She stood her ground. Keron motioned with his head to go back, and the detective and the fishmonger turned and walked away from the house. Not much was said as they returned to Rahway, and the detective wasn't sure how to figure Ross or the old woman.

Sunday, April 3, 1887

Had a person been unaware of the circumstances surrounding this Sunday, he might have thought a holiday was the reason for all the commotion. Shortly after sunrise, long lines of carriages, from every direction, began filling the roads leading into the city. Those without a carriage came on foot, or on horseback, or by any other conceivable mode of transportation. Railroad trains from east and west were jammed with men, women, and children. The Pennsylvania Railroad assigned extra cars to accommodate riders coming into Rahway and one train alone from New York brought in a thousand passengers. Seven hundred and twenty-five excursion tickets were sold at the Elizabeth Station. They came from all over the east coast and from as far west as St. Louis. The streets were filled with all manner of strangers. Farmers, factory workers, and businessmen came, as did well-dressed ladies and servant girls. Policemen from large and small cities were in the crowds. Most came out of curiosity, but here and there could be seen the somber ones who came looking for missing girls. Whoever they were, or whatever their reasons for coming, their destination was the same—Ryno's Morgue.

Undertaker Ryno was as prepared as he thought he could be to receive and handle the expected crowds. He had taken the body from the icebox, which housed it for the last week, and placed it in a coffin with a plate of glass at the head so only the face of the girl could be seen. The entire box, except at the head, was covered with a black cloth. The girl's green dress, torn and still bloodied, was fitted on a milliner's dummy and placed next to the coffin. The hat and black veil were placed on the neck of the mannequin and the fur cape was wrapped around the shoulders. The bloodstained knife, the black satchel, and the items found in the bag were arranged in a showcase next to the clothing display. Also in the case were the basket of eggs, the umbrella, the handkerchief, and the girl's shoes. Late additions to the display case were a large brown button, a plain gold ring, a polished brass ring with red and white glass set in a cluster to look like rubies and diamonds, and a cheap chased ring.

Chief Tooker also had his staff in readiness. The chief himself was positioned at the entrance to the room to take note of any unusual actions or behaviors. Detective Keron was at the exit door to examine anyone who showed the slightest sign of recognition. Sergeant Conger stood behind the case with the responsibility to check the coats of all the men, looking for one with a missing button. Deputies were stationed outside the building to help maintain order, and four more were assigned to the Central Avenue murder site. Tooker also hired Charlie Barber to act as a sort of "Master of Ceremonies" to direct viewers and to move them along.

By the time 8:00 a.m. arrived, close to two thousand were assembled outside the morgue. Already, there was a great deal of clamoring and struggling going on while they waited for admission and as the chief looked down at the mob, he wondered if he had enough manpower to control it. When all was ready, Tooker opened the door, gave a signal, two deputies stepped away, and as if a dam had burst, those at the front of the line were literally thrown up the steps by the mass scrambling behind. Once in the viewing area, Charlie Barber went to work with the skill of a showman. "This is the body of the murdered girl. After taking a careful view of it, pass to the right and see the figure upon which are the dress, cape, and hat worn by her when she was found."

"Pass right along, gents!"

"On the left in the case you will see the knife with which the deed was done. You will also see the handkerchief, the shoes, the egg basket, the umbrella, the rings, and the bag found in the river."

"Pass along, gents!"

"Look at the goods very carefully, and don't go away with doubts. If you recognize the body, any article of clothing, the basket, or the knife, make your case known to one of the officers."

"Pass right along, gents, and make way for others."

"Don't fail to look at everything before you go. Remember, this is the first and last time that all the goods will be on public exhibition."

For the next eight hours, a steady stream of humanity climbed the stairs and filed past the coffin and display cases. The procession became so unwieldy that only twelve at a time were allowed to enter. At 4:00 p.m., when the viewing was officially closed, it was estimated over six thousand persons had viewed the body. Of that number, however, no one recognized the knife or any of the articles. Sergeant Conger spied no coat with a missing brown button. There were no suspicious characters pulled aside by Chief Tooker or Detective Keron, and there were only a handful of visitors who made claims of recognizing the girl. Those were taken aside to present their stories.

Detectives Stanisberg and Wambold of the Newark Police Department looked at the body and then each other and nodded in agreement. Without checking the display of items, they asked Sergeant Conger for the officer in charge and were pointed in the direction of Detective Keron. They approached the exit door where Keron was standing and informed him they could identify the girl. Keron, sensing the identification by two police officers might prove to be important, escorted them to the undertaker's first floor office, a small but private room set up for these interviews.

Stanisberg began the story by stating the girl was Annie Kirkpatrick, a newly arrived immigrant from Scotland. Annie had come to Newark to visit friends. Unfortunately, prior to reaching her destination, she discovered someone had made off with her purse and the thirty-five dollars that was in it. Now destitute, due to the loss of all her money, and disappointed in the search for her friends, she made her way to a police station with hopes of finding assistance. The police, moved by her story, gave her lodging for the night. Stanisberg noted it was Wednesday, March 23. The next morning, Annie was able to make contact with her friends who introduced her to their employer, Mr. Campbell Clark, owner of the Clark Thread Works. Knowing her predicament and the fact she had worked in a cloth mill back in her home country, he gave her an offer of employment. Both detectives noted how she was openly overjoyed at the prospect of a job. She was told to report the next morning, Friday, March 25. Needless to say, she never made it to work, and no one had any idea what happened to her. When photos of the murder victim were shown at the Newark Station, Stanisberg and Wambold recognized them to be the same girl they had put up a week before. The photos were brought to Mr. Clark who remarked how they did resemble Annie Kirkpatrick. Keron wrote everything down and promised the detectives he would investigate their lead.

Mrs. George McGee, Mrs. Kate Dowd, and Mr. E. H. Van Ness, all of Woodbridge, were next to sit in Keron's makeshift office emphatically claiming the girl was Annie Santro, a young Hungarian immigrant. Van Ness, a member of a prominent Middlesex County family, said Miss Santro had been employed as a servant in his home for fourteen months. When the three viewed the body, they were sure they had the right girl. The two ladies were also able to identify the fur cape, the rings, and the satchel. Van Ness was so certain the girl was his former housekeeper; he was prepared to go to the coroner to claim the body for burial. "I've got the right woman," he said. "I knew it as soon as I entered that room. She seemed to rise up from her coffin to meet me." He also made it clear as far as the reward was concerned he would not accept it, but would offer it back for the arrest of the brutal killer. When Keron ended the interview and said he would investigate the matter, Van Ness was incredulous and took offense, feeling the detective doubted his story. The Woodbridge man rose from his chair and left the room in a huff followed by the women. Once out of the office and into the street, Keron could hear the insulted gentleman broadcasting the stupidity of the police.

Mr. and Mrs. August Haas and their two sons waited on line for almost three hours, but when they finally got to see the body, it reinforced their opinion it was Mary, a girl they had met while crossing the Atlantic. The family had given Chief Tooker the gist of the story as they waited to enter the room and now he stood with them at the casket awaiting their reaction. Certain of their identification, the chief brought them downstairs to record the full details.

The Haas' had been visiting in Denmark and were returning to New York City in early March on the National Line Steamer, *The Egypt*. While sailing, the family befriended a Swedish girl, whom they only got to know as Mary. The girl, who was about twenty, was traveling with two male companions. One of the two, a medium-sized, red-faced Scandinavian, with a blonde mustache and goatee, monopolized most of her time and was evidently her lover. Mrs. Haas noted that Mary was full of fun and one of the liveliest among the immigrants who would always join in all the games and dancing. Although Mary spoke both Swedish and English, nothing of importance was discussed other than the girl said she had no relatives in the United States. When they landed at Castle Garden on March 4, the family lost track of Mary and her male friends, and were not aware of their destination.

When Mr. and Mrs. Haas saw photos of the dead girl, they both thought it looked like the girl on the steamer, but it was their eleven-year-old son's reaction that compelled them to come to Rahway. The young lad, not knowing what the photos represented, saw them and asked his parents, "How did you get these pictures of Mary?"

Tooker was very impressed with their account and promised to check the list of arrivals at Castle Garden for the names of the three travelers and to get a lead on where they might have gone. With this, the family left, and Tooker, believing there was something to this identification, went to see the mayor.

~~~~~

Mayor Daly motioned to his chief to be quiet as he entered the office. An interview was just beginning between Assemblyman Frank McDermitt and an Associated Press reporter concerning the elected official's knowledge of the murder victim.

"The last time I saw the girl was about a month ago. She was a domestic who came to my office during the winter for consultation on some legal issue. After several visits, we reached a point in our discussions when I felt she had no case, so I advised her to drop the whole matter."

The reporter paused in his writing and asked, "What was the girl's name?"

"Mary Ann Donahue."

"What would you say her age to be?"

"About twenty-eight or twenty-nine."

"When did you come to realize this girl and the murdered girl were the same?"

"As soon as I saw the pictures, I was sure I knew the girl. I never forget a face. She had the same high forehead, a peculiarly set nose, and a refined face. If I remember correctly, her eyes were blue and she had light brown hair. I believe she had a scar under one eye and wore a number of finger rings."

"Did she say anything during her meetings with you that you feel might connect her to this case?"

"Now that you mention it, the whole thing is starting to flash across my mind. I'm almost sure in one of our conversations, she referred to a Timothy Byrne. She also said she had friends in Plainfield and Rahway."

"I think it would be best at this time if you go and view the body." It was the mayor who interrupted. "They'll be closing at four."

McDermitt, who didn't have anything more of value to offer, agreed and concluded the session. Promising to return with confirmation, the assemblyman, with the reporter close behind, headed for the morgue, certain he would find Mary Ann Donahue.

Now alone with his chief, Daly quietly thumbed through a pile of telegrams and letters stacked on his desk. He looked up at Tooker, "Is everybody going crazy?" Taking several letters in his hand, he continued, "They're from all over the country. This one's from Chicago. The police there think they've got the killer. Here's a good one. The writer says the murderer owns a clothing business right here on Main Street and he killed a foreign girl because she wouldn't go away. It also says the real murder weapon is hidden under a rock near the fence a little north of where the body was found. I sent a deputy to take a look. The letter's signed with only the initials M. L. Listen to this one. 'Dark night. Dark deed. Must be a darkey.' No signature. This one's from Connecticut. It's from a mother who fears the victim is her daughter who ran away from home to meet a man somewhere in New Jersey. This telegram's from Philadelphia. A woman thinks it might be her sister who left Boston by rail on March 20. According to the schedule, the train she was on would stop in Rahway. There's no end to these letters. How many missing girls can there be?"

The mayor gave a weak laugh as he shook his head and then asked Tooker, "How did things go over at Ryno's?"

"With all the people that came through, not very well. I did get one lead that might amount to something. I've got to go over to New York tomorrow to check it out. What's been going on in the rest of the town?"

Again, the mayor gave a weak laugh. "I went around in the afternoon. Everybody was talking about the murder as if it happened this morning. In fact, it reminded me a lot of last Saturday. I ran into old man Tunison over by Chamberlain's Hotel. He told me in all his eighty-one years, he's never seen this many people in town, and he'd bet there were more here today than on any other day in our history. A newspaperman from the *Journal* estimated over six thousand had come to Rahway. Reverend Rollison stopped me, complained that his church pews were empty this morning, and said the same was true in all the other churches. He also warned me that a number of ministers felt it wasn't Christian to keep the woman on display like this and it was my duty to order a burial. Dan Ryno's got the same concern. He doesn't know how much longer he can keep the body on ice. Then I get back to my office and McDermitt comes in with yet another story." The mayor stopped as if to contemplate all he had just said and then asked, "What do you think, Chief?"

"Well, Mayor, I think we should give it another week. Something has to break after today." He paused, "It has to."

Daly was about to reply when one of the deputies walked in. "Glad to find you, Chief. Afternoon, Mayor. We got most everyone to leave the Central Avenue site. We had a tough time moving them along. I'd say there was a couple thousand up there today. You should'a seen 'em. They picked up every scrap of paper or bit of cloth off the ground and examined each shred expecting to find a piece of evidence. Oh yeah, Mayor, we looked for a knife along the fence, but didn't find anything. Then, on my way here, I had to help Marsh and Savage break up a fight on Irving Street between two hotheads arguing over who the murdered girl really was. Things were pretty heated by the time I got there. They started throwing punches and were rolling around on the ground. It took all three of us to calm things down, but we did, and sent them off in different directions."

This time the mayor didn't give a weak laugh, but only said, "Everybody's going crazy!"

Monday, April 4 – Thursday, April 7, 1887

It was inspector Byrnes's modus operandi to keep the particulars of his investigation close to the vest. If he questioned a resident or interrogated a suspect, he would never reveal the slightest bit of information that might give a clue to the lead he was developing. He was known to tell reporters, "Should there be any results to the investigation, the public will be informed at the proper time."

Unfortunately for the New York detective, after several days of investigation, he had little to tell the public and was in fact, as much in the dark as the rest of the hawkshaws. He had his theories and worked them aggressively, but for him, like for the others, nothing materialized.

Byrnes was convinced that if he could discover from where the eggs and basket came, he could solve the case. Following similar theories as Detective Keron, he went to all the chicken farms in Clark and Cranford. He even renewed the search for the man and two women who were seen inspecting henhouses. His search, like Keron's, was for naught. He also made a thorough inquiry into all the general stores and markets in the area where eggs were sold. That too yielded nothing.

Byrnes was certain the murderer was a local man, who after committing the crime, went home and destroyed any evidence. Believing this, he and his partner, Sergeant Frincke, knocked on the doors of all the homes near the murder site. They went from house to house, carefully taking note of any comment, any facial expression, and any behavior that might betray the criminal. Their canvassing proved fruitful and after stringing several clues together, Byrnes was confident enough to make an arrest. In the late hours of Monday night, he was seen bringing a prisoner to the back door of the police station. There was no word as to what was going on or who the prisoner was, but it was surmised that the master sleuth had bagged his prey.

By morning, it was learned that Louis DeCamp, a young rowdy, who lived only a few blocks from where the murder happened, was the man in jail. The story behind his arrest spread quickly. While out questioning the residents on Maple Avenue, Byrnes stopped by the home of Sam Tice, who was one of the jurors for the twice-adjourned hearing. Tice told the inspector that on the night of the murder, he and his wife were rudely awakened by DeCamp as he passed by their house. According to Tice, DeCamp came by his house after a night of revelry, and in a state of drunkenness, stood below his bedroom window and shouted, "Ah, there, Mr. Tice!" Tice's startled wife was said to have exclaimed, "Hear that crazy loon!" From this testimony, Byrnes concluded, DeCamp was out on the night of the murder, in the area of the crime, and in a wild condition, thus making him a prime suspect. Monday night he made his arrest.

It was hard for Chief Tooker to believe Louis DeCamp could commit the brutal deed, and those close to the chief thought he was relieved and even pleased when the case against the young man fell apart. Much to the disappointment and embarrassment of Inspector Byrnes, by noon on Tuesday, suspicions involving DeCamp were cleared and his innocence established. Hearing news of their friend's arrest, witnesses came to his defense with proof that, although he was out late that Friday night, he never went near Central Avenue. Also, by calculating the times he left his friends and when he arrived home, there wouldn't have been enough time to have committed the murder. The alibi was so convincing, Tooker and Keron had no alternative but to release the prisoner. When DeCamp was brought through the chief's office, his bruised cheek and swollen lip gave evidence of Byrnes's third-degree tactics. It was widely known, the New York detective was not hesitant about employing both psychological and physical means to extract answers from his suspects. On seeing Byrnes, DeCamp lashed out with angry threats, cursing him and warning him to stay away from his part of town. The detective's only reply was a cold stare. Tooker, not wanting an altercation, stepped between the two and quickly escorted the young man outside. Reunited with his friends, he promised them, loud enough for the chief to hear, he would get even with Sam Tice.

~~~~~

The release of Louis DeCamp was only the beginning of a busy day for Tooker and Keron. Two women had come to the station requesting time to speak with the police about the murdered girl. One of the women was from Albany and was accompanied by a big, rather stupid-looking boy. She was carrying an official-looking letter that she was anxious to show. The other woman was from Brooklyn. Tooker, curious about the letter, asked to see the Albany woman first and led her to the back room for more privacy.

The woman said her name was Mrs. Barbara Nehmeyer and introduced the boy, who followed closely at her side, as her son, Alfred. Nehmeyer, a plainly dressed, stout, German woman with a heavy accent and little command of English, held out the letter for Tooker to read. It was from the Overseer of the Poor in Albany, New York, who wrote that Mrs. Nehmeyer had seen pictures of the girl and had fears it was her daughter, Mary. He asked if the Rahway officials would please aid her in whatever way possible. As Tooker placed the letter down, Mrs. Nehmeyer said, "Hands and feet. I must see hands and feet." Although the chief didn't comprehend the exact meaning of her words, he issued her a permit to view the body and assigned a deputy to bring her and her son to the morgue.

When mother and son were led into the viewing room, undertaker Ryno brought the cold coffin in from the icebox. Both looked at the face through the glass pane with no expression to indicate if the dead girl was daughter or sister. Again, Mrs. Nehmeyer uttered, "Must see hands and feet. Hands and feet to be sure." Realizing what the woman wanted, Ryno opened the lid and exposed the frozen limbs of the corpse. The woman looked at the hands and began to quiver and sob. She slowly moved to the end of the coffin, placed her hands on the girl's feet, and gently caressed them. Now, almost crazy with grief and nearly fainting, she cried, "It is her!" The son grabbed his mother and held her tightly, and with wide eyes, looked at Ryno and nodded.

The undertaker wasted no time in hurrying them back to the station house. Ryno detailed the scene as it had played out in the morgue and then left the woman and her son with the police for the usual questioning. After the first few inquiries, Tooker and Keron knew the dead girl was not Nehmeyer's daughter. They showed her the bloody clothes, which she failed to recognize. The descriptions she gave of her daughter did not compare at all with the murdered girl. The color of her hair was wrong, the age was wrong, and the height and weight of the girl did not match. When photos of Mary were shown to the policemen present in the office, they all agreed, they looked nothing like the victim. The clincher came when Keron asked, "What kind of earrings did your daughter wear, Madam?" "Small ones. Gold. Small. Mary was little girl, six years when ears were cut. In Brooklyn." This answer ended the questioning and Keron summarized all the discrepancies in her descriptions. Mrs. Nehmeyer was speechless and could only say how she couldn't believe how her eyes would mislead her.

The interview was over, but this did not end the matter with the woman from Albany. In her broken English, she explained how the Overseer of the Poor had paid for her transportation to Rahway and that he thought the authorities here would pay for her return trip. Tooker and Keron couldn't believe their ears and sharply reprimanded her for the outrageous assumption. The disconcerted mother became so pitiful and forlorn that the officers softened their stance, and after a short but animated deliberation decided to give the indigent pair the fare to get them home. Mrs. Nehmeyer, overcome with joy, kissed the officers' hands and bowed several times to each as she tearfully thanked them. With the show of emotion over, the two left, leaving the police with yet another false lead, this one not only costing them time but also some of their money.

~~~~~

The story presented by the Brooklyn woman aroused a bit more interest and would require follow-up investigation. Mrs. Ann Moran claimed the girl was Sophie Hesse, who about a year before, had been working at Dieter's Restaurant where she allegedly stole a diamond ring and other valuables from her employer. The Hesse woman was tried and found guilty and given an eight-month sentence in the King's County Penitentiary. Prior to being sent to the county facility, Hesse spent time in the Raymond Street Jail in Brooklyn where Mrs. Moran was employed as a matron. Moran didn't get to know Sophie especially well but was as familiar with her as she was with the other inmates. Naturally, she lost track of the prisoner once she was transferred out, but she did remember Sophie was scheduled to be released on March 5. The matron probably would have forgotten her completely had she not seen the photographs. As soon as she looked at them, Sophie Hesse came to her mind. To confirm her suspicions, she presented her feelings to a constable at the jail who agreed with her identification. "In fact," she told Tooker, I'm pretty certain the constable came to see the body on Sunday." Mrs. Moran said another person who could make a connection between the photographs and Sophie was the jail's chaplain.

Tooker promised he would send an officer to Brooklyn to get statements from the constable and the chaplain and from any other persons who might recognize the photos.

~~~~~

It was Wednesday, and Chief Tooker was finally able to take action on the story regarding the girl met by Mr. and Mrs. Haas on the steamer, *Egypt*. He gave Sergeant Conger the assignment of going to Castle Garden to find the names on the ship's log and on the entry lists that would match the Swedish girl and her two companions. Once the names were found, Conger was to begin a search for the girl's whereabouts.

~~~~~

Detective Keron volunteered to go to Newark to gather more proof that the murdered girl was Annie Kirkpatrick. Two Newark policemen and the owner of a large mill identified the girl, so this had a chance of being a good lead. Keron planned to stop first at the police station and later to visit the thread mill.

~~~~~

When the reporter from the *New York Times* got off the train, one could easily tell he was both tired and unhappy. Having spent the weekend in Chicago, he came home empty-handed. Shortly after the story leaked that the Chicago Police had arrested the Rahway murderer, the *Times* sent one of their reporters to the Midwest. At first, the communication sent to Mayor Daly sounded good. C. L. Watson, a Chicago native, had been looking for his wife since the middle of March. He had reason to believe she was in Baltimore so he traveled to the East Coast. It was while he was in Maryland that he read about the murder and the girl who no one could identify. Thinking it might be his wife, Lillian, he came to Rahway on Sunday, March 28, to view the body. He was overjoyed to find it wasn't his wife, who had dark brown eyes. Upon returning to Chicago, the police met him with a warrant and arrested him on a murder charge. When the reporter visited Watson in his cell, the prisoner attributed the entire charade to his in–laws who were never in favor of their daughter's marriage to him. Lillian's parents were wealthy and Watson was not, and they were sure Watson only married her to get at their money. Watson told the scribe, "No one can keep me from my wife. She would never leave me voluntarily. When I get out, I'll find her." Whether he did or not, the reporter never learned, nor did he care to. One thing was certain, however. Lillian, wherever she was, was not the murdered girl.

~~~~~

Reports of seeing a tall, mustachioed man wearing an overcoat on the night of the murder had been surfacing since the day the body was found. The young girls in town seemed fascinated by this mysterious rogue and more than a few imaginative females claimed to have encountered the stranger. The police took time to listen to the stories, but had little faith in their believability and credited the accounts to the girls' flights of fancy.

One such story was given to Tooker on Thursday morning by Anastasia Handlon, a young Irish girl who worked for the family of David B. Dunham, owner of a large carriage manufacturing company on Irving Street. Handlon was employed as a servant in his family estate on Milton Avenue near the corner of Pierpont. On Friday, March 25, the young servant was just getting home at nine-thirty in the evening and was sitting in the parlor waiting for Mrs. Dunham to return from a church meeting. As she was watching through the front bay window, she saw a man and woman pass the house walking towards St. Georges Avenue. She watched them until they passed the electric lights near the corner, after which she could no longer see them. She was quite sure they turned right at St. Georges going in the direction of Central Avenue. When asked by the police for a description, Handlon said, "The light was streaming from Mrs. Dunham's window upon the sidewalk and I saw the man plainly. He was of medium height, and wore a heavy, straight, black mustache. He had on his head an old silk hat and the collar of his dark overcoat was turned up to his ears. I did not see the woman's face, but I noticed that she carried a black bag in one hand and a parasol in the other. She walked with her head down, some little distance behind the man, and seemed disinclined to follow him." The police, in the course of the investigation, discovered there had been two young lovers out that night and figured this was the pair Handlon might have seen. At any rate, the authorities were skeptical of this story and felt the young Irish girl was merely exercising her imagination.

~~~~~

Chief Tooker had asked former Police Chief Wright if he would take on the assignment of going to Brooklyn to work on the Sophie Hesse lead. The ex-chief readily accepted. The local murder case had turned into a huge one and Wright, who had been doing some investigative work on his own, wanted a bigger part in it. Walking in the direction of the Raymond Street Jail, he saw a sign hanging from the facade of a building halfway down the block. He recognized the name and considered it an omen of good fortune. Before going to the jailhouse, he would make a stop at Dieter's Restaurant.

Dieter's was a small, neatly furnished eatery with enough seating for about forty. The pungent smell of sauerkraut mixed with cigar smoke hung in the room. A slender, blonde, Germanic woman stood by the cash register and invited Wright to sit anywhere he wanted. It was three o'clock in the afternoon and the restaurant was empty, so the policeman sat at a table near the hostess. As she approached him with a menu, he wasted no time and asked her to look at a group of photographs. The woman obliged, and after she went through the set of six views asked, "Who's the girl?" Wright replied he was hoping she would know, and asked if there were others in the restaurant who would look at them. She called out, "Freda, Rolph, come here." The curtain separating the dining area from the kitchen was pushed aside and an older man, followed by a very pretty, full-breasted girl entered the room. Wright had the photographs lined on the table and asked them if they could recognize the face. Both took time to study the images, picking up a few to get a closer look. When finished, they shook their heads, shrugged their shoulders, and the man said, "So what?" At this point, Wright explained who he was and the story behind the pictures. He then asked if the girl in the photographs could be Sophie Hesse. The name caught the three off guard, but after a moment, they shot out quick responses.

"That's not her."

"Doesn't look anything like her. The wench had hard features."

"It's not Sophie, but it wouldn't surprise me if she was found dead somewhere."

"Who said it was Sophie?"

"I thought she was in jail."

Wright explained what he knew of the identification and left the restaurant satisfied that the staff at Dieter's was positive the photographs were not of Sophie Hesse. He was now wondering what he would discover at the jail.

When Wright arrived at the Raymond Street Jail, he asked the officer at the desk for the name of the constable who went to Rahway to view the body. Much to his surprise, the officer replied that no one, as far as he knew, had made the trip and then added there was little interest in the case because not a single officer knew the girl in the photographs. When asked if he was certain, he replied, "I keep the log on the men and their shifts and I'd know if someone went over to Jersey." Wright next asked if the jail had a chaplain, and if so, was he around. The officer pointed down the hall. "Last door on the left. His name is Bass."

The Reverend J. G. Bass was a middle-aged man who wore a full, bushy beard, had a small, tight mouth, and penetrating, dark brown eyes. The room itself was unadorned, and seated at his desk in his clergy garb, the chaplain made Wright uncomfortable. Once a conversation began, however, Wright realized the minister's stern appearance belied a more gregarious nature.

After preliminary introductions and some casual talk, the policeman got to the subject of the photographs. The minister said he had seen them when they first arrived at the jail. "There was a good amount of commotion that day. Everyone looked them over and over again, but no one had ever seen the girl." Wright then asked the chaplain if he recognized the woman. He answered in the negative. Wright next inquired, "Why would a woman who works in the jail say that you and one of the constables identified the girl as Sophie Hesse?"

"I don't understand. What are you talking about?"

"Mrs. Moran, a matron who worked at the jail, told my chief you could verify her identification."

"What did you say was the matron's name?"

"Moran, Mrs. Ann Moran."

"My good officer Wright, Ann Moran was not a matron in this jail. She was an inmate."

Hearing this, Wright leaned back heavily in his chair and stared past the chaplain to the wall behind. The whole deception came together. He understood. Bass, now also understanding, sighed and said, "I see the time she did with us did little to put her on a righteous path."

~~~~~

Detective Keron was not getting the results he had hoped for as he met with police officers at the Newark headquarters. The identification given by Detectives Stanisberg and Wambold had Keron expecting to find other officers in agreement. Such was not the case. Keron discovered that out of all the police who saw the photographs, Stanisberg and Wambold were the only two who believed the girl was Annie Kirkpatrick. Keron also learned that many citizens came to the station and not one of them remotely suggested it might be the Kirkpatrick woman. The chief of police told him he didn't doubt the sincerity of his two detectives, and held nothing against them for believing as they did, but he was confident they were mistaken.

The story was the same at the thread mill. Because Kirkpatrick had not yet started work there, it was nearly impossible to find workers who saw her, much less knew her. One worker who did, however, was David Andrews, the gateman at the factory. Andrews said he saw her twice and thought he could recognize her. When shown the photographs, Andrews commented, "That's not Annie Kirkpatrick. I'm sure of it."

The number of persons who doubted the Annie Kirkpatrick identification far outnumbered those who thought it was her, making Keron believe he had been chasing another false lead.

~~~~~

Chief Tooker had stayed back in town to continue to interview people with new stories and to keep abreast of the ongoing investigations. As far as the latter was concerned, he had not gotten any good news. Sergeant Conger had returned from Castle Garden without finding anything. After checking through pages of passenger lists, he was unable to find the names of three Swedish travelers who boarded the "Egypt" on the date the ship left port. The only Swedish name he found was that of a woman named Alma Gulbraudsen. No member of the crew remembered anyone fitting the descriptions, nor did they recall a free-spirited, fun-loving young Swede. Conger went through registration lists taken by immigration officials on the date the passengers disembarked and found nothing. He showed the photographs around, even though he realized with the thousands of faces swimming past the officials, it would be a miracle to remember a solitary woman.

The Woodbridge police came by to see Tooker to clear up the Annie Santro lead. They had read in the papers about Mr. Van Ness and his claim that the dead girl was his former servant. They brought proof that he was incorrect. Woodbridge detectives had investigated the story, found Miss Santro alive, and knew that she was presently aboard a ship on her way back home to Hungary.

Almost two weeks had gone by since the murder and not a hint of a solution was in sight. Those who had been so sure of their identifications had been proven wrong. Even Assemblyman McDermitt, who never forgot a face, didn't return to confirm his story as he vowed he would. Tooker was hopeful Wright and Keron would return from Brooklyn and Newark with good news, however, before he left for home on Thursday night, he would learn they too were empty-handed.

Friday, April 8 – Sunday, April 10, 1887

"Sergeant Conger! Sergeant Conger!"

It was still dark when Conger was awakened by a voice calling his name. Although he wasn't aware of the exact time, he knew it was very early and for someone to arouse him at such an hour, it was either a drunken prank or a matter of importance. Half asleep, he got up, and not knowing what to expect, he grabbed his nightstick. He lit a lantern and made his way to the side door. Outside, he saw two men.

"Who's out there?" he called. Somewhere in the distance, a dog started barking.

"George, it's me, David Cox."

"What time is it, deputy?"

"Just past four."

"What's the trouble? Who's that with you?"

"That's just it, Sergeant. I came across Mr. Hubbard here, wandering around in the fields near where the murder was. He was screamin' 'Murder, bloody murder!' at the top of his lungs. Mike Harlan saw me earlier and told me he saw him runnin' down his street screamin' about the murder, so I kept an eye out for him. Look at him. He don't look right."

The man looked up at Conger and said in a serious tone and with conviction, "Someone's out there who wants to kill me. You gotta go out and find 'em, and stop 'em. He's out there. I know it."

Edson Hubbard was a local real estate agent who had been brooding over the crime from the very beginning. His wife was so distressed that she had gone to see Doctor Cladek worried about her husband's mental state. She told the doctor the murder was the only topic on her husband's mind and that he talked about nothing else. She feared he would become sick over it. Conger could see her fears had come to pass and Hubbard had finally cracked.

"What do you want me to do with him, Sergeant?"

"Take him to the station and lock him up. Can't have him runnin' around all night scaring people. It'll be for his own good. The chief'll look into it in the mornin'."

Conger watched as Deputy Cox led Hubbard down the dark street, the silence of the early morning broken only by the intermittent sound of a barking dog.

~~~~~

The third session of the coroner's inquest opened at 10:00 a.m. on Friday, April 8. Once again, the council chambers were crowded. Unlike the first two meetings where the atmosphere was raucous, a feeling of impatience was now palpable in the air. No longer simply curious and looking to be entertained, the citizens came expecting some news that would begin to clear up the mystery and erase the fears hanging over the city. Unfortunately, as soon as Coroner Terrill called the meeting to order, it became apparent that little or no progress had been made and the coroner had nothing of significant importance to present. Terrill was officious in reporting that because there was not yet sufficient satisfactory evidence to bring before the jury, the hearings would not be able to proceed. He did offer a modicum of encouragement, however, stating the police were working on a new clue, altogether different from any previous ones, which might develop into something of value. The suggestion of a new angle excited the newsmen who immediately pressed the coroner for more details. Terrill sidestepped their inquiries and ended their questioning by changing the subject to other announcements.

The coroner reported that a funeral for the unknown girl would be held on the next Monday, April 11, at two o'clock at the First Presbyterian Church. The body would be interred in the Presbyterian Cemetery following the service. He went on to add, because of the decision to bury the body on Monday, the officials agreed to allow another public viewing on Sunday.

Terrill next announced that Samuel Tice, one of the twelve jurors, had been discharged from further duty on the panel. He explained that Tice was being excused at his own request due to his familiarity with William Keech and Clinton Froat, both of whom were still suspects.

None in the room appeared surprised by Tice's removal and many felt he was purposely taken off by the coroner. Not only had his reputation come into question, spread in large part since Tuesday by a vengeful Louis DeCamp, but also it was discovered he had recently spent time in jail.

The three items were all Terrill had on his agenda and before adjourning, he scheduled the next meeting for Friday, April 15. Even though not much was accomplished, reporters left hungry to find out more about the new police lead. The removal of Tice from the jury and rumors that the police were planning to search all the wells and cisterns in Milton indicated the authorities might now be of the opinion the crime was committed by a local. Keech and Froat were under suspicion, but perhaps the police now had their eyes on another Milton resident.

~~~~~

Earlier in the week, reporters had started sniffing around the farm of Dr. Charles Meeker with a special interest in Joe Reifel, a farmhand who worked and lived on the property. Reifel's home was a small outbuilding near the Jefferson Avenue corner of the farm, which he shared with Charlie Henderschott, a laborer who worked at Bloodgood's Mill. A religious sort, Reifel was an ardent supporter of the Salvation Army and was known to many by the sobriquet, "Salvation Joe." His prized possession was a keen-nosed Gordon setter who ran on a long lead within the boundaries of his fenced-in yard. The handsome hunting dog was the perfect watch dog and kept Reifel alerted to anyone's approach even when a hundred yards off.

At first, reporters and detectives interviewed Reifel as they had all other residents who lived in the vicinity of the crime, and only became suspicious of him when he gave contradictory answers to their questions. He altered his responses to questions concerning his movements the night of the murder, his accounts of his roommate's whereabouts, his practice of selling eggs, and the fact he heard no noises on the night of March 25. It was hard for anyone to believe his setter remained quiet when dogs further from the murder site were heard barking. One detective noted on the day he went to see Reifle, the setter started barking when he was still about five hundred feet from the house. The dog became so excited, Reifel came out into the yard, armed with a rifle to not only investigate the commotion, but to also demonstrate how annoyed he had become with all the intruders.

To give the reporters more reason to suspect Reifel, a story was forwarded by a neighbor, an affable Frenchman named Claude Gorisse, that on the night of the crime, he and his wife heard a woman's cries followed by the barking of Reifel's dog. Gorisse, who lived on Jefferson Avenue between Reifel's cabin and the murder scene, also told reporters he occasionally saw Reifel walk past his house in the direction of Central Avenue carrying a basket of eggs.

News of the Reifel connection was reported in all the newspapers prompting Chief Tooker to call the farmhand to his office to conduct his own interrogation. Tooker knew "Salvation Joe" to be a pretty good fellow, although not the brightest of young men. He felt it was very possible Reifel came under suspicion because he talked too much and likely forgot what he said from one reporter to the next. Reifel came to the office with no hesitation and was at ease as the chief went over an array of questions.

"Alright, Joe, what's goin' on?"

"What do you mean?"

"Your name's all over the papers, Joe. People think you might have killed the girl."

"It ain't so! I didn't kill nobody. They're makin' up stories about me."

"Well, you better get your story straight. Where were you that night, Joe? And I want the truth."

"I was at Baumgartner's on Grand. I met Jim Smith there and we walked back to my place."

"I read in one paper you said you were at Baker's that night. Why did you say that?"

"I don't know. I got mixed up on the nights."

"What time did you and Jim get to your place?"

"About nine o'clock."

"Was Charlie Henderschott there?"

"Yeah, he let us in."

"What did you fellas do that night?"

"We played a few hands a' cards 'till about nine-thirty and Jim went home. Me and Charlie said our prayers and went to bed."

"You were up after nine-thirty and didn't hear anything?"

"I didn't hear no screams and my dog was quiet. I told that to everybody who asked. I'd swear to it."

"What about the eggs, Joe? Do you carry eggs around in a basket?"

"I sell eggs some, but Old Man Gorisse is lyin'. He doesn't like me because he says religion's made me crazy. I told him he's a sinner, but he could still turn it around. God will forgive him."

Tooker didn't see any reason to continue. Personally, he didn't think Joe Reifel was the killer. "Alright, Joe, that'll be all. Get out of here and go home, and whatever you do, don't talk to any more reporters."

"I don't plan to. I locked my front gate and put a chain on the side gate. Charlie's making a sign to post on the fence."

Reifel left the office and walked straight home. When he got close to his cabin, he saw a reporter standing outside the locked gate, looking at a freshly painted sign, which read, Trespassing prohibited on these premises under penalty of the law. Reifel smiled to himself and passed by the man with no comment.

~~~~~

It was Friday afternoon, and no one was sure if the story emanated from the Western Union Telegraph Office, from a newspaperman just returning from New York City, or from some completely different source. The Brooklyn Police had arrested a man who confessed to the murder of the unknown girl! The news created great excitement throughout all parts of the city, and within minutes, a score of telegraph messages were on their way seeking more-detailed information. With the local authorities and the general populace waiting anxiously for replies, reporters rushed to the train depot to catch eastbound trains. Perhaps this would be the end of the mystery.

The story awaiting reporters at the Eighth Sub Precinct Station was a strange one, containing enough possibilities to make it plausible and yet enough weaknesses to make it worthless. According to the police, a barber named Theodore Heinzerling rushed into the station and announced he had the murderer in his shop. The suspect, whose name was given as Jacob Flath, had been hired by Heinzerling just three days before. Heinzerling described his new barber to be approximately thirty-two years old, a thin, nervous, dissipated-looking man with restless eyes. He wore a full beard the day he came in to apply for the job, but was clean-shaven, save for his mustache, when he came to work the next day. According to Heinzerling's statements, Flath's first day in the shop went without incident and he demonstrated the skills of a good barber. The second day, however, everything changed. The entire day he seemed nervous and whined about being afraid to be alone. He complained of not being able to sleep because of terrible nightmares, all dealing with violence, murder, and death. Heinzerling said he was concerned about his employee's condition, but did not suspect him of anything until the next day. That morning, Flath entered the shop with a frightened expression on his face and appeared to be laboring under great mental excitement. No sooner did his first customer sit back in the barber's chair than he told of a strange dream he had where he saw the Rahway murder being committed and he himself tangling with the killer. As he cut the customer's hair, he began to ramble like a lunatic and then startled everyone in the shop by wildly shouting, "Oh, so much blood! It was hard, very hard, but she brought it all on herself!" It was at this point, the unnerved Heinzerling, who now thought Flath was the murderer whose guilty conscience had finally got the best of him, hurried from the shop to alert the police.

Jacob Flath was shortly thereafter arrested and brought before Police Superintendent Campbell for questioning. Flath, whose demeanor exemplified a person at least partially insane, began the interview with a scattered account of events over the past few weeks.

"I come from Germany a few years ago. I been for past year working in barber shop in Elizabeth. I stop work on March 21, but did not leave Elizabeth until March 26. On that day, I catch the seven-thirty morning train to Jersey City. I sit next to man who has blood spots on his vest. This man could not button his coat to hide the vest because buttons were missing. The man had scratches on his face and hands. When he saw I was looking at him, he pulled his overcoat collar up to hide his face. When we get to Jersey City, the man disappeared in the crowd. From Jersey City, I go to Brooklyn and take job with Mr. Heinzerling. I have bad dreams the last few nights about the murder. It was a horrible thing. So much blood!"

Chief Campbell suddenly broke in and asked, "Why did you shave your beard off?"

Flath seemed caught off guard by this question, but replied, "Because I want to. For reasons of my own. I cut it off when I reach this city."

Next, Campbell showed him a picture of the murdered girl. "Do you know this girl?" Flath stared at the image and trembled. "I never see her before."

There was a pause. Campbell looked at the two officers who had been stationed in the room and told them to search the prisoner. Several items were removed from his pockets including two pawn tickets, a pair of cuff links and a number of newspaper clippings from German papers. One of the clippings contained an article describing how easily a man's head could be cut off. All the items were stained with blood.

"How is it that everything is covered with blood?" asked a surprised Chief Campbell.

"I got cut on the head in a fight in South Brooklyn. Some dummkopf smash me with a beer bottle."

"Did you kill the girl at Rahway?"

"I kill no one."

The superintendent believed him. The man was definitely unstable in the mind, but he didn't believe he was a killer. He suspected it was the entire mystery surrounding the murder that pushed him past the limits of sanity.

With no further questions, Campbell told the officers to lock him up on suspicion of murder. After the three left, the superintendent sat down and composed a message to be wired to the Mayor of Rahway. "Have suspect…Don't believe he's your murderer…Suspect has connection to Elizabeth…Clues might be there."

~~~~~

The rumors concerning the wells and cisterns in the Milton area proved to do nothing other than add a touch of humor to the case. John Linden, an amateur detective out of New York City, had been observed prowling around the yards and alleys in the vicinity of the crime under cover of darkness, fishing through the contents of cisterns and sinkholes looking for clues. Confronted by police, he told them he was working under the advice of a clairvoyant. Linden explained that the psychic had experienced a vision where the murderer buried his bloody clothes in a deep hole. When it was suggested to Chief Tooker that this was a lead worth pursuing, he replied, "I don't have enough manpower to waste searching through wells. It's all a bunch of nonsense." There were many, however, who disagreed, and felt at this point in the investigation, any lead, no matter how strange the source, was worth exploring.

~~~~~

Since the morning of the murder, a story had been quietly circulating that a handkerchief had been seen lying next to the girl's body. The story originated from one of the first visitors to the site who remained quite sure of what he saw. He believed someone, who was also present

The Case of the Unknown Woman

early on, picked it up and carried it off. Since Chief Tooker, Special Policeman Marsh, and former Chief Wright had arrived before most, there was a suspicion someone connected with the police had lifted it. Several reporters had kept after the story and were informed by sources that a handkerchief actually was there, and found within its folds was a lock of hair. When questioned, Tooker and Mayor Daly both denied the story. They were adamant no handkerchief ever existed nor were their police hiding such an item. Now, two weeks later, on this Saturday morning, it was revealed the local officials had not been quite so truthful.

Prosecuting Attorney William Wilson met with those reporters who were following this lead, and exhibited perhaps the best pieces of evidence yet offered. He displayed a man's handkerchief and a lock of coarse hair, black or at least dark brown in color, which he said was found at the side of the body. On close examination, the hair appeared to have been drawn out by force as the bulb of the hair was on it.

"I had not seen these pieces of evidence until today," Wilson announced. "These items were in the possession of the Rahway authorities, but were not given to me as they should have been. They finally turned them over to me this morning."

One of the reporters asked Wilson, "Why did the Rahway officials conceal them all this time?"

Wilson replied with a touch of annoyance, "I can't answer that question at the present time."

Other questions were thrown at Wilson, but he didn't respond to any. He simply said, "This is all I know of the matter and all I have for you today."

The reporters went away with interesting story lines to consider. Did the hair belong to the murderer? Could the hair color be accurately matched to a suspect? Did Rahway officials doubt William Keech's guilt from the outset because his hair was a lighter shade of brown than the lock of hair in the handkerchief? Was this the only evidence being withheld by City or County officials? Why did the Rahway authorities finally release these items? Once again, more clues only added to the confusion.

~~~~~

Mayor Daly had a bad feeling about the Jacob Flath confession even before he received the telegram from the Brooklyn Superintendent. He knew the news of a killer's confession and arrest would set the town abuzz, but he also knew if the reports proved to be erroneous, the people's ire would be directed toward him and his police force. There had been enough false alarms already, and the citizens were becoming dissatisfied with the way in which the whole official investigation was being conducted. With elections for City offices set for next Tuesday, the mayor was worried they would demonstrate their displeasure at the polls. Some light was needed to solve the mystery, so to help achieve that end, the mayor instructed Chief Tooker to turn over the handkerchief and hair strands they had been holding to the prosecutor.

~~~~~

By mid-morning, Detective Keron had arrived in Elizabeth with the assignment to uncover any facts that might connect the Brooklyn barber to the murder. Keron knew Elizabeth well, so finding the shop where Flath had been employed was not a problem. When the detective entered the shop, he found the owner, two other barbers, and four customers discussing the Flath story, which had appeared in the morning papers. Keron introduced himself and upon making known the purpose of his visit, all were eager to tell stories about the former barber. In each story, Flath was described as moody, irrational, quarrelsome, and unpredictable. The owner said he had to fire Flath because he was often disagreeable to his co-workers and customers. The shop owner told Keron, "The last straw came when he complained that one of the apprentices was trying to poison him. When I told him he was discharged, he flew into such a rage, I had to draw my revolver to drive him out of the shop."

When asked if they thought Flath was the Rahway murderer, they all shook their heads expressing the negative. One customer summed up the group's opinion when he stated, "Flath was bats, but he's not a killer. I can't see him killing that woman. Not the way she was killed, anyway."

Keron's next stop was the boardinghouse where Flath had resided. In an interview with the landlady, Keron learned that on the night of March 25, Flath was in another tenant's room playing pinochle. "There were four men playing cards that night and they played 'til 10:30," she said. She was positive of the date because it was the night he surprised her by announcing he was leaving in the morning. "He left early the next day. He gave me no notice. I'm sorta glad he's gone. He was a very peculiar man. I don't think he had all his senses."

Keron thanked her and left Elizabeth, having found no evidence to connect the strange barber to the crime.

~~~~~

Undertaker Ryno had been in the business for almost forty years and had never felt the tender emotion and genuine pity he had toward the body of the unknown woman. Even when preparing the remains of the poor souls who died during the cholera epidemic in 1849, he was able to keep himself emotionally removed from any of the individual victims. Likewise, when this bloodied corpse was brought to him, he worked on it with the detachment characteristic of a member of his profession, but in the intervening days, he came to feel sorry for and almost protective of the friendless girl. As he gently and carefully placed blooms of white and pink roses around the girl's head, he was annoyed that today, an additional public viewing would be held and the body once more displayed like some freak-show exhibit. He felt contempt toward both the people who came to see the body simply as a Sunday excursion trip, as well as the unprincipled ones who came with schemes to secure a reward. He opposed another open viewing arguing that the girl's facial features had changed markedly in the time she had been in the morgue and he didn't think she now looked like the same girl who was found two weeks earlier. He had serious doubts if anyone would be able to make a positive identification even if they had known her. He maintained it was long past the time for burial and was looking forward to tomorrow when the body would be laid to rest.

The final pubic viewing went just like the previous ones and with similar results. Despite the fact only two day's notice was given and this was Easter Sunday, upwards of two thousand people came and waited on line in the hot spring afternoon, jostling with one another for a chance to look at the yet unidentified face. Chief Tooker, Sergeant Conger, and ex-Chief Wright were again stationed by the bier to watch the faces of all who bent over the body. The clothing was brought back and mounted, and the articles of evidence once more neatly placed in the glass case. The line again moved slowly through the room and from time to time, someone would claim recognition and be pulled aside for questioning. Unfortunately, in each instance, the accounts lacked substantial credibility and it was surmised that most were made on the impulse of the moment.

Mr. E. A. Brickwedell of Hoboken, claimed the girl was his stepdaughter, Theresa Stohr, who left his home on March 10.

Marie Klein of Brooklyn said the girl was her sister, Annasteina, who arrived in the United States from Hungary in March.

Another Brooklynite, John Link, identified the girl as his niece, Mary. Link's identification was negated when he mentioned his niece had a scar on her leg caused by a burn she suffered some years before. The autopsy report gave no indication of a scarred leg.

Daniel Dudley, who came all the way from Lynn, Massachusetts, said the dead girl was his wife Florence. According to his story, she deserted him while they were visiting in Philadelphia in April of '86 and he had recently tracked her down to be somewhere outside of New York City.

Charles Moeckel and his wife thought the girl might be Julia Sinn, the daughter of Mrs. Moeckel from a previous marriage. The Moeckels moved to New York from Wilkes-Barre, Pennsylvania, five months ago leaving Julia at the Pennsylvania home. She wrote to her mother on a regular basis, but the letters stopped after February. Mrs. Moeckel continued to write to her daughter, but received no return letters.

Mrs. Martha Riley of New York City thought the girl might be Maggie Mullen, who left for Middletown, New York, in late February. According to relatives in Middletown, Maggie never reached that destination.

Frank O'Neill came from Troy, New York, looking for his sister, Kate. He was very sure it was Kate until he realized the dead girl's ears were not pierced. His sister's ears were pierced and he noted, "She always took great care in choosing what earrings to wear when traveling."

Hilda Hanson of Passaic believed the girl to be Matilda Carlson, who arrived at Castle Garden on December 9. Mrs. Hanson said Matilda came to Passaic to work as a domestic for the J. R. Sherwood family, who were neighbors of Mrs. Hanson. On January 1, Matilda disappeared. Mrs. Hanson said Matilda carried an umbrella like the one in the case. She also wore an engagement ring engraved with both her initials and those of her lover. When the rings worn by the murdered girl were taken from the display case and examined, no initials were found.

An old German named Frank Wacher came from Paterson to view the body. He claimed the girl, whose name he gave as Katherina Thant, was a fellow passenger on the French steamer *Champaine* out of Austria. The ship arrived at Castle Garden on March 17.

Two additional identifications were given that, although officials had little hope they would prove to be accurate, did require follow-up investigation. Chief of Detectives Patrick Kelly of Philadelphia came to Rahway thinking the girl might be Clara Wilson. This young girl, whose age he placed around twenty-four, had asked for lodging at the Twenty-first District Station House on March 18. She left the next morning carrying a satchel and a basket similar to the ones in the case. Detective Kelly was shown the photographs of the girl, but couldn't be certain of his identification. He left, promising to send two other officers from his force to view the body.

The second identification was even more intriguing. Otto Heisler of New York City identified the girl as Mina Noorz, whom he met on the Red Line Steamer *Westerland* from Saxony. The name Noorz aroused immediate interest. The white handkerchief discovered in the murdered girl's satchel was embroidered with the same name. According to Heisler, Noorz was accompanied by her lover, Max Kinder, a small, but well-proportioned man, who was gruff and disrespectful to her the entire voyage. Heisler was of the opinion he even beat her on occasion. After becoming friendly with the girl, he learned she was going to marry Kinder when they reached America and that they had plans to buy a farm near Newark. She also told her newfound friend she was carrying two monetary drafts, one for $800, and the other for $1,200. Before they reached Castle Garden on January 14, she came to Heisler with tears in her eyes and told him her betrothed had taken possession of the larger draft. Heisler lost track of the pair when they reached shore, but he often thought of Mina and worried about her future with Kinder.

Initially, the story sounded plausible, however, upon examination, Heisler's identification was riddled with problems. When he viewed the body, he complained the face was so bruised and swollen he couldn't be sure if it was Mina. He was unable to identify any of the clothing or other articles and when shown the photographs, he said they didn't look like the girl he met aboard ship. Finally, it came out he was not totally certain of the girl's surname. He said it was more like Noose or Norris. *The New York Herald* reporter who covered Heisler's story from the time he first made his claim in New York, told authorities he would go to Castle Garden to review the passenger lists of the "Westerland."

~~~~~

The end of the day found Daniel Ryno in a bad mood. For six hours, he had stood next to the coffin watching the long line of visitors file quietly past the unknown woman. Few said anything at all, but only glanced soberly at the haunting face and then moved on, satisfied to have seen the curiosity. Those who did speak softly muttered words as, "Poor Girl" or "How Dreadful." He had tired of the procession, and just prior to closing for what he thought was the last viewing, a messenger brought a letter from the office of Prosecutor Wilson. The notice instructed Ryno that the body was not to be buried until an order was issued directly from his office. It also stated that, although the funeral may be held on Monday (tomorrow), the body was to be placed in the receiving vault after the service and later returned to the morgue. It was apparent the County authorities still held out hope that someone from somewhere would appear, recognize the girl, and end the mystery. Ryno strongly disagreed and wondered how much longer they expected him to be able to preserve the body.

Monday, April 11, 1887

The Reverend William Alfred Gay was in his third year as pastor of the First Presbyterian Church, a congregation whose roots dated all the way back to 1741. "Old First" was the city's most influential church community and at forty-two, the young minister felt privileged to be serving as only the ninth pastor in the church's one hundred and forty-six year history. Always involved with issues of the city, the congregation and their pastor were vocal in their opposition to the manner in which the remains of the murdered girl were being treated. Upset by the lack of dignity and decorum during the public viewings and appalled that so many days had passed and the woman was still not buried, the church members appealed to Mayor Daly to do what was decent. The church's cemetery committee had even selected a plot for the final resting place, should the body be interred in Rahway. Although no permission was granted for a burial, the authorities decided the public viewings would cease and a funeral service could be scheduled. It was natural the mayor suggest the funeral be held in the Presbyterian Church and that the Reverend Mr. Gay handle the arrangements.

An hour before the two o'clock service was to commence, the horse-drawn hearse from Ryno's arrived in front of the stately church. In the absence of friends or relatives, six reporters from New York newspapers served as pallbearers and carried the handsome white coffin up the stone steps and into the vestibule. The coffin was set down and Undertaker Ryno unfastened the silver clasps and opened the top portion of the lid to expose the face of the girl. A pane of glass covered the body, which was dressed neatly in a white satin shroud. A group of Sunday school children handed Ryno a beautiful "pillow" of flowers consisting of roses, lilies, and azaleas, which he placed on the closed portion of the lid. The undertaker himself contributed a cluster of callas and roses and a local florist donated green sprays and other assorted bouquets creating the impression the girl, although unknown, was not without friends. A conspicuous silver plate was affixed to the side of the coffin with the inscription:

> Died March 25, 1887
> Cruelly Slain
> A Woman and a Stranger
> Aged about Twenty-Five Years Old

For the next hour, an immense throng from the town and surrounding communities walked past the casket for a last look or to offer a final prayer. Members of prominent families, workingmen and women, the young and the old, all came to gaze through the glass, many pausing to show expressions of deep and undisguised sympathy. County and local members of government were present to pay their final respects. The crowd, which was one of the largest the town had ever seen to attend a funeral, ultimately filled the sanctuary to its capacity.

Two gongs of the steeple bell were the signal for organist Frederick Dunham to play the low dirge to accompany the procession. Pastor Gay led the participating clergymen, who included the Reverends W. H. Ruth of Second Methodist, Jeremiah Cowins of First Methodist, William Rollinson of the Baptist Church, and Carl Albrecht of the German Presbyterian Church, down the long aisle. A solemn Mayor Daly walked behind the clergy, followed by the closed casket borne by the six reporters. Upon reaching the end of the aisle, the ministers stepped up to the chancel area, the mayor took his seat in the front pew with other officials, and the coffin was placed on a bier in front of the pulpit. Two stanzas of the hymn, "Jesus, Lover of My Soul," were then sung by the congregation. Pastor Ruth read the Tenth Psalm, which contained the suggestive verse, "He sitteth in the lurking places of the village: in the secret places doth he murder the innocent." Pastor Cowins offered a prayer asking God to help identify the girl and help solve the mystery, and also to protect those present from being struck by a murderous hand.

Pastor Gay next rose and stood behind the pulpit to give the address. The text he chose was taken from Matthew VII: 2, "Whatsoever ye would that men should do to you, do ye even so to them." The minister looked down at the casket for a few long moments and then, slowly lifting his head and looking out over his audience, he began his impassioned sermon message.

"We meet today under the shadow of a great mystery. In a suburb of this city, an unknown woman has been murdered by an unknown assassin. Silently the victim of this foul deed walked our thoroughfares. In secret, the brutal monster planned the atrocious crime. Unseen by human eye, he struck the blows which hurried an immortal soul into another world. Unnoticed the coward fled, with blood upon his hands, blood upon his person, and blood upon his heart. A few hours passed away and the startling news passed from lip to lip, 'A woman has been murdered!' Following this abrupt statement of fact, came the anxious inquiry, 'Who is she?' But the question remains unanswered and the poor bruised and mutilated body lies in our presence.

"Such horror over an inhumane act, such widespread and continuous sympathy for an unfortunate creature, and such a deep sense of outraged justice, have never before agitated the minds of our people. Our perception of this great wrong, of this almost unparalleled brutality, of this gross insult to womanhood, is something that belongs to consciousness. It is like a blow, which rankles in the breast, rather than burns upon the cheek. Had it been a man who fell that dreadful night, even then every emotion of our souls would have been aroused. Instead, it was a female, evidently a poor, homeless, stranger, and our feelings struggle in vain for an adequate expression.

"In bringing before you the 'Golden Rule,' I make no application of its precepts to the fiend who bears the mark of a murderer upon his brow. I leave him to face the law that he has violated, the woman he has wronged, and the God whose curse rests upon his crimson soul. We turn from the butcher to the butchered and our contempt and loathing are changed to pity. Unknown, saved by the absent friends who call her name in vain, she lies before us in the quiet sleep of death. She drifted into this community. She died here. And she shall rest under the protective wings of Christian sympathy.

"In the first place, we are here this hour to practice the instructions of the 'Golden Rule' because the victim of man's wickedness was a woman. She was helpless. Perhaps she was a stranger in a strange land. Undoubtedly, she was a weary wanderer far from home. Moreover, our hearts melt with pity, as we think of her lonely journey, of her fearful night struggle, of her maidenly terror, of her horrible death. If Jesus were on this platform at this time I am sure that He would say, 'Whatsoever ye would that men should do to you, do ye even so to them. In as much as ye have done it unto the least of these my little ones, ye have done it unto me.'

"Again, we have met in this sacred house, and we give this lacerated body a Christian burial, because we live under the shadow of the cross. We cannot forget the example and the teachings of our Master. The 'Golden Rule' projects itself in the theory and practice of the present. As soon as it was known that this person was to find a sepulcher in Rahway, hundreds of hearts revolted at the idea of giving her other than a suitable burial. Lots were offered unsolicited. The necessary funds were easily procured. Any church in the city would, undoubtedly, have been thrown open. For the spirit of Christ is abroad in the land. We could not help her when she was alive, so we give expression to our sympathy now that she is dead. As we would that others should do for our friends, under similar conditions, so we do this day for one whose friends are strangers to us all.

"But some parent may respond, 'There is no danger of my daughter being murdered like this.' No danger? Then why this long procession of pale-faced friends who have been filing past these remains for two weeks? Why those numerous telegrams and letters, which have come from so many states in the Union? It may seem like a contradiction, and yet this dark mystery has thrown light upon other mysteries. Fathers, mothers, brothers, and sisters by the scores, if not hundreds, have stood by the side of this poor body, fearing, and yet hoping, that here might be the loved one who had so suddenly, so strangely disappeared. Instead of thanking God that we are better than others, let us 'Do unto others, as we would that others should do unto us.'

"A second thought in the same vein. If the assassin lives in our city, and let us hope that he does not, then which of our homes is safe from this red-handed murderer? Let us hope that this atrocious crime may prove a mountain upon the head of the criminal, that it may rankle and fester like a poisoned arrow in his soul, and that the blood of this poor creature may obstruct his vision and haunt his night dreaming, until he shall confess his guilt before his fellowmen, and satisfy the demand of outraged justice with his life.

"I seem to see before me a humble home, where father and mother are waiting for a message that never comes. Eyes are filled with tears, and hearts are heavy, because there are no tidings of the absent daughter. The hours are like days, while days lengthen into weeks, as the lonely parents watch, wait, and hope. But, the child cometh not. The Post brings no letter of love.

"Perhaps there are brothers and sisters; and they too long for some word from the dear one. But the familiar step is heard no more upon the threshold, the well-known voice answers not to the anxious call.

"Absent and unknown friends, she for whom you wait has fallen into the snare of the fowler. The knife of a murderer has done its cruel work. No ear but that of God heard her bitter cry for help. No heart but the heart of the Infinite listened to her last wail of anguish. She fell by the wayside when the night was dark and the air chill and damp. Her dying bed was the cold ground. However, there were Samaritans who passed by that way and they lifted her tenderly from her blood-stained couch. In long processions, they looked down upon her unconscious form and they are carrying her to her eternal home, as you would have done if she died in your arms. Absent, unknown friends, the law that fell from the lips of Jesus is our guide, and we are doing unto others as we would that others should do unto us. We think of you today, strangers though you may be, and we pray to the Father of the fatherless and to the widow's God that He will bless you and comfort you in your loneliness, and that He will give you a double portion of His grace to sustain you while you are waiting and hoping for the dear one whom you shall see no more on this earth."

At the conclusion of the dramatic and eloquent oration, the assembly was profoundly moved as evidenced by the soft weeping heard throughout the sanctuary.

Seventy-year-old William Rollinson, the well-respected and long-time pastor of the Baptist Church, gave the closing prayer asking God to work the conscience of the murderer night and day, to tug at his bosom and goad him to confess. The service concluded with a benediction given by Pastor Albrecht, after which the standing congregation sang two verses of, "Nearer My God to Thee."

The impressive service now over, the coffin was lifted and carried to the waiting hearse. Three other carriages, reserved for the clergy and other dignitaries, and a large number of persons walking behind, followed the funeral coach down the dusty road to the church cemetery. Once inside the old burial ground, Pastor Gay read the words of committal and the body was placed in a receiving vault.

A great number of people were present in the cemetery, but sadly, not a single one of the many who claimed they knew the girl was to be seen. Many lingered around the vault for an hour or more after the heavy door was shut, rehashing all the events and rumors of the past weeks, and only left when the caretaker came to close the gate. With the last of the curious gone, Ryno, acting on orders from Prosecutor

Wilson, transported the body back to the morgue. It would be returned to the icebox for preservation as long as possible or until someone came along to identify it.

Tuesday, April 12, 1887 – Saturday, April 16, 1887

For the first time since the dreadful Saturday morning when the mutilated corpse was found, the murdered girl was not the all-engrossing topic of discussion. On this day, the knots of people congregating on street corners, the groups in neighborhood bars, barber shops and general stores, and the men at their workbenches were debating over which candidates to vote for in the city elections. Every office including the mayor, members of the common council, water commissioners, freeholders, coroner, school commissioners, assessors, and justice of the peace were on the ballot and in this politically active community, there was serious campaigning for each position.

Mayor Daly made it clear he would not attend to any matters concerning the murder case as he planned to put all his energies into working on getting re-elected. Tooker, whose position as police chief would be jeopardized if Daly were defeated, left Conger in charge at headquarters in order to spend the entire day electioneering. Former Chief Wright, who was running for freeholder as a Republican, also took a break from the investigation so he could canvass for votes. Even Undertaker Ryno, on the ballot for school commissioner, was in and out of the morgue to ensure his campaign didn't falter.

However, of all the seats, it was the contest for mayor that would be the most hotly contested. The Democrats had been long waiting this day to remove the man who had bucked the party leaders since his election two years ago on the Democratic ticket. One power broker with a particular dislike for Daly was First Ward Democratic boss

Michael Whalen. Whalen was the proprietor of the First Ward Hotel and Saloon, a popular watering hole for political hangers-on. Located on Main Street directly across from the residence of the mayor, Daly had three months earlier opposed Whalen's application for a liquor license renewal. At the January meeting of the License and Law Committee, Daly presented the committee members with a letter in which he described Whalen's establishment as a public nuisance and Whalen himself as "not a fit person to be licensed." He alleged that persons had been seen going into the hotel on Sundays and leaving in an intoxicated condition. The mayor stated he had received complaints that Whalen's customers frequently vomited on the walkways in front of the building, used foul and unseemly language, and had even exposed themselves in full view of pedestrians and nearby residents. The letter also noted that minors were observed coming out of the saloon carrying pails of beer. These were serious complaints and the law-abiding citizens applauded Daly's effort to "clean up" the city. The Democratic councilmen who controlled the committee, however, disregarded the mayor's protest and granted the application.

Whalen had won the battle, but was outraged by the mayor's interference and pledged to oust him from office. Together with his hand-picked mayoral candidate, James Silvers, a wealthy coal dealer, they set out to discredit the mayor. During Daly's first term, the mayor had made the issue of the huge city debt a top priority. Whalen and Silvers attacked his plan to reduce the debt, arguing it would create greater financial hardships. They also criticized the way the murder investigation was being handled and blamed the mayor for the lack of progress. Whalen sent his political cronies through the neighborhoods spreading the notion that because the mayor had bungled things so badly, the cowardly murderer would probably never be apprehended and the girl would go to her grave unnamed.

Usually a small town election held little interest for anyone outside the community, but with all the reporters on hand, the story was covered in several dailies outside the city limits. The race for mayor remained close throughout the day and by the time the voting was over, it was difficult to declare a clear winner. One New York reporter, trying to scoop his rivals, set off for the telegraph office to wire his editor that Silvers had won. Those who waited, got the correct results. Daly was reelected with a total of seven hundred and five votes, beating his Democratic opponent by the narrow margin of sixteen votes. George Wright became a freeholder, but Undertaker Ryno lost his bid for school commissioner to ice dealer George White by seventy votes.

The Case of the Unknown Woman

Sergeant Conger's report on the day's activities contained several items of interest, two of which put claims of identification to rest. Sergeants Lattimer and Doneghn of the Philadelphia Police Department arrived with a letter of introduction from Chief of Detectives Kelly requesting permission for the two officers to view the body to verify if the girl was Clara Wilson. When brought to the morgue, neither was able to make a positive identification. Otto Heisler's belief that the girl was Mina Noorz was proven inaccurate after the *New York Herald* reporter returned from Castle Garden having found nothing. Carefully checking the ship's registries covering the period from January through March, he was unable to find any names remotely similar to Mina Noorz or her supposed traveling companion and lover, Max Kinder.

For those who came with new claims, Conger recorded their names and a brief summation of their stories while informing them that no action would be taken until after the election. Mrs. Gustav Kakerbeck was in from New York City to share with the authorities her belief that the victim might be Annie Martin, a young girl who lived in her boarding house a few months ago. She did not wish to visit the morgue and simply said she felt it was her duty to report her feelings. Mr. and Mrs. John Hand of Plainfield thought the girl might be Emmie Edsel. They told the sergeant, the girl stopped by their home in January after being chased from her home in New Market by her stern stepmother. Former Elizabeth Chief of Police Robert Yates was annoyed that he would not be able to meet with Tooker, as he was certain he had a good lead. He brought with him a woman who was an intimate friend of Louisa Holm, the person Yates identified as the murdered girl. He and the woman would return first thing in the morning to relate their story.

~~~~~

Chief Tooker pulled his watch from his pocket. It was just past 9:00 a.m. Election Day had been a long one for him, made longer by the post election celebration of which he was a happy and relieved participant. Now, back at his desk and only slightly suffering from the effects of the night's festivities, he sat looking through Conger's report and thinking about the investigation. It vexed him that two and a half weeks after the crime, he was still without a hard clue and he found it incredible that so many people had viewed the body, yet no one could make a satisfactory identification. He knew the line of persons with new claims would continue, but he now faced a real fear that the riddle of the girl's name might never be solved. The thought gave him a dull ache and as he began to focus on the report, a form filled the doorway. Tooker looked up and recognized the man. He knew Yates from his days when he was Chief of the Elizabeth Police and he didn't especially like him. Yates had enjoyed the power that goes along with being in charge of a large city police force and looked down on the officers from smaller towns.

"Glad to see you're back to work." There was a touch of sarcasm in his voice. "I was by yesterday, but they said you were out. May I come in? I think I have the answers you're lookin' for."

"Have a seat."

Before Yates entered, he stepped aside and allowed a woman to go in ahead of him. After both were seated, he presented his account. He had reason to believe the woman lying in Ryno's was a young Dane by the name of Louisa Holm. The woman who was with him was introduced as Mrs. Florence Clink, a close friend of Louisa, both born in the same town in Denmark. Mrs. Clink sought out the Elizabeth Police after reading about the murder, fearing the girl might be her friend whom she had last seen two or three days after March 8. Louisa had been living in Elizabeth with George Benson, a carpenter, but left him because he physically abused her. She stopped by Mrs. Clink's apartment to say goodbye and tell her she was moving to New York City. Mrs. Clink gave her a green dress to wear while traveling. It later came to Mrs. Clink's attention that Louisa had gotten into some minor trouble, was arrested, and spent a few days at Blackwell's Island. She was released around the time of the murder.

"Have you seen the body?" Tooker directed the question to Mrs. Clink, but Yates answered.

"We went to the morgue yesterday, but it was closed. We wasted a whole day here while everyone in your town was playin' politics."

Tooker disregarded the pointed remark and simply said, "The morgue's open today. Let's go take a look."

The group of reporters who were always present to question those who had been in to see the chief was waiting outside on the sidewalk, but this morning it was the reporters who had the news. They rushed over to Tooker as he came through the door.

"A story just leaked out of the county offices that there's a scar on the back of the girl's calf that was never reported in the autopsy."

"What's goin' on? Last week we found out you were hidin' a clue and now it's them."

"Got anything to say, Chief?"

Tooker was flushed, but did his best to keep his composure. "If this is true, it's an outrage. Here I've had men and women coming day after day and I've been telling them there was not a mark or blemish on the girl. We've sent hundreds of printed descriptions all over the country saying the same thing. If someone came looking for a scar, that might have settled it. It sounds just like the type of mark a parent or sister would be sure to know."

"Why do you think the County kept this a secret?"

"Right now I can't say. But I'm sure you boys will get the answers before I do." The sarcasm was now in Tooker's voice.

Having taken Tooker's comments, the reporters hurried out to catch the couple that had just left the office. Tooker decided not to follow. Although the news of the scar upset him, it didn't surprise him. There was a long-standing rivalry between the two towns and from the beginning, instead of an atmosphere of cooperation, there was one of competition. It was obvious to him that the Elizabeth officials, Coroner Terrill, Prosecutor Wilson, and Doctor Mravlag, the physician in charge of the autopsy, were trying to conduct the case by themselves, while ignoring the local officers. Rahway residents were indignant that the Elizabeth group had too strong a hand in the overall investigation and felt it was the bureaucracy of the county that was retarding any progress. Tooker acknowledged this was the reality of the situation, but also realized finding answers would only be made more difficult under these circumstances.

~~~~~

Having been caught in a deception, Coroner Terrill and Doctor Mravlag cleverly deflected any appearance of wrongdoing. When asked by a reporter why a full and complete description had not been given to the public, Terrill responded that it had been done. Asked about the scar, Terrill replied, "I saw the mark as the body was being prepared for the autopsy. I did not think much of it as a means of identification because it was in such a position that I doubted any but her most intimate friends would ever have noticed it, and it is not likely that anyone would ever remember it." Dr. Mravlag played innocent stating, "It is a surprise to me that an official statement of the physical description of the girl has not been given to the public. I think that any intimate friend of the murdered woman might be able to identify her by that scar. It is evidently from an ulcer and several years old. It is perfectly white and very noticeable." Asked why he hadn't pressed for an official public announcement, the doctor stated in a matter of fact manner, "It was not my business. After I finished the post-mortem, my work was done. I thought no more about the matter until the reporters questioned me last night."

The reporters who trailed Chief Yates and Mrs. Clink to the morgue came away disappointed. The woman could not with any certainty identify the body as being the remains of Louisa Holm. In addition, when shown the victim's green dress, Mrs. Clink admitted it was not the one she had given her friend.

~~~~~

The suspicions surrounding Joe Reifel were lessened on Friday by the appearance of two communications. Mayor Daly produced a telegram he had received from Dr. Charles Meeker, Reifel's employer and owner of the estate on which Reifel lived. Although the doctor was wintering in Florida, news of the murder had reached that southernmost state and he had read the reports implicating his worker. He had been sent a photograph of the basket found near the body to ascertain if it came from his farm. His message to the mayor made it clear it was not from his house, nor did he ever see such a basket anywhere on his property.

The second item to put doubt in Reifel's guilt was a letter to the editor, which ran in the *National Democrat*, a local weekly. The letter was from Claude Gorisse, the neighbor who claimed to have seen Reifel pass his home carrying a basket of eggs. It read as follows: "Mr. Editor: There was an article in last Sunday's *World*, which stated that I had seen Joseph Reifel often going to town with eggs, by way of Jefferson Avenue. I was asked if I had ever seen him going to town with eggs and I said I had, but not that way. He always went directly through Hamilton Street or Westfield Avenue. Mrs. Gorisse did not hear cries the night of the murder; she merely heard the dogs bark. The reporters generally exaggerated and misrepresented what was told them."

A story as fascinating as this murder had become, lent itself perfectly to those over-ambitious scribes who were more interested in solving the crime and selling papers then in objectively presenting the facts. These eager writers brazenly embellished their stories to fit their particular angles thus creating sensational stories, but at the same time adding confusion to an already muddled investigation.

This was not the philosophy of the two local papers, *The National Democrat,* and its Republican counterpart, *The New Jersey Advocate*. Published and controlled by Lewis S. Hyer, the *Democrat* had early on made an editorial decision not to give extensive coverage to the murder. Hyer believed the crime put his town in a bad light and the massive publicity it generated would have negative effects. In the issue that came out on the Friday after the murder, he wrote an editorial stating the paper's position. "Some of our readers may be disappointed because we have not devoted more space to the details of the terrible tragedy that has occurred in our midst, by enlarging upon the facts, giving the numerous rumors, and conjectures, etc. concerning it, and making more of a sensation generally. As an explanation, we will say that we do not belong to the class of journalism known as sensationalists. The naked facts are horrible enough, without coloring or dwelling upon them. We have endeavored to note all points that may tend in any way to unravel the mystery, which appears to surround the whole affair—to identify the victim and to apprehend the perpetrator of the dreadful act, in which we hope the authorities and detectives will be successful."

~~~~~

At ten o'clock Friday morning, Coroner Terrill assembled his jury in the Common Council room, and as he did on three prior occasions, postponed the inquest, reasoning he still had no concrete evidence upon which to work. The announcement startled the crowd that had come expecting to hear the progress being made in the investigation. Noticeably more impatient and irritable than they had been at the previous meetings, they shouted questions at the coroner and yelled unflattering remarks at him and the jury members. Terrill understood the crowd's frustration and pointed out that he too was upset by the delay. The next session was scheduled for Tuesday, April 19, and he tried to assure them he would do everything in his power to see that the inquest commenced on that day.

The new date did not satisfy many of the exasperated citizens and Terrill and the jury members had all they could handle to work their way to the exits. As the audience crowded out behind the officials, one angry citizen said to those around him, "It looks like they don't want to have the girl identified at all, for some reason or other." The comment was greeted with nods of affirmation as this attitude was beginning to take hold, especially for those of the cynical nature.

~~~~~

Saturday began with the repudiation of two identifications when the alleged victims walked into town, proving beyond question the accounts of their demise were groundless. Emmie Edsel, the woman who was reportedly chased from her home by her abusive stepmother, was in New York City when she read the stories naming her as the murder victim. Unnerved by the articles, she caught a train to Rahway and upon arrival, noticed several reporters on the platform. She went directly to them, introduced herself confidently, and stated, "I'm alive and want everybody to know it. As you can see, I'm not yet ready to be put on ice!" She asked to see the murdered woman and was escorted to the morgue by the newsmen who sensed a good story. After viewing the body and carefully examining the woman's garments, she commented haughtily, "Good heavens! Did anyone ever suppose that I wore such clothes as that? I've got a little more style about me!"

A few hours later, a man and woman approached Sergeant Conger who was standing outside the police station. The man was unkempt in appearance and looked as though he hadn't slept for days. His female companion was a brown-haired, buxom girl with large blue eyes. Conger, showing no unusual interest in the pair, officiously asked the man what business he had with the police. Conger's demeanor changed completely when the scruffy man said his name was George Benson and the woman was Louisa Holm. Suddenly alert, Conger opened the door and called to Tooker, "Chief, there's some people out here you gotta meet." Tooker looked up from his desk to see his sergeant followed by the two strangers. "What is it, George?" Tooker asked as he focused on the shabby man.

"Remember the story about a girl in Elizabeth who disappeared after she left the man she was living with 'cause he beat her? Well, meet Louisa Holm and the guy she lived with, George Benson. He's the man Chief Yates figured was the killer."

Benson, who was quiet to this point, burst out in anger at the mention of Yates. "I'm gonna sue that cop for damages! He's got his nerve going to the papers tying me to the murder. I couldn't believe it when I read the stories saying I was a suspect. I knew Louisa was somewhere in New York, so I went to find her so I could clear my name. My God, I spent three days and nights runnin' around the city looking for her. Well, I found her and brought her here to prove she's alive and I want you to tell that to the papers."

After answering several questions to prove their identities, the two left, bound for Elizabeth where they planned to hire a lawyer and begin a suit against Chief Yates.

~~~~~

No sooner was one identification discredited, then others were submitted, each warranting at least initial attention. Tooker and Mayor Daly were continuing to receive letters and telegrams on a daily basis, and people from states as far off as Maine, Ohio, and Virginia were still coming to the station with their stories about missing women. William Holle of Troy, New York, wrote a lengthy letter to the authorities with fears the girl might be his niece, Rosa Bada. According to Holle, Rosa left Baltimore for Troy on Tuesday, March 15, but never got there. He calculated that to reach Troy, the train would pass through Rahway. Continuing to supply information, Holle wrote that his niece came to this country three years ago from Germany and lived and worked in Baltimore. Knowing she was homesick and without family, Holle and his wife invited her to come live with them. Overjoyed with the invitation, she responded she would be in Troy sometime in March. Both aunt and uncle couldn't understand why she had not yet arrived or why she hadn't written to inform them of the cause of her delay. When Holle wrote to her employer in Baltimore, he replied he was of the opinion she had left on March 15 by way of the Pennsylvania Railroad.

The story sounded plausible until the girl's description was given. Hair and eye color matched and the girl's ears were not pierced, but Rosa was said to be about eighteen, slender, and well developed. The age and body type did not at all resemble the victim, and the letter was placed in the file with the many others that required no follow-up.

~~~~~

It was around 3:00 p.m., when Mrs. Agnes Space met with Chief Tooker and gave such a good description of the victim, he sent for Mayor Daly and Coroner Terrill to take part in the interview. It was Mrs. Space's contention that the murdered girl was her sister, Mary Dorman, who recently started from Scotland, but had not yet arrived. Had she landed, she was expected to go directly to Mrs. Space's home in Deckertown. She was long overdue. Mrs. Space described Mary as having a medium build, not much over five feet tall, and about twenty-five years of age. She said her sister had blue eyes and brown hair and never wore earrings.

"Did she have any marks or scars on her body?" It was the coroner who posed the question.

"Yes. Mary had a scar on the back of her leg between the knee and ankle. She was cut by a sickle while working in the fields by our home. I'd guess it happened some ten years ago."

The three officials looked at one another and agreed Mrs. Space should be taken to the morgue.

The scene at Ryno's turned out to be the saddest and most melancholy since the body was first displayed. Of the thousands who shuffled past the coffin, none showed more genuine emotion than Mrs. Space. The woman stood quietly looking down at the body, with both hands grasping the side of the coffin. She gave a heavy sigh, her shoulders trembled, and she began to sob. The undertaker, standing next to her, put one hand on top of hers and lay the other gently on her shoulder. They stood like this for several minutes with no words spoken. Mrs. Space took a deep breath and let it out, relaxing her hold on the coffin to wipe her eyes. She reached down and softly touched the girl's cold cheek with the back of her fingers. After another deep breath, she turned to the officials and said sadly, "It is my sister."

The usually austere coroner showed a compassionate side and asked Mrs. Space if she would please look at the scar. "I apologize for this request, but we must be certain." Ryno uncovered the limb and turned it so the mark could be seen. Seeing the white gash, Mrs. Space again began to cry, this time more heavily, and would have fallen had not the chief been near to support her.

Once her composure was regained, the woman was brought to Ryno's office to discuss what other information might be gathered to prove beyond doubt the victim was Mary Dorman. The coroner served as the spokesman. "I feel you've been sincere in all you've told us and the description you gave prior to seeing the remains is most accurate. And, if I may add, to me, you resemble the girl a great deal."

Mrs. Space acknowledged the comment. "We do look alike, however, I have another sister, Jane, who resembles Mary even more. I would like to bring her here to identify our sister."

"I would be most appreciative if you would do that. We look forward to meeting her and hope she will be able to supply us with information to aid our investigation."

Mrs. Space bid the gentlemen a good day and left the morgue. Coroner Terrill, Mayor Daly, and Chief Tooker were in agreement the identification was so complete there was a very good chance the mystery could be over. Yet each knew, with all that had transpired since the case began, it was still too early to give the girl a name.

Sunday, April 17, 1887

The bundles of New York papers were tossed from the baggage car of the Sunday morning local and fell heavily onto the quiet platform. Freight handler Anthony Straub walked stiffly to the stacks and bent over to pick up two piles. In the dim dawn light, his eyes caught the headlines of the *New York World*:

THE RAHWAY VICTIM
She Was in All Probability
Ana Christine Larsen

    The tiered headlines continued down the column, but Straub stopped reading and called excitedly to young Jesse Scudder who was just now getting to the station to pick up the morning papers for his route. Straub called to him, "Hey, boy! Hurry up and get over here!" The boy quickened his pace and reached Straub who handed him a folded paper and told him to take it to the mayor as fast as possible. "Wake him up if you have to. Just make sure he gets this paper." Without pausing to question the baggage man, Scudder lit out on his errand.
    By 9:00 a.m., both Mayor Daly and Chief Tooker had read over the entire text of the *World*'s story a dozen times. The report, which one of the layered headlines stated was the, "Startling result of long and careful investigation by *World* reporters," not only named the victim, but also offered the identity of the murderer, as well as the motive.
    According to the story, a young Danish woman named Ana Christine Larsen arrived at Castle Garden on March 2 (When entry

records were checked, Larsen's name was listed as an arrival.). It was the opinion of the paper that she came to this country for the sole purpose of finding her estranged male companion, Carl Woolf. Larsen had been in the United States three years before and had worked on a farm in Roselle owned by the noted sculptor, Count Leopold Zaleski. It was Zaleski and his wife who provided the basic framework for the story.

Two days after the murder, Mrs. Zaleski and a friend, Mrs. Wohllruck, went to Ryno's morgue to view the body. As soon as she saw it, she became very emotional. She was positive this was the same girl who had worked on her husband's farm in the summer of '84. When Sergeant Conger, who was on duty near the coffin, noticed her reaction and came over to question her, she ran out of the building in tears. The two women quickly boarded their carriage and rode out of town. A reporter from the *World* saw the woman was in distress, and without giving the appearance of having any interest, followed them to Roselle. Once at the farm, the reporter began questioning the Count and his wife and a new angle of investigation was underway.

The next day, Count Zaleski went to Rahway and he too came away quite certain the murdered girl was Ana Larsen. The Zaleskis told the reporter they would not make their identification known to the authorities for fear they might imperil an innocent man. The *World* reporter agreed it would be best to keep their information to themselves.

Count Leopold Chilchen de Zaleski was born in Zalasia, Russia, in 1818, the son of one of the country's most noted physicians. Growing up as a member of Russian nobility, he was raised to be an educated gentleman. He was instructed in the fields of the Arts and Sciences, was introduced to the world of culture, and was also taught the manly skills necessary to become an officer in the army. In time, he became both a sculptor and a soldier. When the Crimean War broke out, he joined the Russian Army and soon became the youngest officer in his regiment. A horseman of superior ability, he distinguished himself in Crimea and in several other wars that followed. In 1871, having grown weary of a soldier's life, Zaleski came to this country and settled on a large farm where he raised horses and created fine pieces of art.

The count was introduced to Ana Larsen in August of '84 by Carl Woolf, who pleaded with the artist to hire him and the girl as they were in desperate need of employment. Woolf had worked on Zaleski's farm some months earlier (January - April, 1884) and was still on good terms with the owner. Zaleski had all the farm hands he needed at present, but feeling sorry for the couple (Woolf told him they were engaged), he took them on, offering only their lodging as payment. Woolf and Larsen were accompanied by a boy in his early teens, who they introduced as the girl's half-brother. The boy stayed the night, but left the next morning for New York where he hoped to find work as a painter.

The couple only worked for Zaleski for four weeks, but in that time, the Count and his wife became familiar with the perverse relationship between the two. It was obvious that Larsen was very much in love with Mr. Woolf; however, the gentleman did not exhibit the same feelings. Woolf was cold toward the girl, often yelled at her, and never demonstrated the slightest bit of affection. On one particular evening, Zaleski overheard the two arguing in the kitchen and heard Woolf warn the girl, "If you don't leave me alone, I promise I'll do something desperate." Surprisingly, his rude treatment and threats did not allay her passion for him.

By the end of August, Woolf went off to find work in New York and Mrs. Zaleski found employment for Larsen in Cranford as a maid in the home of Caroline Furstman. Separated from her lover, Larsen's behavior quickly began to wear on her new employer. She would bother everyone who came to the house, asking if they had any news concerning Woolf. She was obsessed with him, even offering money to anyone who would go to New York and bring back information. Woolf did visit the girl on Sundays and usually brought a young boy with him, who he told Furstman was his brother. The lady of the house found Woolf to be a good-looking and rather pleasant man. It was her belief Woolf and Larsen were married. On these Sundays, he and the boy would only stay until after dinner and then return to New York. Their departure always caused a scene, as Larsen would carry on almost to distraction. After six weeks, Furstman grew tired of her obsession and when Larsen became disagreeable toward her for not giving her time off to go to New York, she terminated her service.

Again, without work, Larsen went to New York, found Woolf and became such a nuisance at his job site over the next few weeks, Woolf's boss had no alternative but to fire the man.

With nowhere to go and determined to be on his own and rid of the pesty woman, Woolf went back to Roselle and once again asked Count Zaleski to give him shelter and a job. The Count and his wife, now somewhat sympathetic toward Woolf for the way Larsen was pursuing him, let him stay. Trying to mediate the situation, Mrs. Zaleski told Woolf it was a scandal the way the two of them behaved and advised him to do the right thing and marry her. The Count agreed and added if marriage was not in his plans, he should go somewhere far off where she could never find him. Woolf told them, "I wouldn't marry her if she was covered with diamonds. If she tries to drag me down, I'll poison her!" Woolf confided in them that he had a relative who lived in Texas and was thinking about going there.

A few days later, just before Christmas, the problem surfaced again, when Larsen appeared at the Roselle Farm. The two began to quarrel and soon the arguing became so heated, the Zaleskis could no longer endure their company and ordered them off the property. That night they left.

The Count told the *World* reporter, "Woolf impressed me with the feeling he was a man who was set on ridding himself of a woman who had made his life a burden." There were more pieces of incriminating evidence. The murder weapon could have belonged to Woolf as the Count had witnessed him using a pocketknife, an item he almost always carried with him. The question of where the eggs came from and why they were carried could be explained because Woolf and Larsen had the unusual habit of sucking raw eggs. "They seemed to really enjoy eating the raw eggs and stole them from my henhouses whenever they had the chance," noted the Count. Zaleski also described a scar on the girl's neck, which Larsen told him was a mark left after an operation to relieve a gland problem.

The remainder of the *World*'s account of the movements of Woolf and Larsen leading to the murder was a combination of fact, opinion, and conjecture. After leaving Zaleski's farm, Woolf was able to separate himself from Larsen who eventually lost all trace of the man without whom she could not live. Search as she might, he was nowhere to be found. Rumors surfaced among acquaintances he had returned to Europe, so in the spring of '85, she sailed for Denmark. Woolf, who was actually successful in his attempt to hide, remained in the area, and in May, began working on D. B. Wade's farm in Union.

For almost two years, all went well for Woolf until March of '87 when he happened to learn that Larsen had come back and was still intent on finding him. On Wednesday, March 23, two days before the murder, Woolf left the Union farm telling Mr. Wade he was headed for Galveston, Texas. The paper speculated that Woolf figured Larsen would return to the neighborhood with which she was familiar. He, therefore, went to Roselle, was able to locate the girl, and promised to return to Europe with her. The pair likely walked from Roselle along St. Georges Avenue and into Rahway enroute to the Rahway Train Station. When they reached Central Avenue, Woolf led the girl to the lonely spot and committed the foul deed.

The Case of the Unknown Woman

~~~~~

"Well, what do you think?" Mayor Daly asked the question of Tooker and Detective Keron who had arrived at headquarters after having read the news. The chief responded first. "I don't know. It sounds like it's possible, but there're a lot of details that need to be checked. Did anybody try to find out if this Woolf fellow really went to Texas?"

Keron had little interest in the account and cut in with a gruff laugh. "The story's ridiculous. Everything's circumstantial. I had dealings with the reporter who wrote the story. It wouldn't surprise me if he concocted the whole thing to make a name for himself."

After a pause, the detective came on stronger. "I still think the crime was committed by someone who lives near Central Avenue. It makes sense! I say we just go out and arrest somebody, anybody who lives in Milton. It'll stir things up. It'll get people talkin'. You'll see, someone will remember something, someone will drop a clue, and one bit of information will lead to another. Before long, we'll find the killer. That's the way it was done in several murder cases I've worked on."

The mayor was quick to respond. "No, I don't want to go into a neighborhood and start harassing people. Besides, remember what happened when the famous New York inspector locked up Louis DeCamp. We all looked like a bunch of fools."

Keron then brought back two names. "What about Keech and Froat? So many things point to them. Why don't we go after them?"

Chief Tooker gave an answer with emphasis. "We've got no evidence to lock them up. We can't go around putting people in jail for nothin'. I agree, they both seem like logical suspects, but we don't have anything hard on them."

Keech and Froat were in fact still prime suspects in the minds of many of the locals and it was not unusual for the mayor to be confronted by citizens who urged him to take action against them. He decided it was time to settle the matter. One way or another, he had to determine whether to arrest the two men or leave them alone. To this end, he instructed Tooker to go to Froat's house and tell him to bring Keech and his other family members to the morgue at eight o'clock that night. He was confident they would not resist coming. From the beginning, they had put forth the appearance of being completely cooperative with everyone regarding the investigation. The mayor planned to interrogate them individually while in the room with the body. It was his feeling that if he could get each family member alone, in the somber setting of the funeral parlor and with the right questions, one of them might become unnerved and come forth with a confession.

~~~~~

Mayor Daly was correct in his belief that the Froats would comply with his request to meet with him that evening. Just before eight o'clock, Chief Tooker escorted Froat, Keech, Mrs. Froat, Nancy Limont, and her two cousins, Mary and Jane Richmond, into the office at Ryno's Morgue. After introductions and some amiable small talk, the mayor took Froat upstairs to begin the questioning in the presence of the body. The atmosphere in the room was enough to rattle even the most unflappable person. The only light was supplied by two wall sconces, their blue gas flames throwing ominous shadows against the walls. Heavy, dark, floor-length curtains closed in the space like a shroud. The corpse, more lurid in the gloomy setting, lay in an icebox with only the face visible through a glass plate. It was difficult to imagine the white, wax-like features were actually human flesh. The girl's hair, soft in life, was now coarse, and the individual strands gave the appearance of an inexpensive wig. The bloody clothes were laid out next to the coffin. The mayor spoke softly, but his voice sounded loud in the still air. "Take a good look at the mangled girl. Go up closer. Did you know this woman when she was alive?"

Froat took small steps to the box and looked long at the cold face. "It doesn't look like the same girl I saw dead on the road. I didn't know her then and I still don't know her."

"Are you sure she was never at one of the parties given at your house?"

"I'm positive I never saw her before. This girl was never in my house."

"Did you see or hear anything unusual that Friday night?"

"No. I was home all night and didn't hear nothin'. There was nothin' different that night. Next morning was the first I heard about it. It's a horrible thing."

"There are people who think you killed the girl."

"I tell ya', Mayor, they got no right to accuse me. They don't like my family and me 'cause we're newcomers, but that'll change. We're movin' back to Elizabeth."

"I wouldn't move too soon if I were you. It'll look like you're running off. Besides, you might be called in to testify."

"Let them call me in. I'll testify. I got nothin' to hide."

Froat answered the remaining questions showing no reservations and was finally led back to the office. The results were no different when Keech viewed the body. Keeping a stolid front, he answered each of Daly's questions giving no indication his responses were anything but honest. He seemed to be truly sympathetic and said, "The man that did this had a hard heart. I hope you capture the rogue so he can be hanged."

The women were far more nervous. Mrs. Froat almost fainted when she was asked to come upstairs. As she neared the body, she trembled violently and called to her husband to help support her. She stood away from the icebox, gave a single glance at the girl, and turned away, an expression of horror etched on her face.

The other women had little to say and stood quietly before the bier. The mayor's questions were answered with one or two words and Jane Richmond was only able to respond with barely perceptible nods. All four of the ladies declared they had never before seen the girl in life. None of them recognized the clothing.

When the interviews were over, Mayor Daly excused the family and simply said, "You can go home now." Alone in the morgue office, Daly considered the events of the evening. There were no discrepancies in the statements; there were no extraordinary developments. No guilty conscience betrayed itself. Not a ray of light was revealed. Ironically, only one thing came out of the session. As far as the mayor was concerned, he now believed neither Froat nor Keech was involved in the murder.

Monday, April 18 – Wednesday, April 20, 1887

The response to the *World*'s article was immediate and one-sided. All of the area papers challenged the story, calling it everything from "a mass of mistakes and inventions" to "a cock and bull story." *The New York Times* called it, "a circumstantial tale of fact and fiction that's the laughingstock of every reader who is familiar with the facts." They continued to say the story was "wholly inconsistent and absurd and was done in such a bungling way as to make it a burlesque on plausibility." *The New York Herald* dubbed it a "fake story" and claimed to have been able to completely explode the yarn by doing an hour's worth of investigative work. *Herald* reporters spent Sunday afternoon uncovering numerous facts to prove the account erroneous. It was ascertained Carl Woolf did secure passage for Galveston and left for that destination on March 16. The knife he owned did not fit the description of the murder weapon. His fondness for eggs came under question when Mr. Wade, his employer at the Union farm, stated in the two years Woolf worked for him, he never once saw him suck an egg. Nevertheless, the finding that completely scuttled the story was the discovery that showed Ana Larsen was really thirty-five years old and was the mother of a grown son.

Rahway officials were quoted as saying they did not put the slightest bit of credence in the story and many residents were insulted and outraged because of the way the poor, helpless, and friendless victim was portrayed. There were also those in town who knew Carl Woolf and were indignant at the insinuations about him. They believed when Woolf got a copy of the newspaper story, he would most definitely initiate a libel suit.

~~~~~

On orders from the coroner, the body of the unknown woman was placed in the white coffin used at the funeral and brought to a vault in the Rahway Cemetery. It would be held there until the time of interment, a date yet to be determined. From this point on, the face of the girl would only be shown to those persons going through the procedure of securing the proper permits.

~~~~~

Had it not been for the criticisms leveled at the *New York World*, the only discussions on Monday would have focused on the impending inquest scheduled to begin the next day. After four adjournments, the town was primed to get the hearings started. It had been hard to accept the official position that the first four meetings could not be held because witnesses were not available or because a clear direction could not be set. Most believed the authorities were waiting for, hoping for, someone to come in with a clue to break the case. There was a rumor going around that the last session was cancelled because Inspector Byrnes was in New York City hot on the trail of the owner of the rubber stamp and would soon return with the evidence to end the mystery. So far, there was no word from the noted New York detective, but the inquest would start tomorrow. The coroner and prosecutor could put it off no longer. At 9:00 a.m., the first witness would be called and the inquest would finally begin.

~~~~~

The dingy upper room of City Hall, which generally served as chambers for the common council, was filled with spectators by the time the jury members entered to take their places. Seats had been set up for them in front of the council desks, which for the hearings were reserved for newspaper reporters. City Clerk Franklin Marsh, assigned the duty of transcribing the testimonies, was at his desk. By the time County District Attorney Wilson and Coroner Terrill entered, it was nearing nine-thirty. Both sat down at the mayor's desk and after riffling through several papers, Terrill called the meeting to order.

Wilson, who would serve as prosecutor and question the witnesses, opened the proceedings by calling the first witness, Alfred Worth, the boy who discovered the body. Caught off guard by being the first to testify, Worth came forward feeling uncertain and appeared awkward as he stood at the lectern. Wilson, unmoved by the boy's uneasiness, began his questions.

State your name and residence.

Alfred Worth, I live on Hazelwood Avenue.

Where do you work?

At Bloodgood's Mill.

Tell us what happened as you went to work on the morning of Saturday, March 26.

I started alone to go to work about 6:15 a.m. At the corner of Jefferson and Central, I saw a cape lying on the ground. I went toward it and then saw the body. I shouted to my brothers who were crossing the Jefferson Avenue Bridge and they came to where the body was. Tom told me to go and notify the police. I met my brother Frank on the way and we both went to Chief Tooker's home and told him what I saw. The chief hurried back with us. Quite a crowd had gathered by that time.

Can you describe the body or any articles at the scene?

The girl was lying on her side. The ground was frozen, but not hard. There must have been a struggle because the girl's dress was torn at the shoulder. Near the body, there was a basket, some eggs, and an umbrella.

Did you notice any footprints in the area?

Yes. I saw footprints leading from the body toward Jefferson Avenue.

Are you sure of that?

Yes, I'm positive they were going to Jefferson.

Did you see a weapon near the body?

No.

Was anything disturbed around the body while you were there?

No.

Did you recognize the girl?

I never saw her before.

Where do you live in relation to where the body was found?

Two blocks away.

Where were you the night before?

I didn't go anywhere after I got home from work. I was in bed about nine.

Do you know William Keech?

I live about 100 yards from him. I only know him by sight.

Did you hear anything strange that night?

No.

Did you see Keech that night?

No.

Did you see any strangers around the home in the days prior to the murder?

No.

That will be all.

The next witness was James Stacy, the photographer. He produced the photos he had taken at the crime scene and was instructed to hand them out to the jury. Wilson then asked him to describe each of the photos. The process took an inordinate amount of time as the jurors went over each picture making inquiries about every conceivable detail. After the last image was finally reviewed, the collection of photographs was submitted as evidence.

Following Stacy, Benjamin Metzger, the man who found the knife, was called to the front.

State your name and residence.

My name is Benjamin Metzger. I live at the Park House across from the train station.

How are you employed?

I am a printer, employed at present in New York City.

When did you first hear about the murder?

At about eight o'clock, the morning of March 26. I heard the news from the milkman who delivers to the hotel every morning.

When did you go to the scene?

I visited the murder scene with Clarence Cook at about eight-thirty. We saw the body and then went back home. I returned later with Alexander Fyffe.

What articles did you notice around the body?

A fur cape, a parasol, a basket with some eggs in it, and some eggs on the ground.

What did you notice in the area around the body?

There must have been a struggle because the ground was chewed up with footprints and the girl's clothing was muddy and torn. I could also see a cut on the arm.

Had you ever seen the girl before?

No, she was not at all familiar to me.

(Items found by the body are shown to Metzger, which he identifies.)

Explain to the jury how you found the knife.

It was becoming chilly and I walked around the field to the left of the body. That's when I found the knife. I'd say it was about twenty yards from the body. There was blood on the grass where the knife lay and also on the blade and handle of the knife.

Did you notice any footprints in the area?

The field was covered with dry grass; I didn't notice any footprints.

(Several knives are shown and Metzger identifies the one he found.)

What was the approximate time you found the knife?

It must have been just before nine-thirty.

Was anyone with you when you found the knife?

There was no one within twelve feet of me.

Was Harry Cadell with you?

Harry was with me at the murder scene, but wasn't nearby when I found the knife.

What did you do with the knife after you found it?

I immediately brought it over to Officer Conger who was looking over the field with Chief Tooker.

Did you bring them to the spot where you found it?

Yes, and I pointed out the spots of blood.

Did you notice any blood anywhere else in the field?

No, only by where I found the knife.

We need to be clear on this. You're saying that you found the knife by accident.

Oh yes, my finding the knife was purely an accident.

Are you familiar with the locality where the body and knife were found?

No, I had never been in that area before that morning.

Do you think Clarence Cook or Alexander Fyffe might know something more than you are telling us?

No.

Have you spoken with either of them since, concerning the knife?

No.

What was the name of the milkman who first told you about the murder?

I believe his name is Mr. Marsh.

Do you know anything more about the case?

Nothing more than I've read in the papers.

Thank you. You can sit down.

Alfred Worth was recalled to look over the same objects just shown to Metzger. He gave a positive identification for each item.
Wilson next called Alfred's oldest brother, Frank, to take the stand.

State your name and residence.

Frank Worth. I live on Hazelwood Avenue.

Were you present to hear the testimony given by your brother, Alfred, and if so, do you agree with it?

Yes.

Can you add anything to his account?

The face of the murdered girl seemed to be pressed to the ground as if the murderer had one foot near the girl's head with the knee on her head at the time her throat was cut. The print of a man's heel was in the ground close to her head and the bruises seemed done by a knee. About ten feet from the body there were many prints as if a fight had taken place. I saw the fur cape and the basket. There were wagon tracks between the curb and the fence and marks of horses' hooves.

Did you ever see the girl before?

No.

Can you tell the jury what you were doing Friday night, March 25?

I was out the evening of the murder. I got home from work about eight-thirty, went downtown, first by way of Westfield Avenue and then Seminary Avenue. I returned home and then went out again about ten-fifteen. I was back home around twelve o'clock.

Why did you go back out after ten o'clock?

I went out at the later hour to see a lady friend home.

Did you go near the murder scene when you were out?

No, I wasn't near Central Avenue.

Did you hear any noises that night?

I heard dogs barking at midnight, but no unusual noises between eight and ten.

Could you tell whose dog was making the most noise?

Bill Brunt's dog.

Do you know William Keech?

I don't know that person.

Did you notice any strangers in the Milton area in the days prior to the murder?

No.

Do colored families live in the Milton section?

Yes.

Do you ever see any of them carrying razors?

No.

Can you explain why you were so late getting out of work on the night of the murder?

On that Friday night, some areas of the mill were still operating until eight o'clock.

That's all.
The process had been terribly deliberate and was moving at a painfully sluggish rate. Almost two hours had passed and the coroner still had six more witnesses to call. Sensing everyone needed a break, he declared a recess until two o'clock at which time the session would reconvene.

The afternoon hearings began with much greater attention to punctuality. Coroner Terrill's only piece of business before calling a witness was to announce the hearings would be adjourned no later than 4:30 p.m. and would resume on Thursday morning at nine o'clock. With the schedule set, Wilson stood and called Harry Cadell to the witness stand.

State your name and residence.

Harry Cadell, Milton Avenue.

How are you employed?

I work for *The Advocate*.

When did you first hear of the murder?

About eight-thirty.

What did you do after getting this news?

I went to the scene of the murder alone, and remained there about ten or fifteen minutes. Then I came downtown and told a reporter about the murder and we went back to the scene.

Were you present when the knife was discovered?

No.

Did you recognize the knife that was found?

I never saw it until it was exhibited at the morgue.

Did you ever see the murdered girl before?

No.

Are you familiar with the Milton Section?

No.

No further questions. Thank you.

Wilson paused to look at his paperwork and called John Dunham.

State your name and residence.

John Dunham, St. Georges Avenue.

What is your line of work?

I'm a coal dealer.

Tell us what you were doing the days prior to March 25.

I was hired to repair a fence on Central Avenue on the left-hand side going toward Madison Avenue. I did the job March 24 and 25.

Did you employ a horse and wagon on the job?

Of course. All my equipment is on my wagon. We stand in the back of the wagon to drive the stakes.

Were there others working with you?

I had a young helper with me.

Did you walk around the area?

I had to walk around a good deal to put up the fence.

When did you finish the work?

About four o'clock on Friday.

Did you notice any strangers while you were working?

No.

Are you familiar with the colored families in the Milton area?

I know some. Most are quiet people.

When did you first see the body?

About eight o'clock, Saturday morning.

Did you recognize the murdered girl?

I never saw the woman before.

Do you think the wagon tracks were made by your wagon?

I'm pretty certain most all the wagon tracks by the scene were made by my wagon.

Did you notice any footprints by the body that might not have been yours?

I saw other footprints on Saturday morning, but didn't take particular note of them. My prints and the boy's would be there.

What size shoe do you wear?

Size nine and I was wearing an arctic overshoe while working on the fence.

That will be all. You can sit down.
At this point, Wilson walked to where the coroner was seated and the two spent several minutes looking through papers and conversing privately. When their conversation ended, the prosecutor asked Dr. Mravlag to give his testimony regarding the autopsy.

State your name and residence.

Victor Mravlag. I live in Elizabeth.

What is your profession?

I am a physician.

Explain your connection with this case.

I came to Rahway at the coroner's request on Saturday, March 26, to perform an autopsy on the murdered girl.

What were the findings of your autopsy?

I conducted the autopsy at Ryno's Morgue with the assistance of Dr. Cladek, Dr. Hough, and Dr. Hodgson. We found it was the body of a female, five feet, two inches high with light brown hair, blue eyes, about twenty-five years old.

We feel the woman came to her death from a stab or cut wound, which commenced at the right side of the throat and cut the windpipe clean through in two places and opened the jugular vein on the right side causing fatal hemorrhage. Aside from this, there were numerous cuts and bruises upon the face, bruises upon the arms, and two cuts on the inner surface of the middle and ring fingers of the left hand.

Excuse me, Doctor. Do you think that the knife that was found could have caused these cuts to the throat?

Yes, I believe that particular knife could do such damage.

Please continue.

We found that the woman had not been ravaged and that she was never enceinte, although she was probably not a virgin.

Did you notice any marks on the body that might help to identify her?

There were two marks, which might prove to be helpful. One was a round white scar two inches in diameter, just below the right knee on the inner side of the tibia. The other was a roundish scar one inch in diameter on the left side of the neck about one and a half inches behind and about one inch below the left angle of the lower jaw. There were no other marks.

What else did you find in your examination?

The feet up to above the ankle were unclean, as were her arms and she was afflicted with vermin. Her left knee was muddy. Her front teeth were sound, but not clean. All her double teeth were decayed. Her front teeth were all her own.

The whole of her right cheek and her right ear were one large swollen bruise. There were three smaller bruises behind the right ear, and bruises over the left eye and over the right eyebrow. These bruises may have been produced by her coming in contact with something blunt, or a knee or foot may have caused them. The hair was pushed up upon her head.

The girl appeared to be of German descent, but the face was so bruised as to render any decision as to her race doubtful.

Do you feel the girl would have had time to scream or make any calls for help?

The murderer was doubtless a strong man, but the girl was so strong as to be able to make a successful resistance, unless she was weakened by fear. There must have been a severe struggle before she was killed, and it is likely that she had a chance to scream.

What is your estimate as to the time of death?

The body was rigid when the autopsy was made. The girl could have been dead from twelve to twenty hours when we first saw her, at 3:00 p.m. on March 26.

Thank you, sir. You've been most helpful.

To corroborate the autopsy report and perhaps to make the findings more acceptable to the local authorities, Wilson next invited Rahway physician, Dr. Walter Cladek to testify.

State your name and residence.

Walter E. Cladek. 52 Grand Street.

What is your profession?

I am a doctor.

Do you agree with the autopsy findings as reported by Doctor Mravlag?

Dr. Mravlag and I conducted the autopsy together and I concur with his report. I do differ on one point, however. I believe the girl may have been pregnant a long time ago for a short time, one or two months, and aborted leaving no evidence. Unfortunately, there were no clear evidences to support any theory.

I believe you made a microscopic examination of the blood found on the knife and around the crime area. Can you tell the jury what you found?

There was blood on the blade and on the handle of the knife. Can't be certain if it was human blood.

Do you have anything else that may be helpful?

There was blood on the interior of one of the woman's pockets, so much that the cloth of the pocket was stiffened.

How would you account for something like that?

I would guess whoever killed the girl went through her pockets to see what he could find.

Thank you, Doctor. I have no further questions.

Again, Wilson paused to look over the sheets he was holding. His next witness was William Rubeck. Of all the witnesses so far, the prosecutor had a feeling Rubeck might be a person in some way connected to the crime or at least have useful information. He had noticed Rubeck sitting in the chambers and it was easy to tell from his nervous manner, he didn't want to be there.

State your name and residence.

William Rubeck. I live in Milton on Maple Avenue.

How are you employed?

I'm a laborer at Bloodgood's Mill.

Can you tell the jury your actions on the morning of Saturday, March 26?

I left home for work at about 6:00 a.m. by way of Jefferson Avenue. When I reached the corner of Central, I turned onto Central and that's when I saw the body.

Just a moment. What time did you say it was?

A little after six.

Mr. Rubeck, if you saw the body a little after six that means you were the first to discover the body.

I don't know if I was or not.

The revelation surprised the jury members and spectators and for the first time during the proceedings, the room came to life. Catcalls came from the audience and a few jurors shouted unnerving questions. The outburst was quieted only when the coroner hammered his gavel and called for order. Rubeck, visibly excited and embarrassed, gathered himself together when he heard Wilson's voice and was able to continue.

What did you do when you saw the body?

I got to about twenty-three feet from it. I didn't know what to think when I saw her lying there. I thought the girl was either drunk or murdered. I was scared. I didn't go any closer to it. I just stood there, frightened. I don't know how long. I went back to Jefferson Avenue and continued on to work. I got there at ten minutes to seven.

Why didn't you go to the police?

I don't know. I don't know.

Did you recognize the murdered girl?

When I saw the girl that morning, I was so scared. I didn't look closely at her face. Since then, I have seen the body at the morgue. I never saw her before.

Did you see anyone else around that morning?

There was no one there when I saw her.

How long would you say it takes you to walk from your house to where the body was located?

About eight minutes.

Do you know Sadie Van Ness?

Yes, she works at the mill. I met her while walking to work that Saturday morning and talked with her.

Did she say anything about seeing a strange man in the area the night before?

She didn't say anything to me about a strange man.

Did you tell Juror Keefe about the murder?

I met Keefe on my way to the mills on Saturday morning and told him about the body. I told him that a girl was lying near the fence on Central Avenue with her dress up to her knees.

Can you tell the jury your whereabouts on Friday evening, March 25?

I got home from the mills at five-thirty. I was home all evening. The daughter of my wife was at home and also a boy named Bert

Harned. I left the two of them up and went to bed about quarter of nine.

How old is Bert Harned?

About eighteen.

What time do you usually go to bed?

Between eight-thirty and ten.

Did you hear any unusual noises that night?

No. I am sure everything was still before I went to bed because I looked out my window a few times for my wife.

Did you hear any dogs barking?

No.

Where was your wife that evening?

She was downtown Friday night and returned home after I had gone to bed. I don't know what time it was when she came home.

How long have you lived in Rahway?

I came to Rahway in 1879, but I've only lived in Milton for eight months.

Do you know James Brunt?

Yes, he lives about a block and a half from me. He keeps a store.

Do you know Frank Smith, Charles Henderschott, and Joseph Reifel?

I don't know Frank Smith, but I do know a "Drum" Smith. I do know Charles Henderschott and Joseph Reifel.

Do you know the location of Dr. Meeker's farm?

Sure, although I've never been on the premises.

Did you ever see "Drum" Smith go there?

No.

Do you know William Keech?

No.

Do you know the Clinton Froat family?

No. I never heard of that family until I saw their names in the newspaper.

What other persons do you know from Milton?

I know Mr. Acken, Mr. Banks, and I know Sam Tice by sight.

Have you seen Sam Tice since he got out of jail?

No. I didn't know Sam got out.

Do you ever attend the parties in the neighborhood?

I never went to any parties. I never had any invitation to any party up there. I never go out much nights. I never hardly travel with anyone.

Have you ever been under arrest?

No.

Coroner Terrill, troubled by the hesitating manner in which Rubeck answered the questions, asked him if he had withheld anything in his testimony. When the witness replied in the negative, Terrill, who believed he wasn't telling everything he knew, directed an officer to keep Rubeck in custody. Shocked, but not uncooperative, Rubeck left the stand escorted by the officer.

The final witness of the afternoon was George Harris, constable and resident of Milton. From the beginning, he was critical of the County officials and the way they were interfering with what he felt should be a local matter. He would testify, but he'd be damned if he would offer any more than basic answers.

State your name and residence.

My name is George Harris and I live on Jefferson Avenue.

What is your occupation?

I'm Constable for the City of Rahway.

How long have you served as constable?

Over three years.

When did you first learn of the murder?

I heard about the crime on Saturday morning from Mary McDonald. I'd say it was around six-thirty.

Did you go directly to the scene?

Yes, I always try to be on hand when anyone tells me something is going on.

What did you find as you inspected the area?

I was very vigilant that morning. I noticed the position of the body where it laid. The head lay up against the fence and the legs the other way. I saw the manner of the dress; I saw the basket that was shown, saw the parasol, saw the hat, and saw the cape.

Can you tell the jury your actions on Friday evening, March 25?

I was out posting bills and when I got done, I stopped by Jake Vetter's butcher shop on Main Street. I left there at about nine-fifteen, got home about nine-forty, had supper, and went to bed.

Did you hear any unusual noises that night?

I heard dogs barking. It sounded like two dogs fighting.

Do you know James Brunt?

Yeah, he runs a store by my house, but I'm not in the habit of going there.

Was Brunt's store open or closed when you came home that Friday night?

It looked like it was shut up for the night.

Do you know Sadie Van Ness?

She's my wife's sister and she boards with us.

Did Miss Van Ness tell you about a strange man she saw in the area on Friday, March 25?

She told that story to my wife. She said she was coming down Central Avenue about six-thirty and met a strange man.

Did she give any description?

I remember she said something about the man having a mustache.

Do you know William Rubeck?

I've known Rubeck for about five months since he came to Milton to get married.

Do you know William Keech?

I have known him only since the morning of March 26 when I saw him at the crime scene.

Do you know the family of Clinton Froat?

Not really. They live next door to me, but I never had reason to talk with them before March 26.

Are you aware that there was a party at Clinton Froat's home on Thursday, March 24, the night before the murder?

I do remember a party there that night.

Do you know any one who attended that party?

No.

Do you know Charles Henderschott and Joseph Reifel?

Yes, I know both.

Did you ever see them around the Froat house?

I've seen both visit that family on occasion.

Do you think any of these persons might have had something to do with the crime?

I have no opinion against anyone.

Can you give this jury any clue at all or a scent that will help to solve this crime?

I think that somebody murdered the girl.

This last comment drew loud laughs from the crowd. Harris left the stand without being excused, and Wilson, taken back by the wry comment, said nothing. Terrill again had to use the gavel to retain order.

Before halting the hearings for the day, Wilson recalled Rubeck for two final questions.

State your name again for the record.

William Rubeck.

Would you tell the jury again how you are acquainted with Sadie Van Ness?

She works with me at the mill.

While walking to work with Miss Van Ness on the morning of Saturday, March 26, did she say anything about seeing a strange man the night previous?

She never said anything to me about seeing a strange man on Friday night. We didn't talk about much. I only walked with her to the corner of Central Avenue that morning.

That will be all for today.

There were definitely discrepancies in the statements made by William Rubeck and his demeanor on the stand gave the impression of a guilty man. However, those who knew him would never believe this meek man was involved with the deed and considered him nothing more than "a great coward."

Tuesday's session ended with questions concerning the story of the stranger on Central Avenue. The coroner planned to explore the sighting in more detail on Thursday. His first witness would be Sadie Van Ness.

~~~~~

The Wednesday morning issue of the *World* set out to justify the Ana Larsen story and criticize its detractors. They explained to their readers, "So many misstatements appeared in all the other newspapers in New York concerning the facts printed by the *World*, that, uncorrected, they might do much to mislead the authorities. It is doubtless the earnest wish of all these newspapers, as well as the *World*, to find and have punished the brutal murderer of this girl, and therefore any carelessness of their reporters in the publication of facts concerning the mystery is to be much deplored."

The paper maintained the story given by Count Zaleski was a "careful and altogether truthful statement" and "the only reasonable theory of the murdered girl's identity." It went on to extol the reputation of the Count as a man respected by his neighbors and a man who is accurate and conscientious. They contradicted the idea that local officials had no interest in the story by reporting Mayor Daly had arranged a conference with *World* reporters and Detective Keron to review all the evidence they had gathered. The *World* was not about to let their story die.

~~~~~

Mrs. Agnes Space, who saw the body on Saturday and stated with certainty they were the remains of her sister, Mary Dorman, returned with another sister, Mrs. Jane Harris. Harris immediately recognized the girl as her younger sibling. Their "positive identifications," however, soon suffered the same fate as all the others that had been issued, when a brother-in-law of the two ladies refuted their claim. Andrew Kirkwood, who was married to a fourth sister, came to see the body and said in the most emphatic language it was not Mary Dorman. According to Kirkwood, he saw Mary as recently as last August before he migrated to this country. His sisters-in-law had not seen the girl for several years so their recollections of her appearance could not be very reliable. "This girl had brown hair," he said, "Nearly black. My sister-in-law's hair is red. The form of the girl is also different. She was too solid for Mary." Kirkwood also told the authorities his wife, who had remained abroad, never wrote any letters indicating Mary was planning a trip to the United States. A final piece of information to cast serious doubt on the sisters' assertion was the fact that Miss Dorman was the mother of a young son. The findings made by the physicians indicated the murdered girl had never been pregnant.

Mrs. Space was shaken by her brother-in-law's statements, but nonetheless, stuck to her opinion. She promised to return with more proof and left saying, "I'll go to my grave convinced the girl is my sister, Mary." Undertaker Ryno told reporters, "I was almost certain on Saturday the name of the girl was known at last and that it was Mary Dorman, the Scotch girl. However, recent developments have proved conclusively that she is not the murdered girl."

~~~~~

The reporters had not yet finished their stories concerning Mary Dorman when a woman arrived with another "lost girl" story. Mrs. Annie Hofman of New York City believed the murdered girl was her sister, Emma Lau, who had been missing since December. According to Mrs. Hofman, her sister fit the description in every particular. Emma

Lau was twenty-seven, had brown hair, blue eyes, and had an old mark just below her right knee, about the size of a twenty-five cent piece. The girl left New York after having a disagreement with her lover. There was, however, nothing different or unusual about this identification to excite the authorities. A report was written up and placed on file.

Thursday, April 21 – Friday, April 22, 1887

Sadie Van Ness walked to the lectern on Thursday morning with the air of a diva preparing for a performance. A number of her female friends were in attendance, and although somewhat jealous that Sadie was the center of attention, they also felt important because they were confidants of the witness and, therefore, they too were looked upon with greater interest. As Prosecutor Wilson approached, Sadie held her head high and gave him a patronizing smile.

State your name and residence.

Sadie Van Ness. I live on Jefferson Avenue with my sister, Mrs. Harris, and her husband, Constable Harris.

How long have you lived there?

Four and a half years.

Where do you work?

Bloodgood's Mill.

Tell us about the morning of Saturday, March 26.

I left for work at about 5:50 a.m. I met William Rubeck as I came out of my house. I had no particular conversation with him. We went along Jefferson Avenue. When we got to Central, he turned down

Central and walked toward St. Georges. I kept on Jefferson and continued to work. It's about a two-mile walk to the mill.

Do you know where Mr. Rubeck went after he left you?

No, after he turned down Central, I could not tell the direction he took.

Did you notice anything unusual about Mr. Rubeck that morning?

No, there was nothing strange in his behavior or appearance.

How long have you known William Rubeck?

About two years.

When did you learn of the murder?

When Thomas Worth came to the mill, he told me about a woman lying on Central Avenue with her throat cut. He said if I had turned my head at the corner, I could have seen her.

Did you see Mr. Rubeck at the Mill during that day?

I did not see him at the mill that morning. I think he was there afterwards, but I did not see him.

Can you tell the jury what you saw on your way home from the Mill on Friday, March 25?

I stopped work at six o'clock. Came home by way of Jefferson Avenue, met a strange man coming down Central Avenue where the girl was found.

What time would that have been?

About six-thirty.

What did this man look like?

He was dressed in dark clothes, was stout and very tall. He wore a black derby hat that sat on the back of his head.

Just how tall do you think he was?

I couldn't say exactly. I think he was taller than the coroner.

Anything else you remember about this man?

He had a heavy mustache, dark in color, wore an overcoat. He walked very erect and proud. He quickened his pace when I looked at him.

Do you know of anyone else who may have seen this man?

My sister, Mrs. Harris, thought she saw the same man in the afternoon.

Have you seen the man since?

I have not seen him since, nor did I ever see him before.

Have you talked with Mr. Rubeck since the murder?

No.

Do you know William Keech or Clinton Froat?

I know that persons of that name live in the locality and that they live within hailing distance from my house, but I do not know them.

Do you know anything about a party at the home of Clinton Froat on Thursday evening, March 24?

I believe there was a party at that home. Alfred Worth told me. Charlie Henderschott told me he was at the party. He said it was a lively party and that there were a lot of new girls there.

How is it that you are acquainted with Charles Henderschott?

He works at the mill.

Was he at work on Friday, March 25?

I could not say for sure. I am certain I saw him on Saturday about noon at the mills. That's when he told me about the party.

Did he mention anything about the murder?

No.

Do you know where Mr. Henderschott lives?

He lives with Joe Reifel on Meeker's Farm.

Have you seen the body of the murdered girl?

No, I do not like to look at dead people, especially when murdered.

If you were asked by the coroner to view the body, would you?

I have no objections to looking at the body, if necessary.

At this point, Coroner Terrill asked Van Ness if she would go to the morgue and view the body. Sadie agreed, but requested that Constable Harris accompany her, as she did not wish to go to the place alone. Terrill had no objection and excused the witness, asking her to be back for the afternoon session.
    The second witness was James Brunt, another person whose name came up at Tuesday's hearing. It was obvious the coroner and prosecutor had no clear direction and no long list of witnesses. The mere mention of a name during someone's testimony might land one on the witness stand.

State your name and residence.

James Brunt. I live in Milton on Maple Avenue, corner of Jefferson Avenue.

How long have you lived there?

Three years.

What is your occupation?

I keep a small grocery store.

When were you informed of the murder?

It was about six-thirty in the morning. My son, Walter, told me.

How soon after hearing the news did you go to the scene?

I went over right after my boy told me. I met John Gettings on the way and told him what happened and we went over together.

Were others at the scene when you got there?

There were several others already there. Frank Worth was there and my brother William was there.

Did you view the body?

Yes, it was the body of a woman with her throat cut.

Did you ever see the woman before?

I thought I had seen the person before with the same face and hair, but I couldn't be certain where or when. I thought I had seen her in my neighborhood, but I'm not sure. I didn't recognize her clothes. I viewed the body at the morgue, but her face changed so much I couldn't form any opinion. However, her face and hair did seem familiar when I first saw her.

Are you acquainted with William Keech and Clinton Froat?

I know them slightly. I've seen Mrs. Froat around, but never spoke to her.

How long have you known Keech and Froat?

I've been acquainted with Clinton Froat since last fall when him and his family moved to Milton. Keech moved in with the Froats two or three weeks before the murder. I see them from time to time.

How would you describe the character of these two men?

Well, the reputation of Froat in this neighborhood ain't very good. I've heard folks say they never saw the man do a day's work. Columbus Banks, he's a colored man I call my informant; he says that Froat is out all hours of the night. As for Keech, I've heard his character questioned.

Anyone in particular make disparaging statements about either?

A man came to see me after the murder who said he was a detective from New Brunswick. His name was Gregory. He asked me who lived in "that" house, referring to Froat's. I told him Mr. Froat and Mr. Keech. The detective said he thought he knew both of them and asked me to describe them, so I did. He told me Keech was a notorious character. I also heard from several persons that Keech would lift things. Once I lost something and inquired around and several people suspected him.

Do you know anything about a party at Froat's house the Thursday before the murder?

I knew there was a party that night. Charlie Lambert came into my store with two other men. I didn't know either of them. Charlie told me they were going over there. And I think I saw two or three strange women come there in the afternoon. I could see from my store that there were several men and women at Froat's that evening.

Do you know what time the party broke up?

No, I went to bed about nine-thirty.

How about the next day? Anything unusual around Froat's house?

Friday morning I saw two or three women going in and out about eight o'clock. I saw them several times during the morning. They were strangers to me. I don't remember seeing them in the afternoon.

Did any of these women resemble the murdered girl?

I don't think any of them had the face or the hair as I remember seeing on the body.

Did you see Keech or Froat during that Friday?

I saw both of them about the house.

Were they ever in the company of a young woman?

I didn't see them with any woman.

How about Friday evening? Can recall anything unusual happening that night?

I went to bed at nine-thirty. After going to bed, I was awakened by my dog at about eleven o'clock. I heard my dog barking terribly. I lay and listened for a long time. It must have been between twelve and one. The dog never acted that way. He was barking as near as I can tell in the direction of the murder.

Don't you think it was your duty to get up and see what was wrong with your dog?

Perhaps it was, I just didn't. I lay quietly in bed and didn't get up. It wasn't until the next morning that I thought I should have gone to see what was the matter. The fact of the visit of the detective and the dog acting strangely makes me think I should have gotten up.

Were there any voices that night that might have awakened you?

No, I didn't hear any people outside. The dog woke me up. Some neighbors heard the dog as well as I did.

As a grocery store keeper, do you buy or sell eggs?

I don't buy eggs. I sell eggs on occasion. I get them from my own chickens.

Did you sell any eggs on Friday, March 25?

No.

Are you positive you sold no eggs that day?

I can swear I didn't.

Did Clinton Froat do much business in your store?

Froat and me dealt very little.

(*Here the witness is shown the basket.*)

Did you ever see this basket before?

It looks like the same one I saw at the murder site.

How long have you been in the grocery business?

Twenty years.

Would you say that you've seen many baskets over those years?

Yes, I've seen many.

Any idea who would use such a basket as this?

I suppose a person on a farm would be likely to use one like it.

That's all for now, Mr. Brunt.

The abrupt termination of the prosecutor's questions surprised everyone in the courtroom. Wilson looked to the coroner and asked to be granted a recess until the afternoon session. Terrill, not quite sure what the prosecutor had hit upon, announced an adjournment until two o'clock.

~~~~~

All the seats in the Council Chambers were filled half an hour before the two o'clock hour struck with spectators curious to find out what Prosecutor Wilson had uncovered during the testimony of James Brunt. Some speculated the mention of the basket gave the prosecutor a lead to pursue. Others believed the answers to his questions about Clinton Froat and William Keech were convincing him the two men were involved and he was building a case against them. The gallery came expecting a dramatic revelation and their restless chatter was stilled when Sadie Van Ness was recalled.

Please state your name again.

Sadie Van Ness.

Since giving your testimony this morning, have you viewed the body of the murdered girl?

Yes.

Do you recognize her?

I cannot identify her as a person I have ever seen before.

Do you recognize any of the articles found by her body?

I do not recognize the parasol, basket, or hat. I never saw them before.

In your testimony this morning, you told the jury that you know Charles Henderschott. Do you know Joseph Reifel?

Yes.

Do you know if Mr. Reifel ever sold eggs to grocery stores in Rahway?

I never heard that he sold eggs to stores.

Have you heard anything at the mill concerning the murder that might be of interest to these proceedings?

I've heard nothing of the murder at the mill.

Are you certain about seeing a strange man on Friday, March 25, as you were returning home from work?

Yes, and when I told my sister, Mrs. Harris, about the person she thought it was the same person she had seen in the afternoon.

Thank you, Miss Van Ness. You can return to your seat.

The prosecutor surveyed the faces in the chambers to be certain the man he was looking for was present. When he saw James Brunt, he called him back to the stand to continue his testimony.

State your name.

James Brunt.

Are you acquainted with Joseph Reifel, Charles Henderschott, and Frank Smith?

No, only by sight. I used to see Reifel going to Froat's house most every day before the murder, and I also saw Henderschott go there.

(Joseph Reifel was here brought in for identification and Brunt said he was the Reifel to whom he referred. Henderschott was also brought in and identified.)

Do you know Frank Smith?

No.

(Smith was here brought before the witness.)

I had seen this man often, and saw him at Froat's house one day since the murder.

What day after the murder did you see Smith at Froat's house?

Probably a week or ten days after, but I can't tell the exact day. I don't remember anything that I can fix the day when Smith was by Froat's.

Did you ever see Mr. Smith at Froat's prior to the murder?

No, I don't recollect.

In the days following the murder, did you notice any suspicious activity around Froat's place?

On Sunday morning after the murder, I got up, went into the store, and was sitting there. I could see from the front of my store right into Froat's house. I noticed Keech standing in front of a window. He appeared to be watching everyone that went up and down the street. When anybody would pass the house, he would step back from the window, and as soon as they passed by, he would step up again to see which way they went. He did this for about two hours. In the meantime, Albert Pierson came by and I called his attention to Keech's actions. He remarked to me, after watching for a while, that Keech's actions were very strange, very mysterious.

Why did Mr. Pierson stop by your shop?

He came to get his horse. His wife wanted to go up into the country.

Continue telling the jury about Keech's strange behavior.

Well, Pierson and me went to the barn to put a harness on the horse and then he went home. When I got back to the store, Keech was gone from the window. About ten or fifteen minutes later, Keech, Froat, Mrs. Froat, some other woman who I didn't know, and a child came out of the house and started up the street toward Short Hills.

Did you notice when they returned?

They were back after sundown.

In your earlier testimony, you mentioned you saw several women around Froat's house in the days prior to the murder. Can you give the jury more information on this point?

They always seemed to have a good deal of company, mostly females. Sometimes the same person came and went. Sometimes they were persons I didn't recognize.

Can you describe the women who came there the Thursday prior to the murder?

Two were young women. One about sixteen years old, the other about eighteen. I can't describe what they wore. I think it was dark, brownish clothing. Their hair was light, complexion white. I don't think either one was over 5'4". They were both stout. The third was older, about thirty-five, maybe more. I think I saw all three leave Froat's on Friday in the afternoon.

Did any of these women resemble the murdered woman?

I think the older one of the first two resembled the murdered woman in the hair. Remember, I was across the street so it was hard to get a good look. That's the only resemblance I saw.

On the night of the murder, what time did you close your store?

Nine-thirty.

Who were some of your late customers that night?

Albert Pierson and Mr. Acken were there, Irving and Alfred Worth, Michael Gettings, Freeman Clark, and I think Ira Worth was there.

Do you know Sam Tice?

No.

Do you know any coloreds in the area who might have committed this murder?

No, I don't know any bad characters of the colored race living in Milton.

Let's move on. Tell the jury how you came to find the black bag.

I found the satchel in the brook behind my barn. I had been to the murder scene and spent about twenty minutes there. It was about seven o'clock when I decided to go back home. While crossing the Jefferson Avenue Bridge, I saw something black lying in the water. I didn't go down to fetch it, but rather went home to have my breakfast. After I ate, I went to the brook and saw the black object. I went down the bank and when I was about five or six feet from the object, I could see it was a handbag or valise. I then went over to where the dead woman was and saw George Wright and told him I found a bag in the brook. He told me to show him. When we got to the spot, Mr. Wright thought we had better take it out for fear it might float away. He picked it up out of the water and we went back to the crime scene.

Do you think this bag could have been thrown from the bridge and end up where you found it?

If the bag was thrown from the bridge, the current would have been strong enough to carry it to where I found it.

(The bag was here brought in for identification.)

Is this the bag you found?

Yes.

Can you tell the jury what you found in the bag?

We tried to open it, but it was locked. When we returned to the field, George saw Chief Tooker and told me to stay back and he brought the bag to the chief. That's when they opened it. I wasn't near when they looked through it, so I didn't see what they pulled out.

Is it also true that you saw what appeared to be marks of blood on the Jefferson Avenue Bridge?

I did see marks on the bridge, but couldn't say for sure they were blood.

After you retrieved the bag and went back to the field, did you take notice of any tracks or footprints or any other unusual signs in the area?

Yes, remember, I was with George Wright, who used to be our police chief, and I stayed with him when he went over the area. We could see a man's and woman's tracks where they had gone across Central Avenue to the place where the cape lay. Then we traced the same tracks from the cape to the spot where the body lay near the basket of eggs. A white pocket handkerchief, a parasol, and a hat were near the body. It looked like there had been a scuffle between two parties. There was a print of a person's knee in the mud. I could also see a man's tracks there, one on each side of the woman's body. We traced the same tracks to Jefferson Avenue and down Jefferson toward Milton. There we lost trace altogether.

Do you know the size of boots or shoes of William Keech?

No.

Is it true that you picked up the white handkerchief that was lying next to the body and that you found strands of hair in it?

Yes, I found in the handkerchief a clump of dark brown hair about an inch and quarter in length all in one bunch. There were probably about fifty hairs. I handed it over to George.

Do you think it was the dead girl's hair?

No, it was darker than the dead girl's.

Does William Keech or Clinton Froat have hair similar to the hair in the handkerchief?

Well, William Keech has quite a long mustache. Froat's hair is lighter than Keech's.

Do you know why or have you heard why Keech and the Froat Family are planning to move out of Rahway?

I don't know why and I haven't heard any stories from anyone.

Did you ever have trouble with Keech or Froat?

No, their relations with me were friendly.

Do you think Keech or Froat had any connection with the murder?

Hey listen, I never thought they were connected. I only thought they acted suspiciously.

Is it not true that you made a complaint to a justice of the peace of this county asking for the arrest of William Keech and Clinton Froat?

That's not true! I have not at any time since March 26 made any complaint to any justice of the peace for the arrest of Keech or Froat. And I haven't heard that any other person was anxious to have either arrested.

That's all I have for this witness.

Brunt stood at the lectern and realized many of the answers he gave had made him look like a fool, or worse, a liar. He also regretted mentioning names of his neighbors and feared he might have put them in jeopardy. He tried to speak in his own defense, but the prosecutor had turned his back on him and was walking away, making him feel very much alone. As the coroner and the prosecutor prepared for the next witness, Brunt left the stand, afraid to look at the audience, lest he see the ones cursing his name.

It was three-thirty and Coroner Terrill announced there would not be enough time before the appointed adjournment hour to fully question the next witness. On the request of the prosecutor, however, the jury was asked to reassemble later in the evening at eight o'clock. It was no secret, Joe Reifel was on the list to be called, and Prosecutor Wilson, who was sure he was on to something, did not want to put Reifel's testimony off for another day.

~~~~~

During the break, Associated Press reporter J. Townley Crane found the coroner dining alone at a table in Chamberlain's Hotel. Crane, a younger brother of the popular novelist, Stephen Crane, was regarded in the profession as a respected journalist. From the day he started covering the case, he had been one of the most persistent critics of the way the investigation was being conducted, and described the authorities as incompetent and derelict. He knew Terrill didn't like him because of his cynical articles, but saw this as an opportunity to goad the coroner into revealing some personal thoughts. He approached the official and asked, sitting down, not waiting for an answer, "Mind if I ask a few questions?"

Terrill, showing no emotion, answered, "Do I have a choice?"

The reporter's questions were fair and objective, although most were edged in sarcasm, and the coroner answered each as succinctly as he could. Whenever he deemed his comments were confidential, he withheld an answer. Nearing the end of his questions, Crane asked if he had any strong feeling about who the girl might be. The coroner shook his head and replied, "No, no, I think it best not to respond to that question." Crane, however, pressed him for an answer. "Look, I won't print anything you say about the girl. I'm just curious what you think. Whose name would you give to the victim?"

Perhaps it was because the coroner did have an opinion and welcomed the chance to let it out, that he gave an answer. "I have confidence in the Mrs. Space and Mrs. Harris identification. Right now this case is being thoroughly investigated and we should have some answers within a few days."

Crane was satisfied with the answer, but did not stop there. "One last question. Who do you think killed the girl?"

"You should know better than to ask me that. You'll get your answer when we find the man. No more questions for today. Now if you'll excuse me, I'd like to finish my meal."

~~~~~

The first and only witness to testify at the evening session was Joseph Reifel. Prosecutor Wilson had been waiting all afternoon for this hour to come and was ready to lay the groundwork for an arrest.

State your name and residence.

Joseph Reifel. I live on Hamilton Street.

How are you employed?

I'm a farmhand on Dr. Meeker's farm.

How long have you lived in Rahway?

Four years.

When did you first hear of the murder?

Saturday morning at ten. Daniel Haley told me when I was walking on Westfield Avenue. He said a girl had been murdered down toward Milton.

Are you sure of the time, ten o'clock?

It must have been at least half past nine.

What did you do after Haley told you?

I went to Larry Baumgartner's grocery store on Grand Street. I stayed there about twenty minutes and then went back home.

Did you stop anywhere on your way home?

No.

What time was it when you arrived?

I can't exactly tell what time I left Baumgartner's or what time it was when I reached home.

What did you do after you got home?

I was home about twenty minutes and then I went over to the place where the body was found.

Tell the jury about your visit to the scene.

I went down Jefferson to Central and after I got there, I saw the body. I went within ten feet of it. I didn't look at the face. I saw her clothing, a fur cloak, a parasol, a basket, and some eggs.

How long did you remain there?

About an hour.

Where did you go from there?

I went to Milton, then I went home.

What did you do in Milton?

I stopped and talked with Clinton Froat a little while.

How long did you stay there?

Only two or three minutes.

Did you talk about the murder?

Yes, he said the case was an awful thing and I said it was too.

While you were there, did you see anyone else?

I saw his boy and his wife. There was another lady there, but I don't know her name.

Can you describe this other woman?

I saw her, but can't give a good description. She was tall, couldn't tell you the color of her hair. I think she had on a calico dress. I never saw her before.

Why did you go to Froat's?

I went to see Froat's boy, William. He promised to come over to my house. When I left, he came with me.

How old is the boy?

Fourteen.

Can you be more clear as to what business you had with the boy?

I wasn't working on Saturday and sometimes Will likes to come over to the farm and keep me company.

How many times had he been to the farm before?

Can't say how many, maybe about five times.

Did you talk to the boy about the murder?

We did talk about it. He thought it was an awful thing.

Did the boy see the body?

Earlier, when I was at the murder site, I saw the boy passing through the crowd, so he probably saw the body.

Was anyone with the boy?

His father and William Keech.

What time did you get home with the boy?

It was one in the afternoon. I know that because I heard the factory whistle.

What time did you say you heard about the murder?

I said about ten o'clock.

How long were you at Froat's?

About four minutes.

Just a moment. You said you heard about the murder at nine-thirty, got back home at ten, went to the crime scene at ten-twenty, and stayed there about an hour. Then you went to Froat's and stayed there all of four minutes. Next, you said you went straight home and arrived there at one o'clock. Mr. Reifel, how do you explain it took you an hour and a half to walk a distance that should take less than ten minutes to cover?

I guess I'm not sure about the times.

What did you do the rest of the afternoon?

I don't think I left the farm again, but I can't swear if I did or not.

How long was the boy there?

The boy went home before dark.

Did you go back to Froat's that day?

No.

Did you see Froat or Keech that day or in the evening?

No.

What time did you go to bed that night?

Not certain what time it was. I don't generally go to bed later than nine o'clock. I'm pretty sure I went to bed by that time.

Did anyone from Bloodgood's Mills stop by your place that night?

No.

Were you at Froat's house on Friday, the day of the murder?

No, and I don't think I even saw him on Friday or on Thursday.

Were you at Froat's party on Thursday, March 24?

No.

Did you know there was a party that night?

Charlie Henderschott told me on the previous Sunday that there was going to be a party and that he was going.

So you didn't go?

No, I stayed home alone.

Are you friends with the Froats?

Not particularly.

Tell the jury about that Thursday night that Mr. Henderschott went to the party and you stayed home.

Charlie left for the party at about nine o'clock. I happened to look at the clock so I knew he left at that time.

Did Henderschott go with anyone else?

No, he went by himself.

What did you do after he left?

I lay down on the settee and slept there so I wouldn't have to get out of bed to let him in.

Do you know what time he returned from the party?

He came home Friday morning at about four-thirty.

Did you see him when he came in?

Yeah, he looked like he needed some sleep.

Did you talk to him at all?

Yes, he said "good morning" to me and said the party was just finishing up. He said they had a very nice time.

Had he been drinking?

No, Charlie's not a drinking man.

Did he tell you who was at the party?

He said Charles Lambert and his wife, Mrs. Froat's mother and another sister of Mrs. Froat, Will Keech, Mary Richmond, Jane Richmond, Mrs. Froat, her husband, and her son. It was only a family gathering.

Do you know Frank Smith?

Yes.

Does he visit you often?

He doesn't visit me. He's never been on the farm.

What are your duties on the farm?

I plow, plant corn, potatoes, peas, onions, lettuce. I raise chickens.

What do you do with your produce?

I sell the products of the farm for the doctor or trade them out for groceries.

Who do you generally sell eggs to?

William Howard, Mr. Fetter, M. L. Baumgartner, and Mark Keefe. I usually sell two or three dozen altogether. Mr. Keefe is the only man I sell a dozen to.

When was the last time you sold eggs to Mr. Keefe?

About three weeks before the murder.

Do you trade some eggs for groceries?

I can't say when the last time was that I traded my eggs for groceries.

Do you know James Brunt?

I know him a little. He keeps a store on the corner, but I've never been into it.

Did you ever sell eggs or take eggs to Clinton Froat?

No.

Did you ever take eggs to Froat's on the request of Charles Henderschott?

No, I don't think I ever took eggs from the farm to Froat's for any reason.

(Here the witness is shown the basket and hat.)

Do you recognize these items?

The first time I ever saw them was on Saturday morning when I saw them next to the body.

Did you ever see the murdered woman before?

I never saw her before; don't know who she is.

Have you seen the knife that was found?

No.

Do you have any objections to viewing the knife?

No. If you want, I'll go to the chief of police tomorrow and ask to see it.

Can you tell the jury your whereabouts on Friday evening, March 25?

I was in Rahway. I left home around eight by myself and went down to Lute Macann's, all the way down Grand Street.

When did you get there?

Can't say.

What did you do at Macann's?

I met Jim Smith there and we left together at eight-thirty to go back to my place.

What time did you get back to your place?

Around quarter of nine.

What route did you travel on your way home?

We went up Grand Street to Westfield Avenue to Jefferson Avenue to Hamilton and we were home.

How long did Smith stay?

After we got home, we played two games of Euchre and then he left. It took about twenty minutes to play. After that, I went to bed and went to sleep. I didn't get up again that night. This is all I know.

Where does Jim Smith live?

Kinsey Corner.

How far is that from your place?

Don't know exactly. I'd say about half a mile.

Did you hear any dogs barking or unusual noises after you went to bed?

I didn't hear any unusual noises that night of the murder.

Do you have any dogs on your farm?

There's one dog on the farm.

If a dog in Milton had been barking, would your dog have reacted?

I don't think my dog could hear another dog barking off in Milton. If the dogs in the neighborhood had made any noise, my dog would've made a noise also and I would've got up to see what was the matter. But he was quiet that night.

One last question. Have you talked to Charles Henderschott about the murder?

Yes, he thought it was an awful deed.

Before Reifel could leave the stand, Coroner Terrill ordered him to remain. Terrill sat up in his chair and spoke firmly, "From your testimony, Mr. Reifel, you have given this court reason to believe you are withholding valuable information. In addition, your inability to give accurate times for your whereabouts and your confusion in the times you spent on Saturday morning, gives the impression you are trying to protect either yourself or someone else. For these reasons I order that you be placed under arrest pending further review." Terrill hit the gavel and adjourned the inquest until Saturday morning at 10:40 a.m.

As the crowd was filing out, there was talk the police had information that would connect Reifel to the crime, and the coroner had him jailed to ensure he wouldn't run off. Some said Chief Tooker advised locking him up to keep him from talking to reporters and adding to the confusion. Whatever the reason, the authorities had their first suspect behind bars.

~~~~~

An unusual procedural wrinkle developed on Friday concerning the burial certificate required by the cemetery authorities. Undertaker Ryno received the certificate signed by Coroner Terrill and found it to be improperly made out. According to cemetery regulations, the coroner was obliged to either record the remains with the name of a known person or to simply write "Stranger" on the appropriate line. Terrill, for some reason, made out the form stating the body was that of an unknown person and in parentheses he wrote, (*Mary Dorman, a native of Scotland, aged twenty-five years*). When asked why he filled it out in this manner, Terrill stated, "I shall regard the body as that of Mary Dorman until it is proven that it is not her. Thorough investigation is being made and it will not be long before we should know the true value of this identification."

Mayor Daly recommended Ryno hold the certificate for a few more days when it was hoped the problem would be resolved. To add to the strange situation, it was rumored Mrs. Space was coming to Rahway to claim the body as that of her sister. It was not certain what the authorities would do should she actually make the demand.

Friday also saw Joe Reifel leave the station house with two deputies who escorted him back to his home. Reporters followed after him, but unable to get him to respond to their questions, they returned to the jail to seek out Chief Tooker. The chief told them, "Reifel was not arrested. He was simply brought to the station house for the purpose of identifying the knife, if possible. This he could not do, of course." That was all Tooker would say. Several reporters continued to snoop around the jailhouse and learned from confidential sources that Reifel was "intensely pumped" for several hours in an attempt to get information out of him. No one was able to find out if any was obtained.

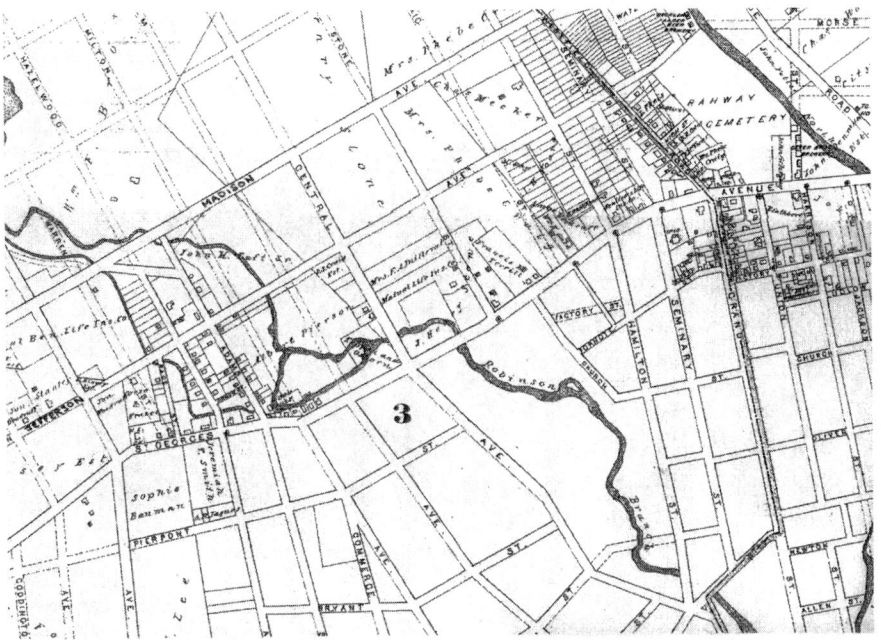

The Milton section of Rahway is shown on the left of this map circa 1882.
(Note: Adams Street was renamed Maple Avenue sometime before 1887)

Crime scene photograph taken on the morning the body was found.

Ryno's Morgue on Irving Street. (Building with the double chimney)

The above is an accurate portrait, published only in the

of the young woman mysteriously **MURDERED AT RAHWAY**, New Jersey, on March 25, 1887. It represents her with every article of dress worn by her, and as she appe d the day before the murder. To any person o persons, who from this clue, may discover the murderer and secure his or her conviction, I will, on proper proof, pay the ove reward.   (Signed.)

Richard K. Fox

AZETTE" PUBLISHING HOUSE,
KLIN SQUARE, NEW YORK.

THIS CIRCULAR AROUND.

City Hall offices and Council Chambers were located on the third floor of the Rahway Savings Bank building.

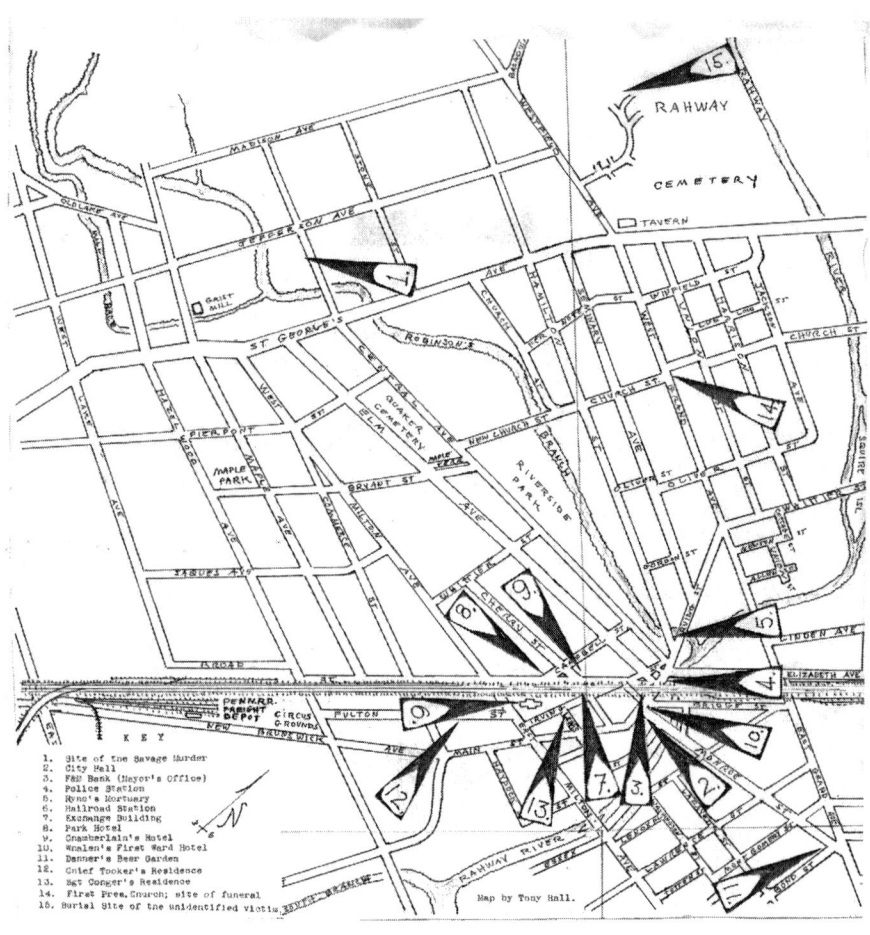

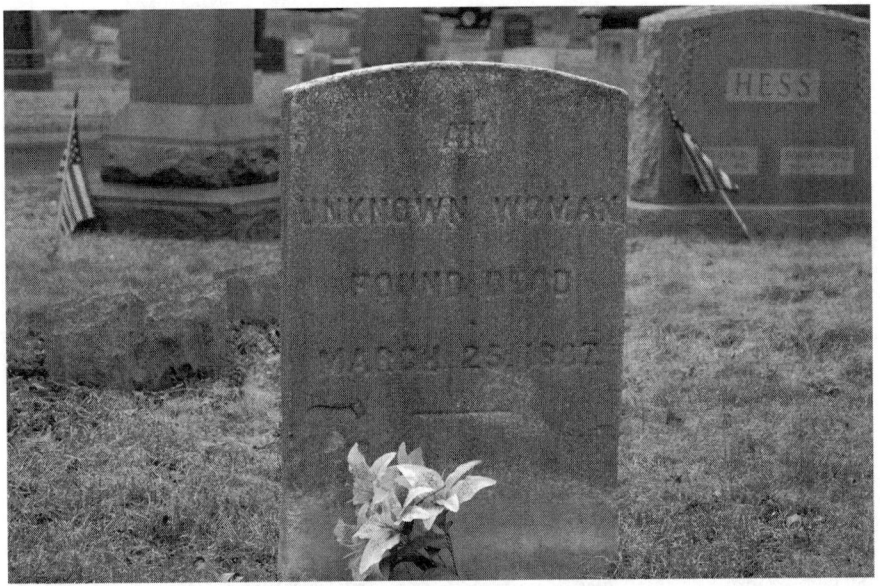

Saturday, April 23 – Wednesday, April 27, 1887

The Saturday morning hearing was called to order promptly at 10:40 a.m. Joe Reifel, who was told to be present, was in the chambers seated next to his roommate, Charles Henderschott. The authorities had gotten all they could out of Reifel and most were satisfied he was not directly involved with the crime. They wanted him to attend in the event he should need to be recalled. Their attention now turned to Henderschott, whose name had come up during the testimonies of several witnesses, and like Reifel, he lived near the crime scene and was friends with the same unsavory characters.

Charlie Henderschott was an illiterate, common laborer, who for most of his twenty-two years never had a place to call home. He was stocky, handsome in a tough way with steel blue eyes and a thick crop of blond hair that when combed down, looked like wet straw. Having been in Rahway only a short time and not one to be sociable, no one knew much about him. No one was sure of his relationship to Reifel or how it was he came to lodge with him. Not even his co-workers at Bloodgood's knew much about this introverted employee. As Henderschott walked to the stand, he seemed uncomfortable in his collarless white shirt, suspenders, and black trousers. He was a man suited for overalls.

State your name and residence.

Charles Henderschott. I live on Dr. Meeker's place in Rahway.

Where are you employed?

I work at Bloodgood's.

Explain how you came to board on Dr. Meeker's farm.

I stopped to stay with Joe Reifel this winter while Dr. Meeker was down South.

How long have you been staying there?

About four months.

How far is it from the Meeker Farm to Bloodgoods?

Don't know.

How long does it take to walk from the Farm to Bloodgoods?

Don't know exactly.

What time did you go to work on Saturday, March 26?

Seven o'clock.

How long have you been employed at the mill?

Four years.

Do you know many people who work at the mill?

I know some, but I'm not very friendly with them.

You must talk with some of them.

I talk only with those who work in my area—Boss Mackey, Mr. Harlan, Joe Fickle.

Do you know Sadie Van Ness?

Yeah, I know Sadie.

How long have you known Miss Van Ness?

I've known her since I started working there.

When did you hear of the murder?

I heard after I got to the mill.

Who told you?

Mr. Harlan told me first. He said a girl was murdered up at Milton.

Did you talk to anyone else about it?

I didn't talk to nobody else.

Have you seen the body?

Yes.

When did you first see it?

I saw the body for the first time on Sunday morning at ten o'clock at Ryno's.

Did you get a good look at the girl?

I took a pretty good look. I noticed her cut throat.

What color was her hair?

I can't remember to be sure.

Was anyone with you at Ryno's?

Joe Reifel was with me.

Can you tell the jury your actions that Sunday morning?

Me and Joe left the farm to go see the body at about nine-fifty. We went directly to the morgue. The last church bells were ringing about ten-thirty. It was about a forty-minute walk. We went into the morgue, saw the body, came out, and I went to church. Joe went to the post office and then went home. I went home after church was over. I got home about half past noon. I stayed on the farm the balance of the day.

Could you tell the jury what you did on Thursday, the day before the murder, after you left work?

I left work at six, got home at six-thirty, got supper, washed dishes, and went to bed.

What time was it when you went to bed?

About eight o'clock.

Do you know Clinton Froat and William Keech?

Yeah, I know both. They live in Milton.

Have you ever been to their house?

Yeah.

Did you go to a party at Froat's on Thursday night?

Yeah.

What time did you leave the farm to go?

I left about eight.

You just told the jury you went to bed at eight o'clock.

I got the days mixed up. I forgot about going to the party.

Did you speak to anyone the next day about the party?

I told Sadie Van Ness about the party and Joe Reifel. Nobody else.

Did anyone go to the party with you?

No, I went by myself.

Did you meet anyone on the way?

No.

Can you remember the names of those who were at Froat's that night?

I can't tell everyone who was there. Charlie Lambert was there, so was Sarah Jane Richmond and Mary Richmond. That's all I know.

Do you know James Smith of Kinsey Corner?

Yeah.

Was he at the party?

No.

Do you know Mrs. Lambert?

No.

Do you know Mrs. Froat?

I know Mrs. Froat. She was there.

Do you know William Keech?

Yeah.

Was he at the party?

Yes.

How many people would you say were at this party?

I can't tell. I didn't count them.

Well, about how many would you say?

I should judge about thirty.

Can you give the jury any descriptions of some of the others who were there?

No, I got nothing to say about any of the others.

How many ladies were there?

Couldn't tell.

What went on at this party?

We had supper. There wasn't any dancing. There was a little "cutting-up" show. Keech blackened up his face and scared the little ones.

What was the reason for this affair?

Mrs. Froat said the party was in honor of Mrs. Lambert who got married. She told me that night that Mrs. Lambert was her sister.

Were you introduced to Mrs. Lambert?

No.

When did you find out there was going to be a party?

Mrs. Froat invited me the previous Sunday.

And you say you knew no one else who was there?

The names I told you were the only ones I knew.

What time did you leave?

It was around five o'clock.

Did you leave by yourself?

No, Mary Richmond left with me.

Were others still there when you left?

We were the first to go. The others didn't seem like they were ready to go.

Where did you and Mary Richmond go after you left?

We walked down to Main Street. She lives at the widow Black's on Main. After I walked her home, I went back to Meeker's place.

What time would you say it was when you got home?

About five-thirty.

Tell the jury what you did on Friday, March 25.

I went to work in the morning and worked all day. Stopped work at six o'clock and went home. Was home all evening.

Was Joe Reifel at home?

Joe was home, but went out for a while. He came back around quarter of nine. Jim Smith was with him.

How long was Smith there?

I don't know. I went to bed.

Did you tell Chick Lawrence and Dick Collins at the mill that Joe Reifel was out all Friday night?

No, I never said that.

Have you talked to Joe Reifel about the murder?

Yeah.

Have you talked to Sadie Van Ness about the murder?

I haven't talked to her since the Saturday the body was found.

Are you aware that Joe Reifel sells eggs?

Sure.

(The witness is here shown the basket.)

Did you ever see this basket?

I saw Chief Tooker carrying it down the street. I never saw it before that.

Are there baskets around the Meeker Farm?

I've seen a basket at the farm, but it's larger than that one. I think Dr. Meeker owns it.

Let's go back to the party at Froat's on that Thursday prior to the murder. It's hard to believe you've told the jury everything you know. Were there any strangers there?

There were some. They were strangers to me at least. There was one strange man there who I heard was from Short Hills.

What types of dresses were the women wearing?

I don't take note of such things.

Was it a very lively party?

I wouldn't say lively, it was only sociable.

What else can you remember that you haven't told us?

I remember supper and the blacking of faces. There was an accordion for music.

Was there a dispute between Froat and a lady or Keech and a lady?

Can't tell ya anything about a dispute. I didn't hear nothin' of the kind.

Is it true that Clinton Froat was walking around outside the house carrying a club?

Froat did go out with a club and paced out front to chase some boys away who were throwing gravel at the windows.

Could you describe the club?

It looked like a police club, about eighteen or nineteen inches long, brown in color, varnished.

Did Keech leave the house?

Yeah, he went out.

(Here the witness is shown the hat found by the body.)

Was anyone at the party wearing this hat?

I didn't see anyone with that hat on.

Were any ladies wearing hats?

Two ladies had hats with high crowns, but there was no hat like that one. I'm sure of that.

Did you go to Froat's house on Friday night, March 25?

No.

Did you ever pay for groceries that were delivered to the Froats?

Yes. My mother boards at Froat's. I pay her board. I paid the driver of Bloodgood's Grocery to take them there.

How long has your mother boarded with the Froats?

Since the Froats came to Rahway.

Are you a relative of Clinton Froat?

No.

Was your mother at the party?

Yes.

Did you have any conversation with your mother about the murder?

No.

Did you ever take eggs from Meeker's Farm and bring them to your mother?

No.

Do you visit the Froats often?

I went over there quite a bit prior to the murder. I haven't gone over much since.

Why not?

I didn't want to go until this thing is settled, as there are suspicions.

When did you hear suspicions concerning the Froats?

I heard the workers talking at the Mill.

Do you think Froat is connected with the murder?

I don't suspect anyone.

When was the last time you saw the body of the murdered woman?

When I saw her at the morgue the Sunday after she was found. That was the first and last time.

Did you ever see her before?

No.

Do you know her name?

No.

Was she at Froat's party?

No.

Prosecutor Wilson stopped here. He had done a masterful job of leading his witness to the point of getting him confused and annoyed. Yet, with all the hammering of questions, Henderschott's answers did nothing to advance the case. Besides his confusion regarding the party guests, all his responses seemed honest and accurate.

Coroner Terrill felt the witness was put through enough for the time being and excused him from the stand. Noting it was a quarter past noon, Terrill adjourned the meeting and told the jury to reconvene at 2:45 p.m. He also advised Henderschott to be back at that time to resume his testimony.

~~~~~

Juror William Brunt sat at a table in Danner's Beer Garden, an East Rahway establishment on the corner of Monroe and Bond, four short blocks from City Hall. He had found the morning session to be slow moving and it had been difficult for him to keep his concentration. He needed a few stiff drinks, but as was the usual situation, he only had money for one. He looked around hoping he might recognize someone who would buy him a round. Most of the customers in the place were workingmen from the neighborhood who came to Danner's for whiskey, beer, and company. Margaret Danner, the proprietress, was an East Rahway native and was wary of patrons from the west side of town, especially if they resided in the Milton section. She considered

Brunt no better than a tramp and didn't like his habit of bumming drinks. However, ever since his appointment to the jury panel, she had become a little more civil toward him. On this day, she bought him a drink, thinking she might get some first-hand information about the trial. The juror heartedly accepted, and being buoyed by the new found attention, asked Danner to join him.

Brunt was just starting to give the tavern owner his perspective on the hearings when Henry Decker entered, spied him, and quickly moved to the table. He got close to Brunt's ear and said nervously, "Bill, come on outside, I gotta talk to you." Not wanting to leave his free shot and not understanding the import of Decker's request, Brunt replied, "What's the matter, Deck? Sit down, have a beer." In the same nervous tones and still close to Brunt, Decker again implored, "Listen to me. I gotta tell ya somethin' I just heard." Brunt now realized his friend was serious, got up, slugged down his drink, and followed him outside.

Decker went a distance from the saloon and when he was certain no one was around to hear, he turned and said, "Johnnie Yose and Caleb DeCamp are tellin' people you owned the knife that killed the girl."

Brunt's eyes widened. "What? That's a lie." Then suddenly more worried, he asked, "Who told you they were bringing my name into it?"

Decker was still excited as he told his story. "I was at Crowell's stable and I overheard one of those newspaper fellas askin' Frank Crowell if he knew anything about you. You know, Frank's on the Council so the guy figured he might know some things about somebody. Frank didn't say nothin', but asked why he wanted to know. The newspaper fella said two men told him that Juror Brunt was the owner of the murder weapon, and he said he was thinkin' about puttin' the story in his paper. Frank told him it was nonsense and wanted to know the names of the two men. The reporter said it was John Yose and Caleb DeCamp. After I heard that I came lookin' for you." Decker paused, "Whata ya gonna do?"

Brunt was scared. He knew this was nothing more than Caleb DeCamp playing tricks to get even with the authorities for locking up his brother, but he couldn't understand why he would pull him into the charade. His mind raced over the past few months trying to remember a time he might have wronged DeCamp. He drew a blank. As far as what he was going to do, he wasn't sure. He thanked Decker for the alert and told him to hang around downtown to see if he could hear anything more. Having forgotten his thirst, Brunt hurried back to City Hall, frantically wondering how he would deal with this unexpected turn of events.

~~~~~

The rumor about the knife and its ownership had circulated rapidly and had not missed the ears of the coroner and the prosecutor. With this new potential lead, Prosecutor Wilson intended to get right to the matter. His plan was to recall Charlie Henderschott and try to rattle him into making a slip about the weapon.

State your name again.

> Charles Henderschott.

Did you ever see a penknife in the possession of Joseph Reifel?

> No.

Does Joseph Reifel own a penknife?

> I think he does.

Did you ever see it?

> Yes.

What does it look like?

> Can't really say for sure.

Does it have a long blade or a short blade?

> I think it has a little, short blade.

How many blades does it have?

> I don't know.

Do you know the color of the knife?

It has a brown handle.

(Here the witness is shown knives, none of which he said were Reifel's.)

Do you own a penknife?

Yes, it's got a brown handle.

How long have you had the knife?

Two or three months.

How many blades does it have?

Two. One big blade and one small.

(Here witness is shown his knife.)

Is this your knife?

Yes.

Is this the only knife you own?

Yes.

Do you know if Clinton Froat carries a knife?

I don't know.

Do you know if William Keech carries a knife?

I've never seen him with a knife.

(Here witness is shown the basket again.)

Have you ever seen this basket before?

First time I saw it was when I saw a picture of it in the *Advocate*. Some of the boys at the mill showed it to me.

As the basket was being displayed, Juror Brunt rose and awkwardly addressed the coroner, "Mr. Coroner, I would like permission to withdraw from the jury so that I may testify as a witness." Brunt had heard enough. He was sure the line of questions was heading in the direction of his name and feared if he didn't act now, he would get mixed up in the investigation and become a suspect. With knowledge of the recent knife rumor, Terrill granted Brunt's request and told him to remove himself from the jury area. The murmurs from the audience that started with Brunt's request were quieted when the prosecutor called for Frank Smith to be brought in to face the witness.

Is this the man who came home with Joseph Reifel on Friday night, March 25?

No, it was his brother, Jim.

That's all for this witness.

Wilson wasted no time in recalling Joseph Reifel. The prosecutor sensed he was onto something and was anxious to continue.

State your name once again for the record.

Joseph Reifel.

On Friday evening, March 25, you went to Lute Macann's and there met Jim Smith, who later went home with you. Is that correct?

Yes.

(Frank Smith was here brought in to face the witness.)

Is this the man you met at Lute Macann's and brought home with you?

No, it's not him; it was his brother.

Did you go to Chief Tooker since the last time you testified to view the knife?

Yes, I did.

Did you ever see it before?

No.

No further questions.

After a brief conference with the coroner, Wilson called the next witness. It was William Brunt. As the former juror approached the stand, it was difficult to tell if he was coming forth as a willing witness, confident of his testimony, or if he was wrestling with some inner dilemma. The courtroom was quiet with anticipation.

State your name and residence

William Brunt. I live on Jefferson Avenue in Milton.

What is your occupation?

Laborer.

When did you learn about the murder?

I was informed on Saturday, March 26, about a body being found. It was about 6:30 a.m.

Who told you about the murder?

My son. I was in the house when he came in and told me.

Did you go to see the body?

I went immediately to the spot and there saw the body.

Was anyone else there when you arrived?

I believe Frank Worth was there, but no one else.

Did you take particular note of the body and surroundings?

I did look at the body and around the area. I saw the woman's throat was cut. I was satisfied she was dead. I saw where the woman had been knocked down and dragged to the spot where she had her throat cut. I saw the basket of eggs there. I could see the print of her bare knee about eight feet from the body and from that I judge she was dragged. I noticed mud on her left knee. I then looked at the eggs and counted them. I counted about ten.

Those were the last words of Brunt's testimony for the day. Juror Josiah Stagg, as if awakened from a sleep, looked at the witness with disgust and cut into Brunt's account with sharp words. "What's he doin' up there? Don't believe a word he says. There isn't anything in him. He's a bum of the worst kind." As the other jurors scrambled to try to quiet Stagg, the gallery burst into an uproar of laughter. The aroused juror had awakened, but not from an idle daydream. He had spent his break in Whalen's saloon over-imbibing in the spirits, and had come out of a drunken stupor. Terrill banged at his desk demanding order, but quickly realized the proceedings could not continue under these strange circumstances. Those who could hear his voice over the ruckus heard him adjourn the session until next Thursday.

~~~~~

It had been four weeks since the body of the unknown woman was found; yet, interest in the murder remained high. The crime scene maintained its magnetic aura, pulling the usual Sunday crowds to the awful spot. The lonely stretch of Central Avenue, which might otherwise have had the charm of a lover's lane, had been transformed into something grotesque. Curious visitors would stand beside the patch of ground where the body had lain, staring and pointing as if the mutilated corpse was still before them. Some claimed that if one looked closely, spots of blood could still be seen. The entire field had been trampled down by the thousands of feet that had kicked through the rough grass searching for clues, and from everyone's lips came the same questions: "Who was the girl?" and "Who killed her?" Two visitors on this particular Sunday afternoon were Mrs. Agnes Space and Mrs. Jane Harris who had an appointment to meet with the authorities on Monday to claim the body of their sister, Mary Dorman.

The Mary Dorman identification was so compelling, that when the two sisters entered the police station, they were received by not only the chief, but by Mayor Daly, Coroner Terrill, Detective Keron and Ryno the undertaker. After brief introductions, the coroner addressed the ladies. "I am anxious to hear if you have new information that might shed light on this mystery and prove the murdered girl is in fact your sister."

"We do," answered Mrs. Harris. "Our brother-in-law, Andrew Kirkwood, knows all about your Rahway murder."

The implication of the brother-in-law caught the officials off guard, and with their interest piqued, they listened more intently as the woman continued. "Andrew has been the ruin of Mary. She was always the prettiest in the family. All the boys were crazy for her. Andrew was married to Maggie, another of our sisters, but he always acted queerly towards Mary. When he left Scotland in August to come to this country, he told Maggie as soon as he found work, he would send money so she could join him. Instead, he wrote letters to Mary urging her to come to the United States. He even sent money to pay for her passage. By February, Mary had saved enough and left aboard one of the Anchor Line Steamers. No one has heard from her since."

The pause in her account gave the mayor the chance to ask, "How can you be certain your sister departed in February? According to Kirkwood, he didn't receive any letters indicating she was planning to come over."

"Andrew's not telling all he knows. I brought a letter Maggie sent my husband saying Mary had left and would be arriving sometime in the middle of March. Andrew knows of this letter. I also have a letter at home from my mother asking if I would see to Mary's needs after her arrival."

Mayor Daly extended his hand. "May we see the letter?"

Mrs. Harris opened her purse and took out a small sheet of neatly folded writing paper. She gave it to the mayor.

The letter was dated March 3, 1887. The mayor read the two lines to himself and then aloud. "Mary sails for New York on March 17. Don't tell my sisters that Mary is married."

Detective Keron made the next query. "Why do you think your brother-in-law is responsible for your sister's murder?"

"I think there was something suspicious about him leaving Scotland so suddenly and Mary knew the reasons. He was fearful she would tell more than would be good for him. When my husband went to Castle Garden to welcome Mary and bring her home, she was not to be found. After asking around, he learned that a girl who fit Mary's description had been met by two men who took her away from the dock. One of the men answered the description of Andrew. I think he must have taken her to a boarding house or hotel for a time and then, under the pretence of taking her to meet her sisters, decoyed her to the lonely spot here in Rahway and killed her."

The most perplexed official in the room was Coroner Terrill. As much as he wanted to believe the murdered girl was Mary Dorman, the fact that she had a child negated the possibility. His voice was firm as he said to the women, "The murdered girl can't be your sister. I wanted to believe it was her, and checked every source I could. I sent cable dispatches over to Scotland inquiring about your sister. It was communicated to me this morning that your sister gave birth to a child when she was fourteen. The autopsy shows the victim was never pregnant."

Mrs. Space, who had been quiet to this point, cut in with emotion, "I don't care what the doctors say. My sister had a child when she was very young so the doctors might be mistaken. Do you suppose I don't know my own flesh and blood? You have only to look at the face of that poor dead girl and then at my own to see the resemblance. We have the same features and build. Every person who saw me at the undertaking shop spoke of how much we looked alike. That girl is my sister!"

Everyone in the room was taken by the honest sincerity in Mrs. Space's conviction and to appease her, and perhaps himself, the coroner directed Detective Keron to find out what he could about Kirkwood in the days and nights surrounding the crime. Terrill ended the interview by telling the ladies the body would not be handed over to them, at least for a few days, until more investigative work could be done.

~~~~~

Had Mrs. Space been the only person who was so exact in every detail and so adamant about the girl's identity, the authorities might have reasoned the pregnancy issue was in error, and concluded the victim must be Mary Dorman and closed the case. Unfortunately, no such solution could be so easily drawn. The Ana Larsen story was being promoted by a number of officials and two new identifications were presented by persons just as strong in their beliefs as was Mrs. Space.

Since their breaking story on Sunday, April 17, The *World* continued to assert their theory in each subsequent issue. Still critical of those papers that blasted their findings, the *World* belittled them for supporting the Dorman identification. "Thus far, there has not been a scintilla of evidence to dispute the identification which Count Zaleski made of the body as that of Ana Christine Larsen. The other identifications made with such positive assertion and seconded so vigorously by even more unreliable champions have all been exploded, particularly that which strove to make the body that of Mary Dorman. Mrs. Space of Deckertown was in error as the *World* pointed out, and it begins to look as though it was brought up now and given notoriety in order that those who have thrown discredit on the *World* identification may, under cover of this false scent, give time to the following up of the clues so generously given (by *World* reporters) on the Larsen case." With headlines reading, "Almost Surely Ana Larsen" and "All Pointing to Ana Larsen," the story was taking on more credibility to the point where the coroner was considering calling on Count Zaleski to give his testimony.

On Tuesday and Wednesday, two identifications were made with such accuracy the authorities were again called upon to conduct interviews. Mrs. Kate Lyons of New York City was positive the murdered girl was an Irish immigrant named Maggie Gormley. According to Mrs. Lyons, a friend of hers, who lived in Elizabeth, employed Maggie as a housekeeper. It was while visiting her friend that Mrs. Lyons became acquainted with the young Irish girl. The two came to enjoy each other's company and on several occasions when Maggie had a day off, she would take the train to New York to see her. The story got more interesting as Mrs. Lyons continued. Maggie's last visit was in late January and on that day, she gave the girl a pair of shoes as a present. Mrs. Lyons identified those shoes as the same ones worn by the murder victim. She also made a second startling claim. The knife found by the body belonged to Maggie. It was her belief that during the struggle, Maggie pulled the knife from her pocket in an attempt to ward off her assailant, but he wrested the weapon from her hand and used it to slash her throat. Mrs. Lyons could not supply any theory as to what happened to Maggie after she left New York City, nor was she able to answer other pertinent questions, but she was insistent in her recognition of the shoes and knife.

Mr. and Mrs. Thomas Clinton of Bridgewater were very persistent in their belief the murdered girl had stopped by their home on Wednesday, March 23, two days prior to the crime. The girl, who spoke no English at all, was with a man who was fully twice her age. In his broken English, the man introduced himself as Charles and said the girl was his wife, Mary. The Clintons described the girl's hair, height, general build, the bag she carried, the rings she wore, her clothes, and the umbrella in every detail matching exactly with the victim and her effects. Both Mr. and Mrs. Clinton gave examples of Charles' cross behavior toward his wife, and Mrs. Clinton had a strong impression the girl was being held against her will. Clinton reinforced his wife's suspicion when he told the authorities of an ominous comment made by Charles. According to Clinton, Charles said his wife wanted to go back to Sweden, but he was against it and he threatened he would cut her throat if she tried to leave.

The Lyons and Clinton identifications left the interviewers with mixed reactions. Coroner Terrill felt the stories were fabricated, based on details that had been reported in all the papers and suggested any follow-up investigation would be a waste of time. It was his feeling both parties were only after the reward money. The others agreed it would be easy for anyone to create a story from what had been printed in the newspapers; however, they felt there was enough in the two accounts to warrant more study. "There has to be an answer," reasoned Mayor Daly. "We can't disregard any identification until we're positive it's no good." The investigation of the two stories would be left open.

~~~~~

By Wednesday, information had come back casting further doubts on the Mary Dorman identification. Detective Keron returned after having had an interview with Andrew Kirkwood, who he located in Paterson, and brought back a written statement accounting for his whereabouts the weekend of the murder. The alibi alleged Kirkwood was in Paterson Friday night (some twenty-five miles from Rahway) and that he left for Jersey City on Saturday morning. The statement was signed by four witnesses. Ex-Chief Wright was assigned to escort Sadie Van Ness to Kirkwood's Jersey City residence to see if she could recognize him. Van Ness had earlier testified she had seen a strange man on Central Avenue a few hours before the murder and the authorities wanted to know if it was Kirkwood. After their meeting, Van Ness could not identify him as the man she saw that evening. The *World* conducted its own interview with Mrs. Harris who was now wavering in her story connecting her brother-in-law to the murder. She said she was distressed over the newspaper reports that she implicated Kirkwood. "What I did say," she declared, "was that Andrew might not have been so positive in his statement that the girl was not Mary." Although her allegations against her brother-in-law had softened, she still insisted the dead girl was her sister.

The major newspapers with overseas correspondents had been sending cable dispatches to Scotland ever since the Dorman identification surfaced, asking for any information on the girl. On Wednesday afternoon, the *New York Herald* received an extensive report giving many details concerning Mary's past, as well as her last days in Scotland. An investigative reporter gleaned his first set of notes from Mary's mother who became deeply depressed when he gave his reason for coming. The old lady struggled as she supplied him with many facts. Mary's parents had eleven children, nine daughters and two sons, of which Mary was one of the oldest. Her father died when she was twelve, making it necessary for the older children to go out to work in order to help support their widowed mother. Mary and two of her sisters found work as housekeepers in the more respectable houses in the area. Mary, who was said to have been the handsomest of the girls, began to attract the attention of all the young men in the neighborhood. She soon became involved with one particular boy and as a consequence of an evening of passionate indiscretion, she gave birth to a child. The year was 1877, when Mary was fourteen years old. The last time the mother saw her daughter was on January 22, at the Grand Hotel in Glasgow, where Mary worked as a maid. It was then Mary said she was preparing to sail to America.

The reporter was also able to locate Samuel Caine, the father of the child, who he found living in a poorhouse. When told of the possibility Mary might have been murdered, the man was totally indifferent. He had had nothing to do with wife or child until 1884 when he finally married Mary, who for several years had complained to him about his lack of support. Caine, a lazy, shiftless sort, agreed to the marriage, but didn't change his idle ways and remained content to let his wife be the breadwinner for the family. They lived this way for about a year until Mary left him, intent on never coming back. He said he saw his wife once more in February of 1886, at which time she told him she was going abroad to be rid of him.

Perhaps the last person to see Mary was Mrs. Elsa Lithgow, landlady at the Grand Hotel, the place where Mary's mother last saw her. The woman said Mary was one of the most perfect servants she ever had and was a clean, tidy, attentive, and civil waitress. If she had a vice, it was her fondness for liquor, but the landlady was quick to add, she had never seen her in a drunken condition. For a reason she couldn't explain, Mrs. Lithgow always felt Mary had a considerable amount of money for a girl in her station of life. Mary left her employment in February.

Although all indications pointed to the fact that Mary left Scotland sometime between the middle of February to early March, no records were found at Castle Garden or on the ship's log that a woman named Mary Dorman had journeyed to America. It is possible the girl registered using an assumed name, but after carefully checking the records and interviewing stewards and ship hands, emigration officials and clerks, nothing was found to give any proof the girl ever sailed or arrived.

~~~~~

The day ended with a strange rumor coming out of police headquarters. In an effort to explore another angle, Sergeant Conger had some three weeks before, taken the eggs that were found lying by the mysterious basket and brought them to his henhouse for incubation. The talk around headquarters was that one egg actually did hatch, and produced a chick that resembled the Plymouth Rock breed. It was suspected Conger's next step would be to try to locate the farm that raised this variety of chickens. The investigation had reached a point where all avenues, no matter how unusual, were worth pursuing.

Thursday, April 28, 1887

William Brunt sat at the back of the council chambers surrounded by empty chairs. Since his aborted testimony on Saturday, his reputation had gone from bad to worse, and today, no one was comfortable sitting next to him. For the past four days, his neighbors had made his life miserable. He was looked upon as a pariah. No one talked to him, no one gave him the odd jobs he counted on for his livelihood, and everyone avoided him. If he entered any establishment, patrons would turn their backs and curse him under their breath. He was warned by a number of the Milton denizens, "If you don't watch what you say, you'll live to regret it." On Wednesday night, rocks were thrown through his front windows.

Brunt was not a likable fellow, and the feeling was he couldn't be trusted, and if he had any loyalty at all, it was to himself. The prospect of him testifying had everyone who knew him ill at ease for they had no idea what he would say or whose name he might utter in connection with the murder. One thing they did know for sure, however. If William Brunt had to save someone's skin, he would make sure it was his own.

State your name.

William Brunt.

Before we adjourned on Saturday, you were telling the jury what you noticed as you surveyed the murder scene. Tell the jury again what time it was that you went to the site.

I went to where the body was found at 6:30 a.m. I was there about twenty minutes looking over the body and surroundings. After that, I went home.

Tell the jury your whereabouts on Thursday, March 24, the day before the murder.

I had been in the woods that day. I came down Central Avenue about four-thirty in the afternoon and saw Mr. Dunham fixing the fence right about at the spot where the body was found. I then went home, got my supper, and went to town. Came back home about eight o'clock.

Did you notice anything unusual going on around Clinton Froat's house that night?

I met my two boys at Baker's Corner and they told me they saw William Keech traveling up and down the street with a club.

After your boys told you this, what did you do?

I went up Maple Avenue toward home with the boys and saw Keech, but I didn't see any club.

Do you think he was carrying a club?

I didn't see it, but I'm pretty sure I heard him sound a club on the sidewalk.

How close were you to Keech?

About thirty feet.

What time would you say it was?

About eight o'clock in the evening.

Where did you go next?

I went home and went to bed.

Did you know about a party at Froat's house that same night?

Yes.

How did you know about it?

My boys told me there was a party.

Was that the first you heard of it?

Yes.

Do you know anyone who attended that party?

No.

How close do you live to the Froat's?

I'd say about a hundred forty feet.

Since you live that close, were you disturbed by any noises during the night?

No. I went to bed by nine and slept through the night. I don't know of anything that happened that night.

Was anyone in your family aroused that night?

No.

How many children do you have?

Four.

And none of them heard anything?

Well, my girl lives in California. Only two of my three boys live with me. They were in the house and went to bed around nine. I went to bed with them.

How old are your boys?

One is fifteen, the other thirteen.

Is it not true that you told persons that you saw a man with a lantern outside your barn that night?

No, I never said that!

Did you see any strangers around Froat's that night?

No.

What are your feelings about Clinton Froat and William Keech?

I have no personal feelings against either.

Did you state you were willing to make a complaint against Froat and Keech?

I was willing to make a complaint against both on the grounds of what my boys said. I was going to base my affidavit on what my boy Willie said.

What did Willie tell you?

He told me that while he was at his uncle's store, he saw a woman that looked like the murdered girl hanging clothes in Clinton Froat's yard.

What day was it that he saw this girl?

Friday afternoon of the murder.

Did you see anything unusual in the actions of Froat or Keech that would make you suspicious of them?

On Saturday afternoon, the day after the murder, Keech and Froat were standing in the window all afternoon, watching my house. I thought they all looked very suspicious.

Did you report your suspicions to anyone?

Yes. Sunday morning I went to the police station and saw Officer Conger. I told him what the boys had said. He said that was his view of it exactly. When he questioned my boy Willie, he stuck to his story to the effect that the dead girl was the one he saw in Froat's house.

Are you now willing to make a charge against Froat and Keech?

No. I was willing to charge Keech and Froat with murder based on what the boys told me at the time. I have changed my mind since last Sunday and will not at this time make an affidavit.

Why did you change your mind about making a charge?

I have no reason of my own why I've changed my opinion against Keech and Froat. I first heard things being said against them on the Wednesday after the murder. It was bad, and I thought they would be very convenient persons to make a complaint against.

So what you're saying is you were suspicious of them because of stories you were hearing?

Their reputations had nothing to do with my suspicions.

Tell the jury what you were doing Friday night, the night of the murder.

I went to bed about nine. At around eleven, I heard somebody go by the house. I heard talking. I looked out my window and saw a person or maybe two in the street. The figures moved away and that was the last I saw or heard. Then, about fifteen minutes later, my brother's dog started barking.

Could you make out with any more clarity what you saw or heard?

No. It was a dark night. The talking was not very loud. My window was down. I couldn't hear distinctly.

Did you think there was something wrong that caused the dog to start barking?

I didn't expect anything to happen that night, but I did feel something was wrong.

You made a request to the coroner to remove you from the jury so you might be summoned as a witness. So far, you have not told the jury anything that might shed some light on this case. What information do you possess that would be of interest to this hearing?

I understand that Calab DeCamp is going to swear in respect to the knife.

Who told you that?

Friends of mine said they saw it in the paper.

Can you now add any new information concerning the knife?

Well, I know Calab DeCamp and George Ayres. George is a painter. I was with them at the Steven's Farm when Ayres was painting his wagon, but I was not asked for a loan of my knife. He never asked me for a loan of my knife. I'll swear he never did. And I never loaned a knife to Calab DeCamp. I have a good memory. I didn't even have a knife on my possession at that time. I didn't see anyone with a knife while we were there.

Was anyone else there who might give credit your story?

I think T. F. Ridge was there.

How long ago did this take place?

About three years ago.

Do you own a knife now?

Yes. I got it about ten years ago.

What does it look like?

It's a white-handled, four-bladed knife.

Is this the only knife you ever owned?

No. About six years ago, I bought a knife from George Harris for twenty cents. It was a brown, wooden-handled knife with three blades. Those are the only knives I own and the only ones I ever bought.

(The coroner then held up a knife.)

Did you ever see this knife before?

No. I never saw anyone have a knife like it. But, if it could be identified, I think I could tell who it belonged to.

What do you mean?

If Calab DeCamp or Johnnie Yose swears to the knife, I think I can swear to the owner. The man who I think owned the knife, if they swear to it, is the man who worked for John Yose on a thrashing machine. If they don't swear to the knife, then this is no clue. If they swear they have seen the knife, I think I know the man that had it.

Are you saying you suspect a man who was working for John Yose to be the owner of the murder weapon?

Yes.

Do you know his name?

I think his name is Jake. I can find his right name by going to the Justice of the Peace up the street. I think the jailer in Elizabethtown could also identify the knife. This same man served time in jail.

Why didn't you bring this information to the jury before you heard about the newspaper story?

I didn't know anything about a knife until then.

Are you presenting this story at this time because there is suspicion going around that you had some connection with the knife?

No! Not at all! I didn't bring it up because suspicion rested on me.

Did you tell the authorities that you could name the owner of the knife?

No. I haven't accused anyone of owning the knife within the last week.

Did you go to see Detective Keron in Elizabeth to tell him this story?

No, I went to Elizabeth on a job. I was delivering blocks for Mr. Ridge. I thought about going to see the detective, but George Wright told me not to.

(At this point in the testimony, Foreman Clark rose from the jury box and interrupted the questioning. The tone of his voice left no doubt he had a strong dislike for Brunt.)

Why are you making a statement in relation to the knife, if you know nothing about it except by hearsay?

I heard stories about the knife and thought there was something to them. I don't know anything else about a knife.

The foreman next addressed Coroner Terrill. "Mr. Coroner, I implore you to grant a recess so the jury members can clear their heads of this convoluted testimony. I have no idea where the prosecutor is going with his questions or what information he hopes to discover from the answers given by this witness. To me, it's all nonsense."

The coroner, although offended by Clark's interruption, had to agree. "I see it's almost one o'clock and I think everyone needs a break. We will recess until two. As for you Mr. Brunt, you will be recalled at that hour to continue your testimony."

~~~~~

Chief Tooker also needed a break after sitting through Brunt's confusing testimony. The chief knew Brunt had assumed a new sense of respectability and power since the first adjourned hearing back on March 30, when reporters hooked onto him as a potentially valuable source. He was a common laborer who never had his day in the sun, so he naturally relished the attention the newspapermen were giving him and went out of his way to answer any and all of their questions. Tooker could easily understand how Brunt could lose track of what he told each reporter over the ensuing weeks. Add to this his propensity for keeping himself out of trouble, even at the expense of others, and it was no wonder he was having a difficult time giving intelligible answers. It was Tooker's opinion that Brunt was irresponsible for any statements he might make, either under oath or otherwise. He wished the man would move out of town and never come back.

On his way out of City Hall, Tooker was met by a reporter who asked if he could join him on his walk. Tooker knew the reporter wrote for the *Elizabeth Daily Journal* and replied as he continued towards his Fulton Street home, "What's on your mind?"

"As Chief of Police, I think you ought to know something. While everyone was listening to that rube, Brunt, a meeting was going on in one of the anterooms down the hall. Five *World* reporters were in there drilling witnesses who are going to be called this afternoon. I recognized two of them. Count Zaleski and his wife. I didn't hang around very long, but it sounded to me like they were going over what they wanted them to say. What do you think of that? Can you believe those guys?"

The chief thanked the reporter for giving him the "heads up" and continued on alone. There was much that bothered him. Where were the County officials going in their investigation? How did the reporters know the schedule of witnesses when he didn't? Who would be the next to come under suspicion by the mere mention of a name? He was tired of all of them and couldn't wait until this whole thing was over.

~~~~~

State your name once again for the record.

William Brunt

This morning, you mentioned Mr. T. F. Ridge. What connection does he have with the murder weapon?

I never connected Mr. Ridge with the knife.

Do you know Jacob Windler?

Yes.

Is he the man you referred to this morning as working with John Yose?

Yes.

So, you're testifying that the knife belongs to Jacob Windler.

No, I'm not. If Calab DeCamp and John Yose said that Jacob Windler owned that knife, I wouldn't testify to it as fact. If they said that he had the knife in his possession at the trashing machine, I really couldn't swear to that either. If they testify to the ownership, then they are the ones that must know. If they testify that the knife belongs to a man named Reamer, I might believe them. If they testify that the knife belongs to a darky in Newark, I might believe that too.

Are you saying the knife belongs to a darky?

No, I said if Calab DeCamp and John Yose said it, I might believe them.

Let me get this straight. You're telling this jury that if Calab DeCamp and John Yose testified that any certain individual owned this knife, you might believe them.

Yes, that's right.

What if they testified that you owned the knife? Would you then believe them?

I wouldn't believe that! It's not my knife, I told you that! Mr. T. F. Ridge can swear he never saw the knife with me. If he tells the truth.

Is it true you told friends that if you did own the knife, you wouldn't acknowledge it to the authorities?

No. Well, I might have said last Thursday morning that if I owned that knife, I wouldn't admit to it. But I was just talking. It's not my knife!

Do you know Henry Decker?

Sure, he sometimes goes on jobs with me.

Was he with you on Friday afternoon, the day of the murder?

Yes, we went to Amboy on a delivery.

Did you come back together?

Yes, we came back in my wagon.

Can you read and write?

I can write my name.

Would you know your signature if you saw it?

Yes.

(A signature was here shown the witness and he stated it was his.)

You may step down for now.

Without delay, Wilson called to the stand Charles Wright, Constable of Union County.

State your name and residence.

Charles Wright of Elizabeth.

Would you please tell the jury your connection with this case?

I am an officer of the county. I was called to see William Brunt on the Monday after the body was found.

What was the purpose of your meeting with Mr. Brunt?

I took a statement from him, which he signed.

Do you have the statement with you?

Yes.

Did Brunt sign it in your presence?

Yes.

(Brunt is shown the signed statement, which he acknowledged bore his signature. The letter was given to Clerk Marsh who was requested to read it.)

"I had been to Perth Amboy, got home between seven and eight o'clock. Decker, that is the man that went with me, came home on the cars and I came home alone on the evening of the twenty-fifth. The boys told me a colored man, John Edgar, had seen someone go in my barn with a lantern. That worked on my mind and I couldn't sleep. About eleven, two parties went past the house. The dog was barking. Then it was along toward four o'clock before I could sleep. I got up about half past four for about half an hour. I think there was a man standing in the road. I had a gun, but didn't know if it was loaded. I got up before six o'clock; saw Tom and Alfred Worth going to work. Alfred came back and told William, my son, that a woman had her throat cut. Then I went there, looked at the body, and saw a handkerchief by her side. I could see she had been dragged to the fence before her throat was cut. That is my opinion. It was nine o'clock when I went to bed. Did not go to the barn to see if anybody had been there. Thought it was of no use. The deed must have been done between eleven and twelve o'clock. The dogs made a great noise up to then. Signed, William Brunt."

Thank you, Constable. I have no further questions for you.

All eyes had turned to Brunt as the statement was being read. From the beginning of his testimony, it was not clear if he would prove to be an important witness or a fool. By now, most in the room had reached the conclusion he had no pertinent knowledge about the mystery, but was only interested in distancing himself from any suspicion. The former juror wished he had never volunteered his testimony and wanted desperately to leave the chambers. Before he had time to devise a plan to get away, however, Prosecutor Wilson called him back to the stand.

Again, state your name.

William Brunt.

In your earlier testimony, you said you woke up several times on Friday, March 25, the night of the murder. Tell the jury again what happened that night as you were trying to sleep.

That night, I didn't sleep at all. After I went to bed, I got up at eleven. Went back to bed and woke up about a half hour later.

Was either of your sons aroused by your getting out of bed during the night?

No.

Did you go out of the house after you got up?

No.

Did you get out of bed after eleven-thirty?

No, I didn't get out of bed until morning.

Just a minute, Mr. Brunt. In your statement to Officer Wright, you stated that you got up at 4:00 a.m. and saw someone in the road.

I made a mistake with what I just said. What I told the officer in my statement is true.

According to your statement to Officer Wright, you stated you came home alone from your job in Amboy and Henry Decker came home later by train. Yet, you told the jury, you came home together.

I made a mistake. My statement to the officer is not correct. I got mixed up on which night Decker came back in the cars.

Are there any other mistakes in your signed statement?

All the rest of it is correct.

Is it true that you told newspaper reporters that you knew the identity of the murderer?

I said to one reporter I knew who the murderer was.

Did you give the reporter a name?

Yes.

Did you name William Keech as the murderer?

I said it was William Keech up to last Tuesday. After Sunday, I didn't say who it was.

Why did you change your opinion about William Keech?

Up to last Saturday, I thought that Keech or Froat had something to do with the murder. Since then, I think it was done by a different party.

Is it true that you've been doing your own detective work trying to solve this mystery?

I haven't done any work or followed any clues connected to the murder since last Saturday.

Why did you decide to try to uncover the owner of the knife?

In my own mind, I never thought to try to find who the knife belonged to until after the suspicions against Keech and Froat began to slow up.

Isn't that about the same time that a certain New York newspaper ran a story connecting you to the knife?

About that time, yes. But, it isn't my knife. I could prove it by T. F. Ridge, Henry Decker, George Brunt, and Mr. Pierson.

Tell the jury what you were doing in Newark last Monday.

I went to a saloon in Newark to see if I could find a man named Jake Reamer.

Where exactly is this saloon?

It's on Broad Street near City Hall on the left-hand side going up.

Were you able to find the person you were looking for?

No, when I got to the saloon, only the barkeep was there. I asked him if he knew Jake Reamer. He said he thought he knew him, but he couldn't place him.

Why were you looking for Jake Reamer?

He is one of three men who I thought might own the knife.

Mr. Brunt, during your testimony, you've implicated several persons with this crime. As of this moment, just who do you think might have something to do with the murder?

It runs in my mind that Jacob Windler did it, but I still hold to the Reamer clue.

Why is it that you suspect Jacob Windler?

Somebody told me he was involved. I have no reason of my own.

Do you think it's honorable for a gentleman to make such a statement without some good reason?

From my evidence today, I wish it understood, I only know what I heard, nothing else. John Yose told Roger Gettings that Jacob Windler was the owner of the knife. Roger Gettings told me about it. I never said Jacob Windler was guilty of the murder.

Before you leave this stand, is there anything at all you can tell this jury that might be of importance to this inquest?

There is nothing more on my mind that I would like to tell before I go. And, don't forget, I asked to be a witness. Nobody called me to testify because they thought I had something to do with the murder.

Brunt was relieved he could finally escape, but before he had a chance to hurry out of the courtroom, the coroner ordered him to stand fast, saying he was not satisfied with his answers. Terrill wanted to be positive Brunt had no connection with the crime and so, he directed Chief Tooker to take the witness to police headquarters for more interrogation.

Few people in the chambers were expecting the next witness. The list of those scheduled to testify was not public information, so when the name Count Zaleski was called out, it caught the gallery by surprise. Not many put much stock in the story the Russian farmer gave the *World* naming the victim as Ana Larsen, so it was curious the County officials thought enough of it to summon him.

Zaleski was sixty-nine years old, but his erect stature and fashionable attire made him appear to be younger and taller. He had heavy, dark eyebrows, wore a full beard and mustache, and had dark brown, shoulder length hair giving him the look of a Bohemian. As he reached the stand, the bespectacled Count reached in a pocket and drew out a folded paper.

State your name and where you live.

Count Leo Zaleski. I own a farm in Roselle.

How long have you lived in Roselle?

Seven years.

(After Zaleski had taken the oath, he handed a letter to the prosecutor, which he wanted read as his testimony. Clerk Marsh was instructed to read it.)

"Ana Christine Larsen was my servant. She first came in the summer of 1884. I believe it was August. She was in my service for about four weeks. I only fed her. I didn't pay her any money. She went to Mrs. Furstman's in Cranford after she left me. She came to my house about two months later around Christmas. She was with a young boy. They were going to Elizabeth. I didn't see her again until I saw her in New York.

"Carl Woolf first came to my place in January 1884. I employed him as a servant. I made an agreement to pay him $4 per month with the provision that if he were good, he would get better pay. I was much pleased with him. He was in my employ from January to April 1884. In total, he got from me $35 besides clothes and other articles. We settled very satisfactorily when he left. I saw him next August when he brought Ana Larsen and begged for shelter. They had a young boy with them. I'd say he was about twelve. Ana said it was her brother. I questioned her once through Carl, she didn't speak English too well, how old her mother was and she said she was sixty-three. I said her mother was like Sarah in the *Bible*."

(Foreman Clark, still perturbed by Brunt's testimony and seeing no reason to listen to this long epistle, again broke into the proceedings.)

Count, who wrote that paper?

It is my statement.

Yes, but I want to know who wrote it out for you?

Why, one of the reporters from the *World* newspaper.

When and where?

Today in his room in the hotel.

Why did you want your statement written out?

Because I understand English imperfectly.

(Juror Clark, clearly exasperated, sat down. There was a pause as the prosecutor considered this new information. He walked to the clerk's desk, took the statement from Mr. Marsh, and after looking over the pages in a cursory manner, continued.)

What made you think the murdered girl might be Ana Larsen?

I saw in the paper the day after the murder that a lady was murdered in Rahway. I thought it might be Ana.

How long had the Larsen woman worked for you?

Four weeks.

How many times had you seen her together with Carl Woolf?

They were at my house four times together.

Do you think they were man and wife?

Of this, I am not certain. They roomed together when at my farm. Ana was really love crazy for him. Every time Carl left, she would give money to anyone to get information about him.

How did they get along when together?

They quarreled always.

The boy you mention in your statement. Do you think he was Ana's brother?

Ana would say he was her brother, but other people thought he was her own child.

Do you suspect that Carl Woolf is involved with the murder?

To me, it is possible.

Count Zaleski, how do you account for the basket of eggs found near the body?

Oh, she liked eggs; that I know. And, she ate them too, at my cost. Before she came with the boy, I had eggs in plenty. When she came, I had none. When she went away, I had eggs again.

When did you last see Miss Larsen?

In 1885 in New York, sometime in March, walking down the street. She was in the company of some half-drunken men.

Did you speak to Miss Larsen?

No. I did not speak to her.

Was one of the men you saw with her Carl Woolf?

No. I didn't know any of those men. To me, they were strangers.

Have you been to the morgue to view the body?

Yes.

Will you swear that Ana Larsen is the murdered woman?

Swear, I cannot do. But, gentlemen of the jury, I will not believe different from what I have stated, until I see living before me Ana Christine Larsen.

Count Zaleski, it's been over two years since you last saw Miss Larsen. How is it that you remember so well?

Why, sir, I am by profession a sculptor. It is my business to study faces. Ana was with me and employed by me. Should I not study her face? Being also a painter, I can judge about color of hair, eyes, and skin. The profile is never changed in a living or dead person. I have taken many busts of dead people, also many casts, and experience teaches me I am not mistaken. After viewing the body, I am certain it is Ana.

That will be all for now.

The prosecutor's next witness was Mrs. Zaleski, wife of the Count.

State your name and where you live.

Mrs. Lambertine Zaleski. My home is in Roselle.

Did you hear the statement made by your husband, and if so, do you corroborate with it?

I agree with all my husband said.

Did you have any conversation with Ana Larsen or Carl Woolf while they were at your farm?

I did, on several occasions. When Carl would visit Ana, it was easy to see she was so in love with him that I had to say to him, that you will have to marry this girl. I told him I would call for a minister and that I would even pay for the service. He said he would never marry her and I told him, she would make him marry her. After all, Carl brought her to this country and it is right for her to be acknowledged as his wife. I asked him what he had against her and he said he could not tell me. He just said he had found something out about her.

Did he ever tell you what he had discovered about Miss Larsen?

No, he never said.

Is there anything else you can tell the jury?

This is all I can state.

At the conclusion of the woman's testimony, a conference between Coroner Terrill, Wilson, and Foreman Clark took place, which lasted several minutes and at times appeared heated, after which the coroner announced there was only time for one final witness before adjournment. He also said it was the wish of the court that the hearings reconvene tomorrow morning at 11:00 a.m.

Due to the strong urging of Foreman Clark, the coroner was persuaded to schedule the fifth session for the very next day. Clark was very concerned and dissatisfied with the way the hearings were dragging on and saw no reason to suspend the testimonies for several days.

Prosecutor Wilson then called Thomas Rasmussen to the stand.

State your name and where you live.

Thomas Rasmussen. I am from Roselle.

How are you connected with this case?

I am cousin of Ana Christine Larsen.

When did you last see your cousin?

It was two years ago in Roselle. At Zaleski's.

Do you know Carl Woolf?

Yes.

When did you last see him?

I saw him at the same time and place.

Can you tell us what you know about your cousin as it relates to these proceedings?

Ana Christine Larsen was married in our country, Denmark. When it was, I can't remember. A son was born to her maybe fifteen years ago. I was present when Ana had her son.

Have you viewed the body of the murdered girl?

Mr. Ryno took me to see the body today. It is not the body of Ana.

How can you be sure?

The Ana Larsen that was at Zaleski's is the same Ana Larsen that is my cousin.

Ana is about thirty-five years of age. I only saw the face and hair of the dead girl, but it looks nothing like Ana. I saw pictures of the dead girl and none look like Ana. Ana's body is much smaller than the height and weight given for girl. Also, Ana wore earrings.

Did you recognize the clothing?

I know none of it.

Can you tell the jury anything else that may refute the claim that the body is that of your cousin?

Last December I was told that Ana was in Denmark. My mother wrote to me that Ana and the boy were both home.

Do you have that letter?

I gave it to Detective Keron.

Is it true that someone today tried to persuade you to give positive identification to the body and clothing?

Yes.

Who was that person?

Count Zaleski.

Has anyone tried to tell you not to identify the body?

No.

Mr. Coroner, I have no further questions.

Rasmussen's last answers drew loud objections from a representative of the *World* who strode to the coroner's desk and demanded permission to question the witness to clarify his comments. Reporter Crane of the Associated Press supported his colleague's request and voiced his feelings. "Let the man cross-examine the witness. Maybe something will finally come of all this." Terrill gave Crane a hard look and demanded order. The coroner thought it would be highly irregular to allow such questioning, but looked to the jury for their opinions. Foreman Clark was particularly opposed and said, "I object to any outside interference in this case. This Larsen story has had a fair show. I must protest against this man's further examination." As it was nearing 8:00 p.m., no one on the jury voiced opposition, so the coroner concluded the hearings for the evening.

Friday, April 29 – Sunday, May 1, 1887

The *New York World* was quick to refute the damaging statements made by Thomas Rasmussen, cousin of the paper's purported victim, Ana Larsen, with a scathing article in their Friday morning edition. It was the view of the publication that after wasting nearly five hours reviewing every minute detail of the inane testimony of William Brunt, the court gave little attention to their most important witnesses. The article denounced the jurors for being "more anxious to get home to dinner" than to perform their solemn duty, resulting in an examination of Rasmussen that was a sham. They condemned Rasmussen himself for plainly contradicting what he told the *World* reporters during their conference session prior to his testimony. The paper characterized him as "an ignorant fellow with a scant knowledge of English, who evidently didn't know what he was swearing to." The article went on to credit the testimonies of the Count and his wife as being the only accurate and truthful accounts presented the entire day, thus giving further credence to their theory.

Another New York daily pictured the hearings in an entirely different light. The *New York Herald* declared, "If there were any who harbored a belief that Count Zaleski's assertion that the body of the victim is that of Ana Christine Larsen, their faith was rudely shattered by revelations in the proceedings of last night's session." They contended the Rasmussen testimony was proof the *World* was orchestrating a presentation to legitimize their story by prepping witnesses with bits of evidence, which were circumstantial at best. They believed there were other possibilities to be investigated and no more time should be spent questioning persons involved with the Larsen story.

The *Herald* also reported that William Brunt was detained by the authorities in the chief's private office until 9:30 p.m., where he was closely questioned about his conflicting statements. According to a source close to the local police, Brunt was subjected to a severe interrogation that frightened him to a point where he began to say anything he thought they wanted to hear. In the end, it was concluded Brunt knew nothing at all that might aid the investigation and was sent home, with the realization he was no longer welcome in the city and that his days in Rahway were numbered.

~~~~~

Like Chief Tooker, Coroner Terrill wanted this enigmatic case to come to an end. He had never been associated with such an uncanny crime where neither the killer nor the victim was known, and where every bit of evidence was itself a mystery. Witnesses were non-existent and those persons called to testify did nothing to piece together any leads worth following. He knew that as each day passed, the prospect of finding answers would become more remote, and once the body was interred, any possibility of naming the victim would be all but gone. Dismayed by the failure of the Mary Dorman identification, Terrill came to acknowledge the Ana Larsen story as the one to pursue. With this plan in mind, his scheduled witnesses for Friday's session included three persons connected to the Larsen account. If their testimonies proved to be strong enough, the jury just might be persuaded to reach a verdict.

~~~~~

State your name and where you live.

My name is Abram C. Miller. I am a farmer. I live in Union Township.

Do you know Ana Christine Larsen?

I know a woman named Ana Woolf, but never knew her as Ana Larsen.

How is it that you came to know her?

She came to work for me two years ago last July 1884, and stayed with me about three weeks.

Can you describe this woman?

She was medium height; her hair was light in color. I think her eyes were gray. I'd say she was between twenty-two and twenty-five years old.

Did she wear any jewelry?

She wore two rings, but I couldn't tell you which fingers they were on. I think she wore earrings.

Have you been to the vault to see the body?

No.

After Miss Larsen, or Miss Woolf as you call her, left your employ, did you see her again?

Ana Woolf came back to my farm one time after she left to get the boy and take him away. She said she wanted to get him a place where he could get more wages.

About how old was the boy?

I'd say about fifteen.

Do you know the boy's name?

Yes, his name was Henry Woolf. I hired him and Charlie Woolf together and after Charlie had been with me awhile, he wanted me to take on his wife to work with us.

Were Charlie and Ana Woolf married?

I think they were married. They roomed together.

Was the boy Ana Woolf's son?

I don't think so.

Have you seen the boy since he left your farm?

No, although I heard from him about a year ago. He said he was in Cranford.

Have you seen pictures of the murdered girl?

Yes.

Do any resemble Ana Woolf?

The profile picture with the hat on resembles her I think, but I'm not very positive about it.

Have you seen the clothing?

No.

(The witness was shown the dead girl's hat, shoes, the egg basket, parasol, veil, and bag, but could not identify any of them.)

Thank you.

Prosecutor Wilson called his next witness.

State your name and where you live.

Louis E. Wenz. I live in Union. I'm a farmer.

Do you know Ana Christine Larsen?

I saw her three times, but didn't know her hardly at all. She stayed at my house two nights after she left Mr. Miller's.

Why did she come to your house?

Carl Woolf was working for me.

Did you have conversations with either?

I never spoke with the girl, but Carl told me that she was his wife. That's about all I know about them.

Do you know anything about a boy?

I saw the boy at Mr. Miller's.

Did Carl Woolf say it was his son?

He didn't say anything about a son.

Can you describe Ana?

It's hard for me to tell how Ana looked. It is nearly three years since I saw the woman.

What about her age or height?

I think she was about twenty-five. Can't judge how tall she was, she was rather stout.

Did you notice if she wore earrings?

I didn't notice.

Have you seen the body?

No.

Have you seen the pictures of the murdered girl and if you did, do any look like Ana Larsen?

I have seen the pictures. There is one picture where the girl has a hat on. That one looks something like Ana.

Have you seen the display of clothes the murdered girl was wearing?

No, and I don't think I could remember what Ana was wearing when I saw her back then.

(The witness was here shown the hat, parasol, veil, shoes, and basket, but could not identify them.)

I have no further questions for this witness.

At this point, Prosecutor Wilson recalled Mr. Miller.

State your name once more for the records.

Abram C. Miller.

You testified that one picture (#2) had a resemblance to Ana Larsen. In what way do you see a resemblance?

The girl's nose in that picture is similar and the hat is one like Ana wore.

Is the hair the same color?

I cannot tell exactly what color the girl's hair was.

Thank you again, Mr. Miller.

The Prosecutor next called Caroline Furstman to testify.

State your name and where you live.

Caroline Furstman. I live in New York City at 480 West 24th Street.

How is it that you may be of help to this case?

I was personally acquainted with Ana Larsen.

When did you last see Miss Larsen?

I last saw her in August of 1884 when I was living in Cranford. I hired her as a servant.

How long did she work for you?

About six weeks.

Can you describe Miss Larsen?

She had set features, high cheekbones, and her hair was a brown shade.

What would you say was Miss Larsen's age?

I should think from twenty-eight to thirty.

Have you seen the body?

No.

(Shown the pictures, the witness said two of them looked like Ana Larsen.)

Did she wear earrings?

I don't really remember.

Did she have rings?

Again, I don't remember.

Did she carry a bag for her belongings?

She had a bag when she first came to me.

If you were shown the bag, could you identify it?

I'm sorry, but if you showed me the bag now, I wouldn't be able to identify it.

Could you identify the clothes she wore?

I can't remember any of her articles.

Did she ever tell you she was married?

She told me she was married to a man named Charlie.

Did you get to meet Charlie?

He used to take dinner with her on Sundays. He always brought a boy with him who he called his brother.

What would you guess to be the boy's age?

Fourteen.

Do you think the boy might have been Miss Larsen's son?

No. Ana never told me she was a mother.

Prior witnesses have testified that Miss Larsen and her companion quarreled a great deal. Did you find that they argued a lot?

When they were alone in the kitchen, I often heard them talking loudly. I can't say they were quarrelling.

Why did Miss Larsen leave your employ?

I liked her as a servant, but she was so infatuated with this Charlie, or Carl as some call him, that she became a problem for me. She would cry and go on after she had been to New York to see him. She was so troublesome, that I had to discharge her.

After she left, did you see her again?

I saw her one time after she left. About three or four weeks after.

Do you know what became of Charlie Woolf?

I helped him secure a position in New York with a mason by the name of Hopper. I don't know if he's still with him.

Do you know Count Leo Zaleski?

Yes. My first meeting with him was when I went to his farm to meet Ana as I was looking to hire her. I was introduced to the Count by a friend of mine in Roselle, who knew I was looking to employ a girl.

Did you see Count Zaleski after you left with Miss Larsen?

Yes, about three or four months after I discharged Ana.

Did you have any conversation concerning Ana Larsen and Carl Woolf?

We had a brief conversation, but I can't remember much of it.

Did he say anything about them being married?

Now that you mention it, I do remember him saying he thought Ana was never married to Carl.

Have you seen Count Zaleski since?

I saw him today in court.

Did you have a talk with him?

No, we had no conversation.

What is your opinion of the Count?

I know nothing in his favor or nothing to his discredit.

When was the last time you saw Carl Woolf?

About two and a half years ago.

Can you describe Carl Woolf?

He had black, curly hair. He wore it rather long. He was very nice looking. He was a short, thickset man. He wore a mustache. I think he had dark gray eyes.

Do you think Carl Woolf could be the murderer?

Oh, no. I don't think he could commit such a crime as this.

Have you been to the vault to view the body?

Yes. I have seen the body. The face and form look like Ana.

Do you think Ana Larsen is the murdered girl?

I don't know for sure. Most of my impressions have come from seeing the photographs. I haven't seen her in almost two and a half years. I will not swear that it is her. I am not positive.

Thank you, Miss Furstman. That will be all.

A recess was here taken until two o'clock at which time three of the local lawmen would be called to take the stand. Some suspected a motive for the day's arrangement of witnesses. If the testimonies of the police indicated they were without valuable leads and definite suspects, the Larsen story might become more believable and change the minds of its detractors.

~~~~~

State your name and residence.

William Tooker. I live in Rahway and serve as Chief of Police.

Can you tell the jury your actions on the morning of March 26?

On that morning, a young man by the name of Alfred Worth came to my house at 6:55 a.m. and said there was a woman murdered on Central Avenue and he would like to have me come right up. Therefore, I went there and found a dead woman with her throat cut. I left Lewis Marsh there in charge of the body, while I came down to telephone the coroner. I also went to notify George Conger and found he had gone up there already. I then went back to the scene of the murder and found Mr. Conger and George Wright, who had found a bag in the river.

Who is Mr. Conger?

George is the Sergeant of Police.

Did you check the contents of the bag?

We opened it and found a velvet sack with lace on the sleeves and bronze buttons down the front, one pair low slippers with heels, one button hook, one ragged chemise, one fur neck gear, one white apron, one bustle with black and red lining, one new plaid skirt, one pair of scissors, part of a New York Herald dated March 23, 1887, one comb and brush, a part of a pair of old suspenders, a handkerchief with the name K. M. Noorz stitched on it, and a rubber stamp with the name Timothy Byrne.

Did Mr. Wright give you the bag?

No. I got it from George Conger.

Did you examine the area around where the body was found?

When we went back to the body, we found one fur cape, a basket containing ten eggs, a straw hat, a parasol, a breast pin, and the shoes, which were later taken to the morgue. The girl was wearing an olive green dress with feather trimming, a dark pair of stockings, red corset, a petticoat of yellow and brown stripes, a knit skirt, a white chemise, red flannel drawers, black elastic garters, three finger rings, and one red horseshoe breastpin.

Did you ever see this woman before?

I took a good view of the body at the morgue. To my knowledge, I never saw that woman before.

How did you come to get the knife in your possession?

Benjamin Metzger walked up to me and said, "Look what I have found!" and he showed me a knife. George Conger was standing there and I told him to put it in his pocket.

(Witness was then shown a knife, which he said was the one.)

What was the time that Mr. Metzger showed you the knife?

I couldn't be sure of the time of day then.

Have you been able to discover the owner of this knife?

No. I have no information to give the jury on this subject.

Do you know William Brunt?

Yes.

Did you hear his testimony regarding Calab DeCamp and John Yose?

No, I was not present to hear what he said.

Did you tell William Brunt that his suspicions were correct and that he was on the right track?

I never said that to him.

Do you think William Brunt is a reliable witness?

I know nothing of his reputation or standing.

Have you spoken to DeCamp or Yose about the knife?

I showed John Yose the knife and he said he had never seen it before. I've let everybody see the knife that asked to see it, but nobody has identified it.

Do you know Jacob Windler?

No.

Do you know Jake Reamer?

Yes. He lives on Haydock Street and I should say his reputation is good.

Have you inspected the handkerchief that was found by the body that contained strands of hair?

I have it in my possession. The hair in the handkerchief was dark, very black.

Was a letter found that belonged to the murdered girl?

I have no such letter and never heard of any.

Do you have any other information to offer the jury?

I feel I told you all I know. There is nothing else of importance I can give at this time.

Thank you, Chief. That will be all. Thank you.

State your name and residence.

George Conger. I live in Rahway. I'm a policeman.

Were you a policeman on the 25th of last March?

Yes.

Can you tell the jury your actions on the morning of March 26?

That morning, I was notified that the body of a woman was found on Central Avenue. It was about quarter of eight. A young man by the name of Worth told me. He said a woman was murdered in Milton on Central Avenue. I went up to the chief's house to notify him, but he had already heard of it and was gone. I then went over to Central Avenue and saw a large crowd of people standing there.

What were your findings at the crime scene?

I saw the body of a woman with her throat cut. Close by her were a basket, umbrella, and a handkerchief.

What time was it when you got to the scene?

I'd say it was shortly after eight o'clock.

Did you talk with anyone?

George Wright came to me and gave me a satchel he said he found in the river.

What do you know about the finding of the knife?

Benjamin Metzger approached Chief Tooker and me and said he found it. I wrapped it in paper and put it in my pocket.

When did you give the knife to Chief Tooker?

I handed it over to him that night.

Was the knife the same one that was just shown to the chief?

Yes.

Do you have any information concerning the ownership of the knife?

No.

Do you agree with the chief's account of the girl's clothing and the contents found in the bag?

I was at the morgue when the bag, clothing, and basket were examined and I think the description given by the chief is about right.

Did you ever see the murdered girl before?

I viewed the face at the morgue and I am sure I never saw that woman before.

What became of the eggs that were found at the scene?

I was given possession of the eggs, and I did have one hatched. I think it will be a black chicken that looks like common stock.

Do you think Clinton Froat or William Keech had anything to do with the crime?

No.

Do you think William Brunt is connected with the murder?

I have never had any suspicion against Brunt. I don't know him too well. I've never heard anyone say anything about him, good or bad.

Were you in the chambers when William Brunt gave his testimony?
I was here for part of it.

Did you hear his statement concerning Calab DeCamp and John Yose?

I heard Brunt say if Calab DeCamp or John Yose could identify the knife, he could name the murderer. I don't believe he could. I don't place any reliability on a statement like that.

Did William Brunt come to the police station and tell you his story about a woman hanging clothes in Clinton Froat's yard?

Yes.

Did you tell him you thought he was on the right track?

When Brunt came into the station house he was so excited, he had tears in his eyes. He told me about his boy seeing the girl in Froat's yard. After he told me the story, and based on what I thought then, I said I thought he was about right.

Do you still think he is about right?

No.

Do you still have any suspicions against William Keech?

No.

Do you have any further information that may be of help to these proceedings?

No.

No further questions.

State your name and residence.

George Wright. I live on Union Street in Rahway.

How are you employed?

At present, I'm a teamster. I was at one time the police chief.

Can you tell the jury your actions on the morning of March 26?

That morning, I received information of the finding of a woman on Central Avenue and reached the scene about seven-thirty. There were about a dozen people gathered around the body. I saw Tooker there. He went down to notify the county physician. After Tooker left, I turned my attention to see what evidence I could find. The first thing I noticed was the tracks of a girl and parties leading from Jefferson Avenue up Central Avenue to where the girl lay. I also found a return track from the body to Jefferson Avenue. I then returned to the body to see what evidence I could find there. That's when I found the handkerchief. I put it in my pocket and then went to see if I could find the knife or whatever weapon with which the deed was done. I hunted the side of the road and then went into the field. When I was there, I met James Brunt who told me there was a carpet sack in the river. He went with me and we found it about 250 feet from the Jefferson Avenue Bridge. I brought it up and returned to the fence near the body. After Chief Tooker came, we took the sack over in the field to get away from the crowd and opened it.

Were there evidences of a struggle?

Yes.

What would you say was the physical stature of the murderer?

I think the man who killed her must have been a large man.

Do you think it was a Negro?

No, I do not.

You mentioned footprints by the crime scene. What size shoe do you think made those prints?

Probably an 8½ or 9.

Did you examine the girl's pockets?

No.

Do you know of any letter being found on the body?

I don't believe any letter was found.

Did you examine the hair that was found in the handkerchief?

Yes. It was black. There might have been fifty hairs altogether. They're about an inch long.

Do you have a theory as to whom the hair belonged?

I would suppose the hair belonged to the man who committed the deed.

Did you ever see the murdered girl before?

I took a view of the face at the morgue. She looks Scandinavian to me. I never saw her before.

Did you hear the testimony given by Chief Tooker?

Yes.

Did you hear the testimony given by William Brunt?

I heard the part where he stated if Calab DeCamp, George Ayres, or John Yose could identify the knife, he could name the murderer.

What is your opinion of his testimony?

I take no stock in any of his evidence in reference to this case.

Have you any reason to suspect Brunt?

The only reason I have to suspect Brunt is his own acts, as he acted like a man who wanted to throw suspicion from himself to another.

Do you know Jacob Windler or Jake Reamer?

I don't know Windler, but I do know Jake Reamer of Rahway. His standing and character are first class.

Do you have any information regarding the knife?

No.

Do you have any suspicions against William Keech or Clinton Froat?

I never suspected Keech or Froat. I have no suspicions against anyone in Rahway, neither do I believe it was committed by anyone in Rahway.

Thank you, that's all I have for this witness.

~~~~~

Wright was the final witness for the day. It was difficult to tell what impression any of them had made on the jury. The first three had known Ana Larsen and testified she resembled the murdered woman, however, not one of them was positive enough to swear the two were the same person. As a result, it wasn't clear if their remarks would convince the jury to finally name the victim. The only information revealed by the police officers was that they were now no closer to solving the mystery then they were on the morning they found the body.

Coroner Terrill was troubled by the lack of progress and realized the need to bring the inquest to a conclusion. Before adjournment, he made several announcements. Addressing the assembly, he said, "At least one more witness will be called at the next meeting, which I've scheduled for Monday, May 2, at 11:00 a.m." He paused for a moment and then said with a tone of finality, "Unless there is an important development over the weekend, it is the desire of this court to conclude the inquest after the Monday session." Then looking at the jurors, he continued, "I would therefore ask the jurors to come to that session ready to consider a verdict." The words were no sooner out of his mouth than a protest was sounded from the reporters' area. It was J. Townley Crane. "Mr. Coroner, you can't be serious! What kind of a verdict do you expect these men to reach?"

Terrill replied with anger in his voice, "That will be all, Mr. Crane! You're out of order! I will not tolerate such outbursts. Your opinions of this court are well documented. We read them each day. If you cannot control yourself, I'll have the constable remove you, and I'll consider not allowing you back in this courtroom." Crane looked at the other reporters in amazement and walked out of the chambers.

The coroner closed the session by reporting the victim's body would be buried on Tuesday, May 3, in the Rahway Cemetery at three o'clock in the afternoon.

~~~~~

For readers of the *World*, the Rahway mystery was a mystery no longer. With the bold headline in their Saturday edition, "ALL SAY SHE IS ANA LARSEN," the New York daily heralded the news that their reporters had broken the case. The self-congratulatory article praised the work of their staff writing, "By reason of the untiring and intelligent efforts of the reporters of the *World*, unaided by the police authorities and opposed by the representatives of other journals, it has been made clear that the girl murdered was Ana Christine Larsen." The paper based their conclusion on the testimonies given on Friday by their three witnesses whom they described as "perfectly respectable and certainly truthful." From the paper's perspective, after carefully examining the photos of the victim, all three testified to their strong resemblance. They also all connected Larsen to Carl Woolf, their alleged murderer. In singing their own praises, the editors boasted, "Even Foreman Clark, that prince of skeptics, was convinced and admitted that the proofs of the girl's identity were very strong."

The main competitor of the *World*, the *New York Herald*, gave them no credit, but continued to dismiss their story. In their column they wrote, "The witnesses failed entirely to identify either the pictures of the dead woman or her clothing." It was difficult for the *Herald* to understand why the coroner was still wasting everyone's time with a story that had been refuted by almost all reasonable people.

~~~~~

Just as the Larsen story was starting to sway opinion, identification was made to again cloud the entire case. Mr. and Mrs. Samuel Eichorn came to Rahway on Friday looking for their niece, Mary Link. They were accompanied by a Detective Hartright of the East New York Police, who had been searching for the Link woman since she had been reported missing in November. After obtaining permission to view the remains, Undertaker Ryno brought them to the morgue. He removed the coffin lid allowing Mrs. Eichorn to get a full view of the body. She nervously approached the box and closely scrutinized the face, the color of the hair and the body's shape and structure. She turned to Ryno and exclaimed, "Yes it is Mary. That is my niece. I am sure of it." The woman then asked if she could see the right leg of the girl to point out a scar she was sure would be there. Ryno removed the white stocking covering the limb and exposed a scar about the size of a silver dollar between the back of the knee and the heel. Mrs. Eichorn said quietly, but with conviction, "Sure enough, that is Mary. That is the mark of a burn she got when she was living out in New York. She spilled some boiling fat."

Ryno's interest in this identification was heightened when the woman said her brother, John Link, had been in Rahway early in the month to view the body and recognized it to be his niece. He returned to Brooklyn unsatisfied after being told there was no scar on either leg. Ryno couldn't specifically remember the man, but he did recall turning a number of persons away because they mentioned marks on the body. It wasn't until Wednesday, April 13, that the local officials learned the County's autopsy report neglected to note a scar on the victim's leg. Although Ryno had been through many false alarms in the past month, he thought it best to take the Eichorns to see the mayor.

In the presence of Mayor Daly and Chief Tooker, Mrs. Eichorn presented the interesting history of Mary Link. "Mary came to the United States in 1883 and after going through the process at Castle Garden, went to East New York to stay with her elderly uncle, John Link, and his wife. Like most girls who come to this country, Mary came to work and make money and then to find a husband, so a good portion of her days was spent looking for employment. She had been with my brother only a few weeks when an employment agency found her a position as a domestic for a family in Cooperstown, Pennsylvania. Mary worked out there for about two months and then returned to my brother's. She also stayed with my husband and me a good deal. She worked at various jobs, but none for long. I guess she was let go each time because Mary wasn't the tidiest person, I can tell you.

"In August of '84, me and Sam came home one day and found Mary sitting in the living room with a young man who was a stranger to us. She introduced him as John, the blacksmith, and surprised us by saying, 'What do you think of this fellow? He will be my husband some day.'"

Mayor Daly cut into the woman's story and asked, "What was the man's last name?" He was ready to write down her response.

"The funny thing is, she always referred to him as John, the blacksmith. I never heard his last name."

"Do you know how or where they met?"

"I really don't know. Mary didn't talk about him much and I didn't think it was my place to pry. I think she once said he was from Newark."

"Can you describe him?"

"He was probably in his middle twenties, stout, healthy looking enough to be a husband."

"Go on with your story please."

Mrs. Eichorn had to pause to remember where she left off and then continued. "In the summer of '85 another agency gave her information about a job at the home of George Danner here in Rahway. I lost track of her after she took that job. The last I heard from her was a letter she wrote, which was dated July 5, 1885. In that letter, she said she might be leaving for other employment and asked if I had received any word from John, the blacksmith. She sent her love and said she'd write again in about six weeks.

"When November came and I hadn't gotten a letter from her, I wrote Mr. Danner. I received his reply early in the New Year saying Mary had left his place at the end of September. It was his impression she was going off to New Brunswick. I was concerned about my niece, but I didn't become worried until last November when, after not hearing from her in over a year, I decided to notify the police and report her as missing. Now, unfortunately, I have found her."

The mayor had one final question for Mrs. Eichorn. "Was your niece the type of girl who would go out late at night on a lonely stretch of road?"

"Mary was a brave girl. She was proud of her strength and was not afraid of any man. She would go out at night anywhere, without any fear."

~~~~~

George Danner was owner and operator of the East Rahway drinking establishment where his wife, Margaret, had given a free shot of whiskey to William Brunt. When confronted by Chief Tooker and Sergeant Conger, Danner obligingly answered their inquiries and was frank in his assessment of Mary Link. He described the girl as having light hair with a reddish hue, grayish eyes, and a turned-up nose. He said she was at least 5'7" and had a robust figure. "The girl had such a hefty build, the regular customers referred to her as Big Mary," he added with a smile. He told the two officers she worked for him for about three months and he eventually let her go because her methods of housekeeping were less than satisfactory. As Danner put it, "She was slovenly and wicked."

When Tooker asked if he had viewed the body, Danner said he was at the morgue the Monday after the murder.

"Did you recognize the girl?"

"I thought I had seen the face before, but I couldn't remember where."

"Do you think the murdered girl could be Mary Link?"

"I'd say there was a resemblance. But remember, it was almost two years ago that I saw her last."

"Did you recognize any of the effects that were on display?"

"Mary had the same kind of satchel that was in the case and she wore clothes of the same style."

Tooker was bothered by one thing Danner stated earlier and now came back to it. "George, are you certain the Link girl was 5'7"?"

"She was at least 5'7". Ya see that shed over there? The height of the door is exactly 5'8". One night a few of the customers wanted to have some fun and made a wager if Big Mary could pass through the doorway without stoopin'. To settle the bet, we got Mary to stand in the doorway. Her hair touched the frame!"

As Tooker and Conger were leaving the tavern, a beer maid came after them. She addressed the two in low tones. "When Mary was here, I roomed with her. The bag they found was the same kind Mary had. And something else. Mary never wore earrings." With that, the girl stepped back into the building.

Of all the clues just gathered, Tooker felt only one was useful in proving or disproving the Mary Link identification. He came away from Danner's Beer Garden quite sure the victim was not Mary Link. The murdered girl was only 5'2".

Monday, May 2, 1887

The columns in the Monday morning papers all but totally defused the notion the victim was Mary Link. Reporters had worked on the new identification theory all weekend and uncovered enough discrepancies to debunk the story. Those reporters, who followed after Mrs. Eichorn, found that the woman was not positively certain about the location of Mary's burn and could only say for sure that of the facial features, only the lips and nose of the murdered girl resembled Mary's. When asked about her size, Eichorn again stated her niece was a large girl, about 5'7" in height. She also gave the shoe size of Mary to be much larger than the foot of the victim.

Detective Hartright was also questioned by the scribes. He commented that the examination made by Mrs. Eichorn at the morgue "had not been all that careful."

The *Times* summarized the Link identification by writing, "On the whole, the Mary Link theory is one of the lightest, which has been spun since the Rahway murder occurred. The positive identification given by Mrs. Eichorn is worthless." If Coroner Terrill was looking for an important development to surface before the last session, it didn't emanate from the Link story.

~~~~~

The final session of the inquest was called to order at eleven o'clock. The one witness scheduled to testify was Daniel Wade, the last person known to have employed Carl Woolf. Coroner Terrill wanted the girl buried with a name and if the jury was to ultimately conclude she was Ana Larsen, it was Wade's testimony that might be used to tip the scale.

State your name and where you live.

My name is Daniel Wade. I live in Union.

What is your line of work?

I'm a farmer.

Are you acquainted with Ana Larsen?

No, I never heard of her before these hearings.

Do you know Carl Woolf?

Yes.

Can you describe Mr. Woolf?

He's a man about my height and weight, wore his hair short.

What would you calculate his age to be?

I'd say he's about twenty-five years old.

How did you come to know Mr. Woolf?

I first met him May 6, 1885, when he came to work for me.

Is he still employed by you?

No, he left my place on March 16 of this year.

Can you tell the jury anything about the background or character of Carl Woolf?

He worked at Count Zaleski's before he came to me. As for his character, I thought Carl was a square man. He was very pleasant, had no bad habits, almost always in the house evenings.

Did he ever mention Ana Larsen?

I never heard that name from Carl.

Did you ever see a woman come to visit him?

Never.

Do you know if Mr. Woolf kept company with women when away from the farm?

Don't know of any women he associated with.

Did Mr. Woolf carry a knife?

Yes, it was a white-handled jack knife.

Did he own other knives?

That's the only one I ever saw him with. He might have owned a dozen more, I don't know.

When Mr. Woolf left your farm in mid-March, did he say where he was going?

He said he was going to Texas.

Did he give you a reason for wanting to go there?

He said he was going to visit a cousin and maybe stay in Texas.

Did he mention where the cousin's home was located?

I believe he once said it was somewhere in the interior of the state.

Do you know if he ever actually left for Texas?

I took him and his trunk to the Roselle Depot to catch a train.

Did you see him purchase a ticket for that destination?

No, I didn't go with him to the window when he bought the ticket.

On what train did he depart?

I don't know. I left before the train came in.

Do you know how much money he had with him?

I'd say he had about seventy-five or eighty dollars. I know he had at least $33.00.

How is it you know he had that amount?

I paid him that much the morning he left. I would guess he had some more from his savings.

That will be all, Mr. Wade.

Having heard the testimony of farmer Wade, the coroner addressed the ten men remaining on the jury. He began by expressing his thanks to each of the gentlemen for giving their time, attention, and energy to the case. He then told them he had nothing more of importance to present, and felt it would be non-productive to continue the hearings. He went on to say a copy of the verdict and all evidence would be sent to the Grand Jury where Judge Van Syckel would review the entire proceedings to determine if further action would be necessary. He also wanted to make it clear that although the inquest was going to end, Prosecutor Wilson would retain full authority to continue the search for the murderer. Terrill next charged the jury to complete its work. "You have heard the witnesses and the evidence is fresh in your minds. From this you must draw your own conclusions and it will rest with you to say whether or not there has been a positive identification. You will bring in a verdict accordingly." Understanding the task set before them, the jury members retired to a small room behind the chambers.

~~~~~

Mayor Daly spent a busy morning meeting separately with two women, who both implored him to help persuade the coroner to allow them time to testify. Mrs. Mary Lacy, a local resident who had moved into Rahway four years ago from Philadelphia, had read in Saturday's papers the story concerning Mary Link and came to support the identification. According to Mrs. Lacy, while living in Philadelphia, she employed a German girl by the same name. From the beginning, she had had no interest in the events surrounding the murder, saying she lacked feelings of morbid curiosity, and had never even gone to view the body. When she read the name, however, it struck her memory. Although she had never seen the remains, she gave the mayor a good description of her servant that was a pretty fair match to the victim. In an effort to convince the woman the victim was not Mary Link, the mayor went over the findings, which discounted the identification. Not certain if she was satisfied or not with his explanation, Daly still sent her off saying he would not recommend bringing her before the jury.

His second meeting was with Mrs. Agnes Space, who was back in town, still insisting the murdered girl was her sister, Mary Dorman. She pleaded with the mayor to make arrangements so she could tell her story to the jury. She said if given the chance to speak in court, she would swear positively and under oath that the girl was her sister. Daly reminded her of the reasons her story was not accepted and regretted having to tell her, he would not act on her request. Mrs. Space, a gracious and reasonable woman, understood the mayor's position. She thanked him for his time and said she would return tomorrow for the burial. With that, she left leaving the mayor alone to wonder if the authorities had reached the correct conclusion in regards to Mary Dorman.

The mayor had no idea how this mystery would end or if in fact, it would ever end. He had agreed with Coroner Terrill that the inquest should be concluded and personally felt it had dragged on for too long. He was tired of being teased by the potential case-breaking clues that eventually led to nothing, and felt his citizens too were growing weary of the rumors and suspicions circulating against their neighbors. Perhaps, he thought, the stream of people coming forward with identifications and names of suspects would cease once the inquest was over and the girl buried. The thought was comforting, but in the back of his mind, he sensed this mystery was not about to go away.

~~~~~

At 12:30, the jury called for the coroner, an indication they were ready to come out of closed session. With this signal, the reporters scrambled to their places and waited anxiously for the jury to return. The chambers also quickly filled and were quieted as the jury members entered and took their seats. It had taken them only forty-five minutes of deliberation to reach a verdict. Coroner Terrill wasted no time and asked, "Gentlemen of the jury, have you agreed upon a verdict?" Foreman Clark rose and responded, "We have. After careful consideration, we find that said unknown woman came to her death by stab wounds in the neck, said wounds being inflicted by some person or persons unknown."

Everyone in the room, save the jurors, was caught off guard by the foreman's words. For a few moments, no one moved or uttered a sound. Had they heard right? Could it be, after all the phlegmatic question and answer sessions the inquest was to end like this? One spectator, not sure how to react, broke the stillness and started to laugh as though the verdict was intended to be comical. The tension broken, laughter broke out in other corners. Terrill grabbed for his gavel, but before he could use it, the courtroom was again quieted by Associated Press reporter Crane, who fired harsh invectives at the jury. "Is this some kind of a joke? I can't believe what I just heard! This verdict is a miscarriage of justice! All of you, you Mr. Prosecutor, and you Mr. Coroner, should be reprimanded for the way this inquest was conducted from the very beginning!"

Terrill attempted to regain order by shouting back, "You are out of order! Constable, remove this man immediately!" Then, to put an end to the uncomfortable situation, Terrill rapped the gavel repeatedly and announced, "This court is adjourned!"

Crane, however, did not yield, but continued to lash out at the jury and coroner even as they were filing out and the Constable was moving toward him. "You did nothing but waste everyone's time! You failed utterly! This was a complete travesty!"

As the jurors and coroner were exiting, the inquiring reporters followed them outside, pressing for details and explanations. One of the first facts uncovered was that eight of the ten jurors voted to pronounce the remains unidentified, while two voted to identify the body as Ana Larsen. Upon learning this, the *World* reporters went after the two jury members for comments that might give them a favorable spin on the verdict. They found a willing confidant in W. T. Miller, a juror who had earlier indicated his belief in the Larsen theory.

"I am satisfied that nearly every man on the jury believes the body is that of Ana Larsen. The trouble is that the evidence is all circumstantial and there is no positive proof that Ana Larsen was in Rahway the night of the murder. Even on circumstantial evidence, a verdict would have been brought in had it not been for the peculiar testimony of Ana's cousin, Tom. His testimony that he was in Denmark when a child was born to Ana impressed the jury. My fellow jurors took the physicians' evidence that the woman had never given birth as conclusive on that point. I think the witness meant to tell the truth, but he doesn't understand English very well and was a little confused. When he left the stand, I supposed he would be recalled the following day or I should have insisted on cross-questioning."

The *World* was also able to get a quote from the coroner, which indicated his support for the Larsen story. Terrill stated, "If the girl is not Ana Larsen, the *World* has discovered one of the most peculiar series of coincidences ever brought to my attention." He then added, "It's the most plausible theory yet advanced."

A *Times* reporter stopped Terrill as he was trying to make his way out of the crowd and asked him for his opinion of the verdict. The coroner answered curtly, "I'm glad the thing is done with."

~~~~~

The work of the jurors was not officially completed, however, until later in the afternoon when the ten jurors again met in the room where they had formulated their conclusion. Coroner Terrill had earlier requested the gentlemen return to sign the official papers that would be forwarded to the Grand Jury. As Clerk Marsh read the document, several of the jurors were made uneasy by the formal, legal language. Phrases such as "good and lawful men," "inquire on the part of the State of New Jersey," "upon their oaths," and "jurors set their names and seal," made these men realize, perhaps for the first time, the gravity of their work. Therefore, it was with some trepidation that a number signed their names to the verdict, which when read aloud, sounded inane.

Terrill himself was upset with the way the inquest ended and was worried his reputation would be tarnished when the higher court read the verdict. He was certain they would view it as a complete farce. He needed to extend the argument that his work and the work of the jury were hampered by witnesses and reporters who made solving the case next to impossible. To this end, he encouraged the jurors to prepare a second verdict that would illustrate the problems they encountered. He explained to them how William Brunt's testimony was completely counterproductive, and because of his spectacle on the stand, others were afraid to say anything, much less testify. Terrill suggested it was even likely he committed perjury.

Foreman Clark, who had no use for Brunt, agreed with the coroner and added, "The man should be in jail for what he did."

Terrill also had issues with the reporters and pointed out how they had complicated the investigative work. He had a personal dislike for Townley Crane and singled out the Associated Press reporter as a main culprit, saying, "I should have fined Crane for contempt."

As the discussion went on, the men came to agree on the wording for a supplementary verdict, after which the clerk was called upon to put it to paper. He was instructed to pen the following: "We do further find that one William Brunt and J. Townley Crane have both, during the progress of this inquest, so conducted themselves in such a manner as to be a bore and troublesome, and earned the reputation of being first-class cranks and, therefore, ask that the said William Brunt and J. Townley Crane be apprehended and held in the County Jail for three months."

Terrill signed the additional verdict along with nine of the jurors. H. O. Houston, the tenth member, refused to sign and stated, "Let's be done with the whole affair. This will only make for more trouble."

After the jurors were dismissed, the coroner sat down to write out a list of fees for his services since the morning of March 26. He included amounts for swearing in of jurors, issuing subpoenas, swearing in of witnesses, fees for conducting each session, and even mileage. His total came to $126.12. He would bring the bill with him when he returned to Elizabeth and file it with the Union County Clerk. As far as he was concerned, his duties in Rahway were over.

~~~~~

Of all the letters received by the mayor, the one he was about to have read to him would prove to be one of the most interesting. The letter was delivered to Daly in the afternoon and as it was written in Danish, he sent word to Chief Tooker to find someone in town who could do some translating. It was not long before the chief brought local merchant Peter Thruelsen to the mayor's office. Reading the letter first to himself to get an understanding of the context, he could not hide the expression of wonder on his face as he twice looked up at the mayor as he read.

"So what does it say?"

Thruelsen read, "I expect to arrive in Rahway in a few days to see the officials and explain where I was at the time of the murder. I have not been in the area for several years since Count Zaleski beat me with a shovel and told me if I ever stepped a foot upon his property again he would have me arrested and punished." The interpreter stopped and then said slowly, "The letter is signed Ana Christine Osterberg, maiden name Larsen."

Tuesday, May 3 – Wednesday, May 4, 1887

Fewer than forty people were standing outside the receiving vault in the Rahway Cemetery waiting to pay their final respects to the unknown girl found dead over a month ago. Most in the group on this warm spring day were curious women, some with their young daughters, whose little hands they held tightly in their own. About a dozen men were among the number, however, the city fathers and jury members were noticeably absent. Six New York reporters were also at the scene having requested the duty of carrying the coffin to its final resting place. Mrs. Kate Lyons, who still maintained her firm belief the girl was Maggie Gormley and that she was murdered with her own knife, stood with Mrs. Bonney, a friend, some distance from the others.

At three o'clock, a carriage halted at the entrance of the graveyard and four passengers alighted. A mild breeze wafted lightly through the rows of tombstones as Pastor Gay, Undertaker Ryno, Mrs. Agnes Space, and her friend and legal advisor, Mr. Lytell, walked up the path toward the vault. Mrs. Lyons was standing to the side of the path, and seeing the attention given to Mrs. Space, glared fiercely at the woman as she passed. As they got closer to the waiting group, comments were heard remarking how much Mrs. Space resembled the victim. The voices were soon hushed and everything became still as Ryno unlocked and opened the heavy iron doors of the vault. The crowd immediately pressed forward and could see in the shadowy light, the white coffin resting on its bier. Ryno removed a panel covering the face of the girl and moved back as he invited the mourners inside for a final viewing. Those strong enough to enter, gasped as they looked at a face now shrunken and discolored, and quickly exited the crypt, their eyes wide and wet with tears.

Mrs. Lyons and her companion waited until the general group was done and then passed through the doors together. Upon seeing the face, Mrs. Lyons cried out, "Oh, Maggie! Oh, God! It's a shame to bury the girl without a name! Oh, God, if her mother were only here!" The two women came out of the vault crying and shaking. Mrs. Space was last to enter. Standing beside the coffin, unable to raise her head, her lips began to tremble and tears trickled down her cheeks. She whispered a short prayer, and then turned, and left the body.

The viewing over, Ryno closed the lid and instructed the reporters to carry the casket to the gravesite, some seventy-five yards away at the western end of the cemetery. Mrs. Space and Mr. Lytell walked behind the pallbearers, followed by the rest of the party. Mrs. Lyons and her friend trailed the procession, wailing and moaning as they made the sad journey.

Pastor Gay had gone ahead to the lonely grave and waited somberly as he watched the slow marchers. The gravesite had been selected by the elders of the church, who had deep concerns whether or not the girl had led a virtuous life. Unable to be certain, they decided to donate a plot fifteen yards removed from the nearest grave and on the other side of a graveled walking path, the sole plot on that side. The friendless girl would have no company, even in death.

When they reached the open pit, the reporters placed the coffin on the lowering ropes and moved to the side. As Ryno and an assistant started to lower the box, Mrs. Lyons implored, "Are you going to bury her without a name?" The undertaker looked at the woman, and without a word, nodded, and continued to lower the coffin. Visibly affected, Mrs. Lyons cried out, "Oh, God! Oh, Maggie! Put into the earth like a dog!" With this, she and Mrs. Bonney dropped to their knees in prayer.

A sense of decorum returned when the minister stepped forward to offer appropriate and consoling remarks. "We meet around an open grave. For weeks, the mutilated body has been the focus of many eyes and the subject of protracted investigation, but the shrouded form is nameless. The assassin still skulks in the gloom, while those who loved the living are not here to pay their last tribute to the dead. Poor unfortunate, sleep on, until the voice of Deity shall call the dead from their quiet sleep. Find here a home where the violets and daisies shall bud and blossom, the evergreens chant their requiems, the birds carol the livelong day, and the insects sing from eventide until early morn, and may the loving Father, the gentle Savior, and the protecting spirit comfort the absent mourners with the consolation of the blessed Gospel of Jesus Christ our Lord."

After giving the words of committal, Gay grabbed a handful of earth and sifting it through his fingers, let it fall into the grave. The action caused Mrs. Space to weep loudly and cry out the name of her sister, Mary. Mrs. Lyons, perhaps exhausted from so much crying, could only stammer, "Why bury the poor girl with no name when her name is Maggie Gormley?"

Thus, the unusual burial service was over. The people remained until the grave was almost half filled and then left the cemetery. Pastor Gay and Undertaker Ryno escorted Mrs. Space and her lawyer back to their carriage, the woman unshaken in her belief the girl was her sister. Mrs. Lyons went straight to the mayor's office beseeching him to take up her cause. Daly gave her no help. Besides having little faith in her theory, he told her the matter was no longer in his hands and sent her to Elizabeth where she could state her case before Detective Keron and Prosecutor Wilson.

~~~~~

The *World* had some explaining to do. The jury did not declare the murdered girl to be Ana Larsen. Furthermore, the story was in the rival papers concerning Larsen's desire to visit Rahway, proving beyond a doubt she was not the victim. In their Wednesday edition, the *World* attempted to rationalize their reporting of and belief in the Larsen/Woolf story. Following the headline, "Now Quite Certain That Ana Larsen Is Not the Rahway Victim," the paper stated how they had employed every possible agency as they pursued the facts and tracked every available clue to the most extreme limits. They noted how they had utilized the cable to Copenhagen to secure information to support the case. The article also stated that they trusted the identifications of Count Zaleski, his wife, and the others who knew Larsen and Woolf personally and felt their testimonies were the most accurate and truthful. Finally, they maintained they had actually helped the investigation by exploding many theories and identifications that at first seemed plausible and would have otherwise distracted the authorities.

The article concluded with fresh information received after Monday's verdict. Cables arrived from Denmark with news that Larsen was married to a seafaring man named Albert William Osterberg. On April 4, she and her son, Johannes, took passage on the steamship *Trave* for the journey to America. The ship arrived on April 15. When ship records were checked, both names were found on the list of passengers. The Ana Larsen investigation had come to an end.

Wednesday, May 18, 1887

In the two weeks following the burial of the unknown woman, interest in the murder had waned, leaving the citizens of Rahway grateful to have life in their city back to normal. The identifications had stopped, most of the reporters had gone off to other assignments, and a number of the principal participants were no longer in town. William Brunt, tired of being abused by everybody, moved to Cranford, taking his two sons with him. Clinton Froat and his family had packed up and returned to Elizabeth a few days prior to Brunt's departure. William Keech, the strange, one-eyed man many connected to the crime, left with the Froats to start a new life. On the day he departed, Keech was philosophical as he told a reporter, "The affair cost me many a day's suffering, but a good conscience and plenty of hard work will straighten me out." In all, no fewer than a dozen people had moved away from the Milton section on account of the murder.

~~~~~

During those same weeks, the only matter of any interest was the pending Grand Jury session scheduled for May 18 at which time the Court would review the two verdicts filed by the Rahway jury. From the moment they were announced, the absurd verdicts were widely ridiculed, and it wasn't difficult to imagine how the Grand Jury would view them. When one of the Rahway jurors tried to explain the second verdict by suggesting it was written up as a joke, the criticism toward the entire group became more heated. One person who didn't take the "joke" lightly was Townley Crane, who was threatening a libel suit in order to vindicate himself. Public opinion was on the side of the reporter as the area newspapers, including the local *National Democrat*, came to his aid, characterizing Crane as a gentleman highly esteemed in the profession. On the other hand, they portrayed the Rahway jurors as buffoons. It was likely the Grand Jury would see both parties in similar fashion.

The Court met as scheduled and it came as no surprise that their presentment carried both a harsh reprimand and a caution "never to do this again." They condemned the action of the Rahway jury stating, "(They) brought discredit on themselves and trifled with the solemn duty they were sworn to perform." The Court was especially troubled by the second verdict, which requested jail time for William Brunt and Townley Crane. In their opinion, this supplementary verdict was "uncalled for and criminal in its nature, and while deliberating as a body, they had no authority to incorporate it in their findings."

Copies of the presentment would be served upon each of the jurors. With no further action recommended by the higher Court, the work of the jury in the Rahway murder inquest was officially completed.

Monday, June 6 – Monday, June 13, 1887

Officer J. W. Conley closed the cell door of the Iuka, Illinois, jailhouse and turned the heavy key in the lock. He paused as he took a long look through the barred window at his prisoner, not sure what to make of him. He was a small man, maybe 5'2", and one hundred and twenty pounds, with heavy auburn hair. Conley guessed his age to be about twenty-five. Earlier in the day, the man, who gave his name as Casper Strombach, had walked into the sheriff's office to confess to the murder of a woman in Rahway, New Jersey. Strombach had come to the station accompanied by his employer, John Bowman, who gave Conley all the particulars of an interesting story.

Bowman's account began with Strombach entering the tiny Midwestern town asking around for the names of any German businessmen who might be hiring. Strombach, who hailed from Munich, Germany, had been in America for five years and still felt more comfortable in the company of his countrymen. When directed to the blacksmith shop owned by Bowman, he went to see the smithy to ask for a job. As it turned out, Bowman did need help and offered the newcomer work and lodging. It was Wednesday, June 1.

The next three workdays went by without incident. The man was genial and was proving to be a good worker. By Saturday afternoon, however, Strombach's manner changed. For no apparent reason, he became moody, giving Bowman the impression he was wrestling with some inner conflict. On Saturday evening when Bowman questioned him, he abruptly left the room. There was no work on Sunday, and Strombach kept to himself most of the day. At supper, genuinely concerned about his helper's state of mind, Bowman again made inquiries.

This time, Strombach didn't leave, but gave a long sigh and with a sad look, said, "I had done something bad back east and am tormented almost to death." Bowman then listened with shocked attention as the man sitting across the table from him presented a tale of murder.

"The whole horrible affair started the morning I boarded a ferry to cross over to Jersey. My plans were to go by rail to Elizabeth where I was thinking I might find employment. While I was sitting alone, a man I did not know approached and asked if he could join me. Having no reason to object, I invited him to sit. The man introduced himself as John, and from his accent, I could surmise he was a Swede. He inquired about my plans for the day and after telling him, he asked if I would consider going a few stops further to Rahway. He had an appointment to meet a handsome girl at that place and thought I might be interested in meeting her. 'My intentions are to lead the girl astray,' is how he put it. The possibilities aroused my curiosity and I agreed to go along.

"We reached Rahway Station around four o'clock and walked for about a mile until we reached an area of open fields. We were there only a short time when we spied the girl coming toward us. She was carrying a basket. The Swede told me to wait while he went to talk with her. They were together only a few minutes when the girl suddenly turned away and started running. The Swede called out to her, 'Clairy, I want to talk to you!' but the girl didn't stop. The Swede cursed loudly and started after her. I followed, and by the time I reached him, he had caught the girl and was struggling with her to keep her from running off. In the struggle, she must have scratched his face or something because he flew into a rage. Twisting the girl's arm behind her back, he brought her to the ground and holding her down, reached for a length of fence post he found in the weeds. With the club in hand, he struck down two or three hard blows to her head. The body went completely limp. I walked to where the girl was and stood over her. I wasn't sure if she was dead or not. The Swede was panting and rubbing his cheek. Still trying to catch his breath, he said to me, 'Finish the job!' The words startled me, but somehow I knew what the command meant. My mind was in turmoil after the frenzied drama I had just witnessed, so I can't explain what happened next. I dropped to one knee, took out my knife, and cut the girl's throat. After that, the Swede and me hurried away and boarded another train back to New York. I got drunk and stayed that way for several days. When I finally realized what we had done, I knew I had to get away to try to forget about the deed. But, the trouble is still in my head. The girl's face haunts me, even in my sleep. There's nothing left but to turn myself in and confess. It's the only thing that might put my mind at peace."

There was firmness and yet a hint of uneasiness in his confessor's reply. "I think come morning, we better go to the police." Strombach didn't answer, but gave a few faint nods and then looked away.

The basic story having been told, Officer Conley had only a few questions to ask Strombach before taking his written confession.

"You claim you didn't know the girl at all. Is that right?"

"I never saw her before."

"And yet you killed her. Why?"

"I don't know. I can't explain why. I just did it."

"Do you still have the knife?"

"No, I needed some money so I sold it."

"Who did you sell it to?"

"I don't know the man. It was in some town in Indiana."

"Where abouts in Indiana?"

"I think it was around Vincennes."

"This accomplice you call 'the Swede,' do you know anything about him?"

"When we were drinking, he told me he lived in the Bowery on 4th Street. He mentioned some names of people he knew, but I don't remember any."

"Where did you live in New York?"

"Several places. Nowhere in particular."

"What did you do for work?"

"I am a musician. I go into saloons and play and patrons give me money."

"Do you have any family back east?"

"None."

There was no emotion in Strombach's responses and the officer found his matter-of-fact attitude disconcerting. Conley was finished with his questions and called for John Phillips, one of the more educated men in town, to help write out the confession.

> "Casper Strombach comes and makes confession to John Bowman and J. W. Conley, that on the 18th day of March, 1887, at Rahway, New Jersey, in the afternoon that he the said Casper Strombach and his friend John, a Swede (he cannot recollect his surname) did kill and murder a young lady about 17 years old, named Clairy. We met her outside of town and killed her by the roadside. My friend John struck her with a club and

I cut her neck with a pocketknife. I therefore demand that J. W. Conley, a constable of the County of Marion and State of Illinois, take me into custody, and have me dealt with according to law in the matter above stated, and I hereby surrender myself into his charge. I hereby make the above confession to John Bowman, J. W. Conley, and John A. Phillips of my own free and voluntary will and no act of compulsion on their part."

The document was signed and the alleged murderer brought to his cell. Conley planned to ride the ten miles to Salem, the largest town close to Iuka, to confer with the police in that place. It was just possible they might have more information concerning this east coast murder.

~~~~~

The information at the Salem sheriff's office related to the Rahway murder was a surprise to Officer Conley. News of the unsolved crime was known in the larger communities, but had not always reached the outlying rural burgs, so he was fascinated by the size of the file on this case. Leafing through the photographs, wanted posters, and reward notices, he began to realize he was part of something bigger than he had ever imagined. It was hard for him to believe the prisoner back in his jail was a notorious killer, and it gave him a feeling of pride that he had something to do with his "capture."

The Salem authorities were also excited, but wanted to investigate the matter more fully before sending communications to Rahway. To this end, they sent a delegation to Iuka with photographs for the prisoner to identify. Among this group was a physician who would give Strombach a medical examination and also make an evaluation of his mental condition.

By Friday, they were satisfied they had the right man. When Strombach was shown the photographs, he recognized each to be the girl he met and killed. His answers to the doctor, who was disadvantaged at having no knowledge of the actual particulars of the crime, sounded rational and truthful. During the entire exam, Strombach gave no sign of mental confusion nor was there any indication he was not in full control of his faculties. It was, therefore, the doctor's professional opinion that the man was sane. With the signed confession, the prisoner's identification of the photos, and the doctor's diagnosis, a dispatch was prepared and sent.

"Confessed murderer secure behind bars...Advise if you want prisoner brought to New Jersey...Reward offered for arrest will be accepted...Will send further details."

~~~~~

Although the celebrated Inspector Byrnes had disappeared from the local scene, he had remained very active in New York City investigating potential leads. Since the middle of May, he had been following clues involving a German zither player who he considered an important suspect. Byrnes had gotten most of his story from Louis Schwarzenbeck, a porter at the Windsor Hotel, who said the musician had admitted to the crime before he left for the West. He gave the man's name as Casper Strombach.

Schwarzenbeck met Strombach in early April while the latter was lodging at the Windsor. Strombach had no job and spent most of his hours practicing his instrument, often in the company of the porter. When he was finally out of money and could no longer afford the hotel, he moved into a boarding house in Brooklyn on Humbolt Street. On a visit to the Windsor to see his friend, Schwarzenbeck told him to go and play at Schubmann's bowling alley and saloon on Division Street where patrons might throw him pennies if they liked his music. The zither player took his advice and soon became a favorite entertainer at the saloon. To supplement his tips, Strombach ran errands, practiced sword swallowing and ventriloquism, and ate cockroaches for a price. When thirsty, he would bet he could eat three of the insects for a schooner of beer.

On March 23, Strombach again came to see the porter and said he was going away for a few days to look for work. He also asked him if he could borrow his long-bladed knife as his instrument was in need of tuning and repair. Schwarzenbeck told him it wasn't safe to carry around such a knife, but, even with the warning, let him take it.

Strombach returned five days later, but he was not the same man. He seemed to be afraid of everything and commented, "I feel as though I were shot through the head."

About a month and a half later, on May 17, Strombach came to the hotel in an excited state and told his friend he was going to leave for the West and that he was changing his name to Charles Edelman. He then confessed to the crime. "You must not tell anybody. I murdered a girl at Rahway. I killed her on March 24 and they found her the next day." When Schwarzenbeck questioned him about the identity of the girl and why he killed her, Strombach gave the full story. "She was from Chicago, but her parents were dead. I made advances and she gave me a great push. I was drunk and I pulled out my knife and stabbed her. First on the cheek and then on the throat—clear across. From the left, I cut her throat all the way."

He held out a handbill bearing a sketch of the murdered girl and noted, "It's a good picture, but the eggs were left out."

He gave Schwarzenbeck two pawn tickets, one for his zither, and one for a pair of trousers. He also wanted to return the knife, but the porter, thinking it might be the murder weapon, refused to take it back. That was the last time Schwarzenbeck saw the man.

The next day the porter went to Schubmann's and asked the proprietor if someone could get in trouble if he knew something about a crime and didn't report it. The owner wasn't sure, but hinted a person could get five or six years in jail for withholding evidence. Hearing this, Schwarzenbeck went to report what he knew to Inspector Byrnes.

During his investigation, Byrnes also interviewed several neighbors of Strombach who lived on Humbolt Street. Everyone he talked to found Strombach to be a sociable fellow and anything but bloodthirsty in his manner. They didn't think he was crazy and never noticed anything in his conduct or speech to suggest he was insane.

Byrnes kept all information on his leads within his agency and had sent two detectives to follow the suspect's trail. Little did he know, his prey had stopped running and was in the custody of the Iuka police.

~~~~~

By Monday morning, news of the telegrams from Illinois had become public knowledge in Rahway, reviving the excitement that had abated over the last month. There were those who thought there was considerable credence to the story, while others figured another lunatic had fashioned an account to satisfy his deranged mind. Whatever their opinions, they all clamored for the authorities to investigate the lead, no matter the cost in time or money.

Mayor Daly was incensed that news of the confession had leaked. If this story followed the pattern of all the others before it and was proven false, his city would again criticize the handling of the investigation and he would be held responsible for its failings. As it was, he had little faith in the story. In a second telegram from Illinois, details of the suspect's story were forwarded that didn't fit the facts. There were contradictions in the date of the murder and the age of the girl and because it was believed the murder weapon had been found, the story of a long-bladed knife was doubted. The most obvious discrepancy, however, was the time of day given for the murder. It was generally accepted the crime took place in the hours just before midnight and that it was not possible to have occurred at four in the afternoon. Nonetheless, the authorities agreed they had to conduct an investigation in order to satisfy the public's need for a definite answer.

In the discussion of whether to bring the prisoner to New Jersey or to send an officer to Illinois to question him there, it was decided to send Detective Keron and, therefore, spare the cost of transporting the suspect. When figures were drawn up, it was estimated an expense of $300 would be accrued if the prisoner were brought back East and sufficiently examined. The cost to send one lawman would be considerably less. Mayor Daly felt his chief of police should go, but since the County was picking up the bill, he acquiesced in favor of the Elizabeth detective.

The authorities were also miffed by the mercenary attitude of the Illinois officials who seemed overly anxious concerning the reward money and how it would be divided. In their second dispatch, they asked if they would be required to share a portion of the reward with officers sent to fetch the prisoner. No reply was made. The County would wait until Keron completed his assignment and ascertained if Casper Strombach was indeed the killer they were after before they divvied up the bounty.

Sunday, June 19 – Monday, June 20, 1887

Salem, Illinois, located seventy-two miles east of St. Louis, was an important railroad town on the Chicago and Eastern Illinois Line, and was the county seat of Marion County. Earlier in the week, the alleged murderer had been transferred there from Iuka and placed in a larger, county jailhouse, one more fitting a criminal of his stature. Being from New York and a suspected killer, Strombach was treated with a curious level of respect by the sheriff and his family who gave him hot meals and plenty of bottled beer to drink. They also took him on an excursion about the town, even stopping at a local barbershop to treat him to a shave and haircut.

Detective Keron arrived at the Salem Depot at 6:25 p.m., glad to be able to stretch and walk around in the fresh Midwestern air. He had been confined in railroad coaches since he left Elizabeth on Saturday morning and was looking forward to cleaning up before meeting with the police and their prisoner. After inquiring about a good place to lodge, he was directed to the Park Hotel, just a few blocks down Main Street on the corner of Broadway and Schwartz. It was getting late, but he was planning on having an initial session with Strombach before turning in.

By the time the refreshed detective arrived at the jail it was almost eight o'clock. Sheriff William Matthews and one deputy were the only two in the station. They described to Keron the circumstances behind Strombach's surrender in Iuka, his outline of the events of the murder, and the results of the medical examinations. Keron could tell they were sincere in their belief that they were holding the man who had committed the horrible crime. In their opinion, everyone involved in the investigation found Strombach to be rational and sane, and felt he was honestly contrite over his deed. According to the two officers, there had been nothing in his actions or demeanor to suggest his story was anything but the truth.

The preliminary information having been given, Keron requested to see the prisoner, and Strombach was immediately brought into the office. Strombach looked none the worse for wear after spending a week in jail and appeared at ease and almost confident as he entered the room prepared to tell his story to yet another official. He was holding several sheets of paper in his right hand. Keron's practiced eyes surveyed the man from head to foot. He didn't give the appearance of a killer.

"It looks as though you've been treated pretty well since your confinement."

"Yes, the officers have been very kind to me."

"What are those papers you've got?"

"Just some drawings I've penned since I've been in jail. It helps pass the time."

Keron reached for the papers. They were sketches of trains, ships, and other scenes of various kinds all done with a fair degree of skill.

"These are quite good. Are you an artist?"

"No, actually I'm a strolling musician by profession."

"Are you one of those musicians who play for people in the parks and in the fancy restaurants?"

"Oh, no, I mostly play in saloons."

"What are the names of some of the places you play?"

"They're just small places in New York. You wouldn't know any of them."

At this point, the detective decided to change the subject and get down to business. "Do you know who I am and why I'm here?"

"They told me policemen were coming from New Jersey to take me back, and I'm ready to return East and take my punishment. I won't give you any trouble."

"Before we talk about going back, I'd like to hear what happened the day you killed the girl. I want you to start from the beginning and tell me everything you can remember."

Strombach had agonized over the story so many times he knew it by heart. He told how he left New York on March 18, met a stranger named John, the Swede, got off the train at Rahway and together walked to the outskirts of the city. He explained that they met a girl and when she tried to run away, the Swede overtook her and clubbed her several times. He described how he cut the girl's throat. He gave the time as three or four in the afternoon. No mention was made of the satchel, the parasol, or the basket of eggs. Strombach finished with his return to New York, his departure for the West, and his subsequent arrest.

Keron was quiet for a few moments and finally said to the sheriff, "That will be all for tonight. It's getting late. I'd like to see the prisoner again tomorrow and if you would, ask the other officials who examined this man to please be present."

The Elizabeth detective left the jailhouse and headed back to his hotel. He was positive Strombach wasn't the person who committed the crime. The man he just interviewed seemed intelligent, well schooled, and spoke rationally on all subjects except the murder. Tomorrow Keron would prove his story false and try to figure out the reason for his deception.

~~~~~

Five Salem officials including Mayor Henry Hall, Sheriff Matthews, the County Judge, and two physicians listened for almost half an hour as Keron presented the particulars of the murder. He went over descriptions of the girl and her possessions, details of the crime scene, articles of evidence, and general features of the area. He noted the approximate time of the murder. He also described the train station as a dark brown, brick building located in the business district. Now familiar with the facts, the officials were ready to judge the prisoner with a keener perspective. As Strombach was brought into the room, Keron was sure the self-confessed killer would stumble through the questions, thus proving to all present his story was counterfeit.

"I need you to answer some more questions about the murder and I want you to be as specific as possible with your answers."

"I have no reason to avoid answering any questions. Visions of the awful act are always in my head. I can't get rid of them."

"Are you certain you came to Rahway on Friday, March 18?"

"It was a Friday. I think it was the eighteenth."

"What reason did you have for going to that town? Were you planning on killing somebody?"

"Oh, no, not at all. As I told you, my plans were to go to Elizabeth to seek employment. During my travels I met a man who would change the course of my life."

"Are you sure you arrived at the Rahway Depot in the middle of the afternoon?"

"Yes, it was around three or four o'clock."

"Could you describe the station?"

"It was a large, brick building, painted white."

"We have yet to find witnesses who saw two men get off the train that day at that time and no one saw you at the station after you committed the crime. Your clothes must have been bloodied, yet no one took notice. How do you explain that?"

"No one was around to see us. The depot is on the outskirts of town. There weren't any houses or shops nearby."

"You said you met the girl in the open fields. Was the field close to any road?"

"No, it was pretty much just fields. No roads were around there."

"What did the girl look like?"

"She was a short girl with a medium build."

"How old do you think the girl was?"

"She was a young girl. I'd say about seventeen."

"Do you remember what she was wearing?"

"She was wearing a hat. I think her dress was green."

"Was she carrying anything like a bag or purse?"

"She had nothing with her that I can remember."

Keron paused to reach in his pocket to pull out two items. He unfolded a white handkerchief. "This was found by the girl's body. Did you see it fall from her hand?"

"I didn't see anything like that."

"You say the Swede struck the girl's face several times with a fence post he found on the ground. What did he do with it after he beat the poor girl senseless?"

Strombach had to think a moment before he could answer. "I'm not sure. He must have thrown it to the side."

"If he dropped the piece of wood by the body, someone would have found it and given it to the police. How do you explain the fact that no club was found?"

Strombach gave no answer.

Sensing the man's confusion, Keron pressed harder, "Describe for us the knife you used."

"It was a knife with a long blade. I guess you'd call it a hunting knife."

"That's an unusual kind of knife to carry if you were going to look for employment. Why did you bring it with you that day?"

Strombach had never considered the question and again took time before he quietly answered, "I don't know. I just had it with me."

"What did you do with the knife after you cut the girl's throat?"

"I kept it, but I don't have it anymore. I had to sell it when I needed money."

The second item Keron had was the white-handled knife believed to have been the murder weapon. He held it out. "Did you ever see this knife before?"

"No."

Keron turned from Strombach and addressed the officials. "Gentlemen, after hearing Mr. Strombach's answers, I think you will now agree he is not the man we are looking for."

Surprised and caught off guard, first by the questions concerning the club and the knife and now by Keron's statement, Strombach asked with honest amazement, "How can you say that? I killed the girl and I demand you take me back!"

The detective responded without emotion. "Your mind has been playing tricks on you. I doubt if you were ever in Rahway, and you certainly didn't kill that girl."

"I did kill her! Why else would I think about it all the time?"

"You probably read about the murder too much in the papers. Constantly thinking about a thing can work in your mind."

Strombach said nothing. His eyes seemed to go blank and he became transfixed in thought. When he finally spoke, it was as if to nobody. "I can still see the girl so perfectly lying next to the fence with the blood pouring from her throat. Every day, I'd walk past the Bowery Museum and see her in the window. It all looked so real. I'd stand and look until I couldn't bear it any longer. How did they know I did it? What a cruel way to punish me until I broke down and was forced to confess."

The room was quiet as everyone focused on the prisoner and his strange ramblings. Keron understood and gave his interpretation. "Do you see what's happened? A museum display of the ghastly spectacle has affected his mind."

Strombach, still in his meditative state, continued as if to himself, "Take me back East. I must go back and atone for my crime."

There was no pity in Keron's response. "You just want to go back to New York at someone else's expense. I'd bet that was your plan from the start."

The accusation woke Strombach from his trance. "That's not true! I could go back on my own. I could return the same way I came."

"And just how was it that you got out here?"

"I paid my fare from New York to Philadelphia. Then I rode on the trucks of freight cars the rest of the way."

"You're no better than a common tramp. Go back to New York anyway you can. You're not coming with me."

Realizing free passage was no longer a possibility, Strombach went into a panic. "I killed a girl and must pay my debt to society. If you don't take me back, I'll kill myself to serve justice. Let me have your revolver so I can do it! I beg you."

Keron's reply was again without empathy. "I think I would let you have it, only I'm afraid you're crazy enough to use it." Then, addressing the officials he said, "Gentlemen, my work here is done. Thank you for all your help. I must be going."

As the detective was rising to leave, Sheriff Matthews asked, "What are we supposed to do with him? We have no reason to hold him."

"I leave the prisoner in your custody. I'm sure you'll do what's right."

Mayor Hall made the last request. "I wish you would take him back with you. This is no longer any affair of ours."

"Mr. Mayor, we have plenty of cranks in the East right now. We don't need another. You must have an asylum somewhere out here."

With those final words, Keron left the station and went to the telegraph office. His message to Mayor Daly was a short one. "Strombach is not the man."

~~~~~

The telegram from Keron was not the only one Mayor Daly would receive from the Midwest that day. Another communication also arrived from St. Louis sent by a Mr. John Rhodmaker who thought the victim might be his daughter, Mary. According to the message, the daughter left Missouri three years ago and had been working in the area around Rahway for the past year. She wrote home regularly, but her letters stopped after March 25.

Both telegrams were troubling news for the mayor. The Strombach arrest in Illinois and the Rhodmaker note indicated the murder story was making its way further west and that could only mean inquiries and identifications would start coming in from a new audience in search of lost girls. Things had quieted down in the month and a half since the unknown woman was buried, and Daly felt a revival of interest would do nothing but upset the town. Expectations were high among many citizens that the arrest made out West would end the mystery. The simple fact that an officer was sent on the long journey to bring the prisoner back was proof the authorities were sure they had their man. Returning to his office with both telegrams clutched tightly in his hand, the mayor wondered what the reaction would be to another false alarm and another name to add to the long list of missing women.

Monday, July 4 – Tuesday, July 5, 1887

Rahway awoke on the Fourth of July to the sound of church bells and cannon fire, signaling the beginning of a day of celebration, which would feature a parade, oratory exercises, and fireworks. The churches, which were asked to toll their bells from seven to eight in the morning, would ring them again from noon to one and from six to seven. Members of the G. A. R. Post #27 would fire the artillery piece they used at the Battle of Gettysburg during the same hours. The festivities were scheduled to begin at 10:00 a.m. with a parade that would start at Irving Street and Elm Avenue and after winding its way along several streets, end at Maple Park, corner of Maple Avenue and Bryant Street. The program at the park would include a reading of the Declaration of Independence by Postmaster Gilbert R. Lindsay and a keynote oration presented by Pastor Ruth of the Second Methodist Church. Maple Park would also be the viewing spot for the evening's fireworks.

    The city had not had an Independence Day celebration on this scale for the last dozen years, so the entire town was filled with a holiday atmosphere. Most of the houses, especially those on the parade route, were adorned with American flags or other patriotic displays. Stores in the business district were decked out with red, white, and blue bunting. It promised to be a busy day for the merchants, and one establishment in particular, Michael Hermes' saloon on Cherry Street, was drawing a crowd from the time it opened. The reason for the unusual excitement was a large, colorful sign posted next to the entrance which read:

> See "Mystery" the Rooster
> Hatched from an Egg Found In the Unknown Woman's Basket
> Only 10 Cents - 2nd Floor
> Also on Exhibit, a Chinese Chicken, a Talking Crow,
> and Two Tame White Mice

 The two men responsible for the attraction were Ike Crane and Johnnie Winans, who figured they could make a little money for themselves and at the same time do a favor for their friend, Sergeant Conger. Conger still believed the basket of eggs, and now the rooster, were the best clues in the murder mystery. The rooster, having grown enough so its breed was recognizable, had large feathers on its legs and appeared to be of the English Leghorn variety. For the past several weeks, the police had searched henhouses in all the surrounding towns for fowl of that type, but none were to be found. The sergeant reasoned the more people who saw the rooster, the better the chance of finally discovering the farm from which it came. With this purpose in mind, he gave his friends permission to show it on the Fourth. Conger also agreed to allow Crane to bring the rooster to the State Fair at Waverly in September, where it would be seen by a much larger audience.

 Since Crane and Winans were regulars at Hermes' saloon, the owner let them set up their display in a vacant room above the tavern. The attraction proved to be successful, at least from a financial standpoint. From the time the exhibit opened, there was a line to get to the second floor and it was estimated several hundred people paid their ten cents to see the strange relic of the unsolved crime. Unfortunately for Conger, no one could identify the bird.

~~~~~

For most of the day, the weather had been hot and oppressive, but the night air was more agreeable as Mayor Daly strolled among the spectators watching the sparkling rockets burst in the black sky. He exchanged brief pleasantries as he moved from one cluster of people to another, and felt satisfied as everyone had favorable remarks concerning the entire celebration. Daly was content and would have rested well that night had he not been approached by Mark Keefe, who asked to speak with him on an important matter. The mayor followed as Keefe led him out of range of anyone who might overhear his words. Before they got too far off, Daly stopped and asked, "Where are you taking me, Mark? What do you want to talk to me about?"

"Mayor, I've had something on my mind since the inquest ended, but didn't want to say anything to anyone. I thought about going to you or Chief Tooker a couple of times, but whenever I started, I changed my mind. When I saw you tonight, I decided I had to tell you."

In the flashing light of the fireworks, Daly could see Keefe was serious. "Well, good God man, tell me. What is it?"

Keefe's voice was stoney. "I know where the basket came from. The one found by the girl's body. I know who owned it."

The words silenced the mayor. The murder had not been on his mind since the Illinois arrest was resolved. News that the suspect was not the killer was one more frustration for the citizens, but it almost seemed they expected to be disappointed. Daly had even started to believe the whole affair was over and would soon be totally forgotten. He never expected such a revelation. When he finally spoke, he said quickly and quietly, "Don't say anything more. Meet me in my office tomorrow at ten. I want to hear everything you've got to say."

Keefe replied he'd be there, turned away, and walked back toward the crowd. Daly stood alone and watched as he disappeared into the darkness. As he considered where this development might lead, the intermittent booming that had earlier sounded so festive had now become an ominous portent.

~~~~~

Mark Keefe arrived at the mayor's office at exactly ten. Keefe was one of a handful of respected residents of the Milton section and was connected with some of the best families in Rahway. Employed at Bloodgood's as their night watchman, he was considered by most, including Mayor Daly, to be a thoroughly reliable individual. In the recent inquest, Keefe served on the coroner's jury.

"I have to tell you, Mark, I was enjoying a perfectly fine day yesterday until you pulled me aside. I couldn't sleep all night wondering what you were going to tell me. So, what is it? What do you know about the basket?"

"It really bothers me that I have to tell you this, Mayor, because I thought by now the owner would have come forward on his own. But he hasn't, and I can't keep silent any longer.

"The whole thing started back on an evening last February. I was in Stu Baker's General Store and saw his mother mending the cover on a small basket, refastening the lid to the sides with a bit of white cord.

When she finished, she proudly showed it to Stu and me, looking for our approval. I was impressed by her workmanship and called to Baker's clerk, a young fellow named Billy Burns, who came over and also commented on how nicely the job was done. It was only a trivial incident so I didn't think anything more about it.

"Then the murder happened. Like everybody, I went to the scene, saw the body and the objects near it, but didn't recognize any of it. I went home and was sitting in my dining room when I saw Burns coming from the direction of the crime, so I went out to ask him what he thought of the murder. He said it was horrible and then he asked me if I remembered the basket that was next to the body. I told him I didn't. Burns said he was pretty sure he knew it and then walked off.

"After the encounter, I started thinking about the basket and soon became convinced I had seen it before, but couldn't remember when or where.

"A few days after the inquest ended, I went out riding with Stu Baker and I mentioned the basket and how I couldn't get it off my mind. Stu made no reply and started talking on another subject and the matter was dropped.

"Near the end of May, while doing my rounds at Bloodgood's, the episode at Baker's hit me like a thunderbolt. As I looked back, the pieces came together. I remembered showing the basket to Burns and his comment to me the morning he came back from the body. I also remembered that Paul Price, another friend of mine, was in the store that night. And, there's something else. When I went to the field to see the body, I met Paul, and I can almost swear he also made a comment about knowing the basket. He might be able to verify all this.

"Like I said, Mayor, I didn't want to say anything because Stu Baker is my friend and I was waiting for him to say something. I don't know why he hasn't. I mean, even if the basket was the one from his store, it doesn't mean he had anything to do..." Keefe's words trailed off as he realized what he was about to say.

Daly knew where Keefe's words were going and he was also disturbed by the thought. Implicating Rahway citizens was something he had tried hard to avoid; yet, this story demanded his investigation.

"I can see how this might be tough on you, but we need to pay Baker a visit. I think it would be best if just the two of us go. I'll pass the information on to Chief Tooker if and when the time comes. I want to keep this quiet and I don't want the newspaper people getting wind of it and blowing it out of proportion. It might not lead to anything anyway." Daly was seriously hoping it wouldn't.

~~~~~

The Baker family had operated a general store on the corner of St. Georges Avenue and Maple for the last thirty years. The store offered the usual fare of groceries and dry goods, and since the passing of Mr. Baker, son Stuart added a corner saloon where he served malt and spirituous liquors. Baker and one clerk were all that was needed to handle the regular business and both worked most of the hours. His current employee, Billy Burns, had been with him since the fall. If Baker was away or additional help was needed, his mother would lend an experienced hand. Baker was married, but his wife, a shy, timid girl, was uncomfortable dealing with the public and was hardly ever seen in the store.

Baker was checking over his stock of liquor bottles as Mayor Daly and Keefe entered. When he realized one of his customers was the mayor, he came from behind the bar and approached the official with an outstretched hand. "Mayor Daly, what brings you out here?" Before getting an answer, he said lightheartedly to his friend Keefe, "Why didn't you tell me you were going to stop by with the mayor?" Again, not waiting for an answer, he turned back to Daly and said in the same light tone, "I hope I got what you're lookin' for."

Baker's neighborly manner had no affect on his visitors who were noticeably uneasy as they tried to figure how to broach the purpose of their coming. There was an awkward silence and Baker began to sense something was amiss. He looked at the expressionless faces and asked, "So what do you want? Can I help you with anything?" This time there was a slight edge to his voice.

Daly saw no reason to procrastinate. "I've just been informed that you might know something about the basket found by the unknown girl's body."

A look of confusion came over Baker's countenance. He studied both the mayor and Keefe and not certain if they were playing with him or not, said, "What are you talkin' about? Who said I knew anything about that basket?"

Keefe, who had been uncomfortable from the time he entered, said anxiously, "Stu, don't you remember the night your mother stitched that basket and showed it to us? And we all said it was a fine job."

"No, I don't remember any basket. What is this? Is this some kind of a joke?"

"Stu, how can you not remember? Your mother was working on the basket over there and we were sitting there. Billy saw it. I think Paul Price did too. You must remember."

Baker made no reply to Keefe, but instead said to Daly, "I don't know what you're tryin' to do here, but I don't like it. I don't know nothin' about any basket."

The mayor, knowing he had more questions that needed to be answered, tried to be conciliatory. "Take it easy, Stu. Don't get excited if I ask a couple of questions. I'm just trying to get something straightened out. I'd like to talk to your clerk if he's around. And if your mother's in, would you get her too?"

Baker was still annoyed, but the mayor's manner relaxed him. "I'll call them both if you want, but you're wasting your time."

Billy Burns was a plain looking, twenty year old, who gave away his lazy nature by the way he moved. He shuffled into the room followed by Mrs. Baker, neither giving any indication of being impressed by the presence of the mayor. Mrs. Sarah Baker, who was called Aunt Sarah by most of her customers, still had all her wits about her, and after years of waiting on the rough Milton clientele, had the reputation of having a sharp tongue. She declined Daly's invitation to sit when he offered her a chair. "I don't have time to sit," she said curtly. "Stuart said you wanted to see me. What's this about?"

Daly didn't appreciate the woman's tone and skipped any further pleasantries. "It's come to my attention that the basket found by the murdered girl might have been a basket that was in this store. Is it possible it might be the same basket you repaired one night a couple of months back?"

Mrs. Baker was quick with her response. "I don't know who told you that, but it's a lie. You sure the person wasn't drunk? Or maybe it's somebody still after that reward."

"You mean you don't remember stitching the cover of a basket and showing it to your customers?"

"Why would I spend time fixin' up a basket? We got plenty of good ones in the store."

Daly looked at Keefe who couldn't believe Mrs. Baker would refute his story. Keefe asked her almost pleadingly, "Aunt Sarah, don't you remember showing me a basket you worked on? Think back. It was sometime last February. Me and Stu were sitting right over there."

"You're not the one tellin' these tales, are you, Mark? What's wrong with you?"

"Come on, Aunt Sarah, I saw you working on that same basket."

"You're crazy!" She glared at Keefe for a long moment and then, as if struck by an idea, continued. "Oh, I see how it is. You know what I think? I think you're still upset because you and the rest of your jury bunch couldn't solve that crime. But, you're makin' a mistake bringin' your friends into it. You got some nerve! And you're supposed to be Stu's good pal. Now you're hangin' around with the mayor, gettin' to be like all the others who think they're better than us. You're nothin' but a louse! If I had my way, you'd be taken out back and horse whipped."

Having vented her anger, the old woman abruptly left, leaving the group silent. Daly said nothing to stop her. He turned his attention to Burns.

"How about you, Billy? Did you see Mrs. Baker mending a basket?"

"I don't remember nothin' like that."

Keefe, stunned by another refutation, came at the clerk with more passion. "How can you say that? We called you over to look at the basket. You saw it. How can you say you don't remember?" Waiting for an answer and not getting one, Keefe hit on another point. "What about our conversation the morning the body was found? You asked me if I knew the basket. You can't tell me you don't remember that."

Burns eyed Keefe quizzically and responded, "I don't know what you're talkin' about. I never even saw you that mornin'."

Keefe was dumbfounded. "What's the matter with all of you? What are you trying to hide?"

Stuart Baker, who to this point had remained quiet, took offense at Keefe's accusation. "You better get out of here before I bust you one. I don't know what you're up to, Mark, but don't bring it around here. Now get out of my store before I take up my mother's advice."

Keefe had no idea how to respond and walked out. Daly was also ready to leave, but had one more question for Burns. "One last question, Billy. Do you have any relatives named Timothy?"

"I don't know too many of my relatives or even how many I got. Of the ones I know, I never heard tell of one named Timothy."

Daly met Keefe outside the store and told him he would continue to investigate the basket story. Keefe was still dazed by what had just transpired, and could only thank the mayor before starting down Maple toward his home.

As Daly sat in his buggy, he considered the strange meeting. He wasn't satisfied with the Baker denials and he found it hard to believe Burns. As for Keefe, he didn't think he was a liar, and he couldn't think of any reason why he would concoct such a story other than to honestly try to unravel the mystery. By the time he reached the center of town, he decided he would share all that happened the last two days with his chief of police. He didn't like the idea, but he also realized he would have to inform Detective Keron. From here on, he knew it would be hard to keep the story under wraps.

Friday, July 8 – Friday, July 15, 1887

As Mayor Daly briefed Detective Keron regarding the new disclosure, the Elizabeth detective couldn't help but feel a sense of satisfaction. From the very beginning, it had been his belief the murderer lived in the vicinity of the crime and was a person who was familiar with the area. Because Mark Keefe's basket story involved individuals from Milton and a general store in the proximity of the scene, he felt his theory was vindicated. "It looks to me like a definite solution is imminent and I suggest we proceed with dispatch. It is imperative we bring Mr. Keefe to Elizabeth to give his statement under oath. I'll make arrangements with the justice and you contact Keefe. I'll try to schedule a time for Monday. Once that's done, we can interview the persons he named and anyone else who might help solve the case. This could be the break we've been waiting for."

~~~~~

Since earlier in the week when the mayor and Keefe went to Baker's General Store, all manner of gossip began to emanate out of Milton. The horde of reporters who had been covering the murder from March 26 had dwindled after the victim was buried, but for those who stayed on, rumors about the basket were fodder for good copy. Thinking something of substance might develop, they hurried to the neighborhood looking for Mark Keefe. The reporters knew Keefe from his work as a juror, and because he had been open and accessible to them during the inquest, they expected him to be a cooperative source. To their chagrin, they were surprised to find him tight-lipped. Keefe knew the mayor wanted to keep the story out of the papers so he was obligated to comply with his wishes. Just as important, was a second reason for remaining quiet. He had been warned by his wife and friends that he would make enemies if he started giving out names.

Unable to extract information from Keefe, the reporters went after other people who were mentioned in the rumors. Paul Price, who Keefe claimed had made comments about the basket, wanted nothing to do with the matter and did his best to hide. A house painter by trade, he was finally cornered while up on a ladder. Resigned to speak, he not only denied talking with Keefe at the murder scene, but he swore he never even saw him the entire morning. Columbus Banks, another Milton denizen, told reporters he recognized the basket from seeing it in Baker's store. He said Aunt Sarah had it hanging on a post and kept onions in it. A story was going around that Baker sold the basket to a colored man a week before the murder. There were whispers that Keefe, Baker, and Burns all knew the victim and for three days prior to the murder, she had been staying in Baker's barn. One source told a reporter that Baker raised several different breeds of chickens and some were similar to the one hatched by Sergeant Conger. According to other sources, Billy Burns was so scared the authorities were closing in, he was either going to tell everything he knew or go on the lam. Some had heard Baker was going to shoot Keefe on sight.

The mayor's hope of keeping the basket clue out of the papers was not to be. As the reports began to circulate in the area dailies, the level of anxiety heightened for the residents of Milton. No one felt safe from the possibility of being thrown into the scandal by an offhand remark and neighbors were once again looking at each other with suspicion. The crime story the mayor thought had died had resurfaced, and the specter of the unknown victim was back to haunt his city.

~~~~~

Mark Keefe had no misgivings as he got out of the mayor's phaeton in front of the Elizabeth Courthouse where he was about to swear to the truthfulness of his account. During the ride from Rahway, he confided that after thinking over all his recollections, he was more positive than ever that they were accurate. "I can't believe Stu and Billy would deny every single detail of what happened that night. That's what makes me so suspicious. If they had only acknowledged being shown a similar basket, I'd have some reason to believe I might be mistaken. If Billy at least agreed he spoke with me on Saturday morning, I might wonder if I was correct in what he said. But, they deny everything like it never happened. And I can't understand why Aunt Sarah would say she never repaired a basket. The whole thing makes me mad. I'm dreadfully sorry about all of this, but it would only be worse for me to keep quiet and act against justice."

Keefe's sworn statement before Justice David Hetfield and witnesses Daly and Keron, included all the details he had previously given the mayor. He was specific about Mrs. Baker mending the basket and showing it to him, her son, and the clerk. He outlined the episode when Burns told him he knew the basket's owner. Keefe also stated under oath that he was with Paul Price when they were viewing the body and added, "Paul pointed to the basket, and said, 'Aunt Sarah.'"

With the signed affidavit in his possession, Keron planned to be in Rahway on Wednesday to meet with Price and Burns and confront them with Keefe's official statement. He was sure he was on the right track to finding the killer.

~~~~~

Paul Price read the document, tossed it on the table, and said to Detective Keron, "Mark Keefe has lost his mind. I don't know if he's right or not about what happened at Baker's, but the part about me just ain't true. There were a lot of people walkin' around the body and most were sayin' stuff, but I never saw Keefe and I never said nothin' about the basket. I'm sure of that. I don't know what's got into him, but you can go back and tell him he better watch out if he says things about me. I'm gettin' sick and tired of people botherin' me because of him."

Keron didn't know how to figure Price. While checking his background, he had learned Price was friends with both Keefe and Baker, but had no particular allegiance to either. Why he would refute one and protect the other made no sense. Keron lifted the statement from the table and stared at it as he asked, "Why would Keefe swear to all of this if it wasn't true?"

"I don't know. All I do know is the part about me is a damn lie. It never happened. Maybe he got me confused with somebody else. Like I said, there were a lot of people around."

"What's your opinion of the connection between the Bakers and the basket?"

"To tell you the truth, I don't believe a single word that's written on that paper."

"Would you be willing to make a statement under oath? I think it would be a good idea if you did."

"I don't want to get dragged into this any more. But if that's what I need to do to clear my name, I guess I'd do it."

"As long as you tell the truth, you won't have any trouble. You'll be notified when I want you."

"Good. Maybe then everybody will leave me alone."

Keron's interview with Price was over. If he were telling the truth, Keefe's entire testimony would be in jeopardy. While listening to his responses, Keron's trained eyes and ears had tried to pick out something to suggest he wasn't being totally honest, but he was unable to detect anything. There was no hesitation in his voice, no faint change in his expression, no awkward gesture. The interview did little to help the investigation. Keron's next move was to have a talk with Billy Burns, but before going, he returned to the police station and asked Chief Tooker to accompany him. Tooker knew Burns and would know how far to push the young clerk in order to get the answers for which they were looking.

~~~~~

Burns lived in a makeshift, three-room cabin just outside of Rahway in Clark. His father had built the shack in 1880 after he had abandoned his wife and two children in Pennsylvania and migrated to the area. The elder Burns lived by himself until the spring of '86 when his son unexpectedly showed up at the door. Not long after Billy moved in, his father disappeared again, leaving the boy alone and on his own in the strange place. Unskilled and uneducated, menial jobs were the only ones available. Lazy and undependable by nature, the job at Baker's was his fourth since coming into the area. Billy had gotten to know Baker from hanging out in his saloon where he would often stay long into the night and drink to the point of drunkenness. When sober, Burns was quiet and unassuming, but with alcohol in his belly, he became loud and boastful. The Billy Burns Inspector Keron and Chief Tooker were about to encounter was the former.

~~~~~

As Chief Tooker read Keefe's statement aloud, it was difficult to tell if the import was getting through to Burns. During the entire reading, he remained silent and expressionless, even when Tooker emphasized the parts referring to him. Still quiet after Tooker finished, Keron asked, "Well, Burns, what do you have to say?"

Burns had his head down and was looking at his hands. He said without looking up and without emotion, "It ain't true. None of it's true. I never saw no basket and I never talked to Keefe."

Tooker didn't like his answer. "Come on now, Billy, you can do better than that. I think you know more than you're telling us."

"There's nothin' more to tell."

"Sure there is, Billy. You know about the basket. And I'd bet you know something about the girl."

Emotion showed on Burns's face at the mention of the girl. He looked scared. "I don't know nothin' about that girl. I got nothin' more to say about any of it."

"What's the matter with you? Don't be a fool. You'd be smart to open up. Tell us what you know!"

"I told ya, I got nothin' more to say. I don't know nothin' more."

Keron took the affidavit from Tooker and held it under Burns's nose. "This is a signed statement given under oath. A man gave his solemn word that everything on this paper is true, and you're saying he's a liar. Why should we believe you?"

Burns didn't know exactly what to say. All he could do was repeat, "I got nothin' more to say."

Keron became more forceful. "Mark Keefe swore to the truthfulness of his story. Would you pledge your word that what you're telling us is the truth?"

"If I had to."

Keron had disgust in his voice and shouted back, "That answer's not good enough. What's wrong with you, boy!" Keron folded the paper and put it in his pocket. "Chief, I'm in agreement with you. This boy's not telling us the whole story. I think we should take him to the station house."

The last suggestion caught Burns's attention. There was a touch of surprise in his voice. "Am I under arrest?"

Keron's reply was firm. "That depends on what you're going to tell us."

~~~~~

Following the afternoon interview, Burns was brought to the station house and locked in a cell to await further interrogation. Detective Keron, who was familiar with various methods used to induce prisoners to open up, suggested they take Burns on a nighttime ride and question him at the site where the body was found. Mayor Daly agreed to the strategy and told the detective a carriage would be ready at nine o'clock.

Daly and Keron were waiting when Burns came from around the back of the jail followed by Chief Tooker. A yellow moon hung heavy in the Thursday night sky, and the mayor thought this was a perfect night for the intended ride. Because the moon was full, the electric streetlights would not be turned on, lessening the chance someone might see them as they traveled through town. He was satisfied the trip could be made and the questioning done without arousing attention.

Central Avenue on the night of the brutal crime could not have looked much differently than it did as the four men approached the dreadful spot. They said nothing and stopped when they reached the wooden fence. An aura of awe was still palpable and the men remained quiet as they looked through the darkness out over the open field. Finally, it was Burns who broke the stillness. "What's the idea of bringin' me here?"

Tooker snapped back. "Keep your mouth shut. We'll ask the questions."

"That's right, Billy." It was Keron's voice. "All we want from you are the answers. We brought you out here because we thought maybe if you came back to the scene of the crime it might help you remember some things."

"I got nothin' to remember. I told you that."

"Well, you better start remembering. We know you saw the basket at Baker's and we know you had a conversation with Mark Keefe, so why don't you come clean and tell us everything you know."

"Maybe Keefe's not tellin' the truth. Ever think of that?"

Again, it was Tooker who answered sharply. "Watch what you say, boy. I told you, we ask the questions. And, as far as Keefe's concerned, we sure as hell put more stock in his word than we do in yours."

"Just a moment, Chief." The mayor wanted to try a calmer approach. "You know, Billy, this murder has disrupted the whole town and I want it to end. If you know anything that might help solve the mystery, it's important you tell us. We want to know about the basket. Tell us what you know about the basket and we'll all go home."

Burns shook his head. "I don't know nothin'."

This time it was Keron who snapped back. "Damn it, Billy. We've wasted enough time on you already. You're going to find yourself in a lot of trouble if you don't talk. People are saying you killed the girl and you're getting ready to run off." Keron paused and raised his voice. "Did you bring that girl out to these fields, cut her throat, and leave her bloody body right there?" He pointed to the spot.

"I didn't kill nobody!"

"Then tell us who did!"

"I don't know, I don't know!"

"Was it Baker? Are you protecting him because he's your boss?" Burns was silent. "Don't be afraid to talk. You know about the basket. Who took it from Baker's store and killed the girl?"

"I'm tellin' you, I don't know!"

"There's a lot of rumors out there, Billy. They say you knew the girl. Did you know the girl, Billy? You must know who the girl was!"

"I don't know who she was and I didn't kill her!"

"Let me tell you something. If we don't get to the bottom of this, you're the one who might hang. You're a newcomer around here. Nobody knows much about you. You work in a place not far from here. You know something about the basket." Keron stopped and waited for a response. There was none. When he continued, he brought up a new point. "A rubber stamp was found in the girl's bag with the name Byrne on it. That's close to your name. How do you spell your name, Billy?"

"I don't know. I never spelt it. You know I can't read or write."

"The way I see it, you've got a big problem. If people can spell your name any number of ways, it might appear that you're the one who owns the stamp."

Burns hadn't cracked, but he was scared. Even if the accusations weren't true, they did make him appear guilty and he didn't want to hang.

"I don't care what people say or what you think, I didn't kill the girl and I don't know who did. That's all I can tell ya."

Realizing there wasn't anything more to gain in continuing the questions, Keron let out a breath and asked, "Would you swear to everything you're telling us? Would you give your word as a man that your story is the truth?"

"Yes."

"In that case, we'll take your statement tomorrow. And, Billy, we've heard you're thinking about leaving town. I wouldn't do that if I were you."

With no further business, Daly, Keron, and Tooker returned to the carriage. Burns was left to get home on his own.

The next morning, Burns was taken to the mayor's office where he placed his mark at the bottom of a sworn statement contradicting the one given by Keefe. Before going back to Baker's, he went to the office of the *National Democrat* to tell the editor he had not run away as some parties were reporting and had no intention of doing so. He wanted it put in the paper.

Monday, July 18 – Thursday, July 21, 1887

Seventy-eight-year-old Alexander Osborne stood in Mayor Daly's office with a folded copy of the *Newark Evening News* under his arm. Daly remembered the white-haired, old gentleman from when he lived in Rahway, but hadn't seen him since he moved to Newark almost ten years ago. His haggard features and shabby attire made the mayor wonder if it was the same man. Once a prominent citizen and former school commissioner, he had been a man of wealth whose worth was said to be in excess of $400,000. Unfortunately, a series of foolish Tennessee land speculation deals cost him his fortune, and by the mid 1870s, most of his money was gone. He eventually left Rahway and ended up in Newark, a dependent of that city, living in an almshouse. Daly couldn't imagine what business brought him to town and was taken aback when the old man said, "I read in this paper about Mark Keefe's story, and I came to tell you it's true."

After all the events of the past months, Daly had conditioned himself not to get too excited over any development, but this one fazed him. The mayor recalled Osborne had a reputation of being an intelligent man with strong convictions, and a man who could be stubborn when crossed. Trying to appear as nonchalant as possible, Daly asked Osborne to elaborate.

"Last February, I came to Rahway on an invitation from Moses Acken. Moses and I were neighbors for years and hadn't seen each other for a long time, so he invited me to come to his place for a couple days. One evening, I walked over to Baker's store and when I went in, Mark Keefe was examining a basket and showing it off to Stewart Baker and his clerk. I heard Keefe compliment Aunt Sarah on her fine stitching.

The incident never crossed my mind until last week when I read the story in this newspaper. That's why I came in today. What Mark Keefe said really happened. I was there."

Daly no longer knew who or what to believe. Was Osborne on the level or did he have hidden motives? The mayor was curious to find out what the old man had to say, although he doubted any of his answers would necessarily bring him closer to the truth.

"How is it that you know Keefe and Baker?"

"Mr. Mayor, remember, I lived in Milton for a good many years. Mark Keefe walked past my door on his way home from Bloodgood's almost every day. I knew Baker from the store. I did a lot of trade at Baker's."

"Were you very friendly with either one of them?"

"No, I wouldn't say so."

"Did you ever have any problems or disagreements with either?

"No."

"Is there any reason you might be angry with Baker?"

There was a perceptible pause before Osborne answered. "No."

"You do realize, because your account supports Keefe, it makes Baker out to be a liar."

"I have nothing personal for or against anyone."

"Was there anyone else in Baker's that night that could substantiate what you saw and heard?"

"I don't recall any others being there. It was late and the store was pretty empty. It was a quiet night, not much going on. That's why I went there. Just to talk to some old neighbors."

"I hope you're not offended by my asking you this, but are you aware of the rewards being offered for solving this mystery?"

"If you're suggesting I came for financial gain, I am offended. The thought might be on your mind because of my present condition, but you embarrass me by asking outright. I am here today so that justice might be done. That's all. I want nothing more."

"That's all any of us want, Mr. Osborne. My apologies for being so forward, but I'm sure you can understand my reason for asking." Daly rose from his desk indicating the interview was over. "Before you go, is there anything else you can tell me that might be helpful?"

"No. I've told you everything I remember from that night."

"One last question, Mr. Osborne. If I ask the detective in charge of this case to come in to take your statement, would you sign your name to it?"

"Yes, I would."

Mr. Osborne gave his statement in front of witnesses on Tuesday afternoon relating the same story he had given the mayor the morning before. After he put his signature on the document and was excused, the mayor, Detective Keron, and Chief Tooker remained to review the puzzling developments. Each day since the basket story had leaked, reports were coming forward both supporting and refuting Mark Keefe's original account. Besides Osborne's confirmation of the events in Baker's store, Columbus Banks also offered details supporting Keefe. He had told reporters he had seen the basket some months before hanging from a nail in Baker's store, and more recently he told Sergeant Conger he was present at the murder site and overheard the conversation between Paul Price and Keefe regarding the basket. The stories were adamantly denied by Baker and his mother, Billy Burns, and Paul Price, the latter two having sworn to their statements. As the three men discussed each of the principals involved, they realized it would not be easy to resolve which of them were being truthful and which were being guided by personal situations and prejudices.

Old Mr. Osborne was in dire financial straights and might have been enticed by the reward money to fabricate his tale. In doing some background work, it had also been learned that after Osborne lost his fortune, he worked off the charity of others until he could right himself financially. Stewart Baker gave him a line of credit and allowed him to run up a bill that covered several months. He finally cut him off when he realized Osborne was making no effort to secure an income nor was he giving any indication he was ever going to pay his debts. On the day Baker told Osborne he would no longer extend his credit, the old man became furious, cursed the owner, and stormed out of the general store. A number of witnesses were found who attested to the scene.

Columbus Banks, who proudly stated his full name was George Washington Christopher Columbus Banks, was an elderly colored gent whose reason and rationale were often clouded by his advanced age. Chief Tooker recalled a story a reporter told him, which illustrated Banks's unusual thinking process. A few days after the murder, the reporter had questioned Banks regarding his thoughts on William Keech's involvement with the crime. Banks told the man, "I don't think Keech coulda done it. Dat girl's neck was cut clear from ear to ear. Keech only got one eye and a man with one eye could only make a cut on one side." Some Milton residents contended Banks might be getting even with

Baker for not allowing him to loiter in the store with his white customers.

As far as Billy Burns was concerned, no one knew much about him and few could be found who had anything good to say on his behalf. When his three former employers were questioned, they all had similar evaluations. They said Burns showed little interest or initiative in whatever task they gave him, and from the time they hired him, they each had the feeling that he wouldn't be kept on for very long. One of them questioned his character and said he never felt he could trust the young man. For some reason, however, Baker took a liking to Burns and gave him a job. Burns had been with Baker for almost eight months, and it was generally believed by those who frequented the store that if forced to take a side, Burns would be loyal to his employer.

The Paul Price rebuttal was the one the authorities couldn't figure. Not a single underlying motive could be found to cast doubt on the truthfulness of his account. He had no special connection to Baker and no investigator could uncover any problem he might have had with Keefe. If his version of the story were the truth, the connection Keefe made between Baker and the basket would be difficult to prove.

The three officials had to admit the link between Stewart Baker and the basket was far from solid. Keefe's accusation, which had sounded so reliable a few weeks ago, was now fraught with doubt. Although seemingly honest, the challenges against it seemed just as honest and the supporters of his story were not the best of witnesses. Throughout the investigation of Baker, none of the rumors or suspicions surrounding him had led to anything. Mayor Daly was beginning to question the entire story and was reaching a point when he would suggest dropping Baker as a suspect.

~~~~~

Reporters from the *New York World* had returned to Rahway immediately after the basket story broke, intent on solving the mystery. This was the paper's chance to get even with their critics and rectify their reputation, which had been tarnished by the Ana Larsen debacle. Their scribes could be seen throughout the city and were especially aggressive in covering any and all angles. One reporter had learned that Stewart Baker was often seen at picnics held at Danner's Beer Garden and went to check out the eastside tavern. After spending several evenings at Danner's, he found most customers either said they had no knowledge of Baker or were simply reluctant to talk. Finally, however, he hit upon a willing confidant. John Walsh, a local plumber, said he had a story to tell and would agree to meet at the bar on Wednesday afternoon.

Danner's was usually quiet during the early afternoon and Walsh felt it would be a good place to have a private conversation. After quitting time, the room would be alive with workingmen stopping in for a couple of drinks before making their way to their homes. Now, the bar was empty and although it was a bright August day, the interior was dark. The reporter and Walsh sat at a corner table. There was a glass of beer in front of each man.

After sitting for a time in awkward silence, the *World* reporter opened the conversation with a complaint about the heat. "I thought when I came inside it would be more bearable, but it's just as hot in here." Walsh made no reply. The reporter lifted his glass and took a drink. "So, why did you want to meet with me? What do you know about Stewart Baker?"

Before answering, and perhaps to give himself courage to go on, Walsh took a swallow of his beer. When he spoke, it was in a low tone, wary that the hollow room would amplify his words. "Danner has some of the best picnics in the area and people come from all parts of town. There's a lot of girls at the picnics and the men come to have some fun with 'em. Baker has been to most of them."

"But Baker's married. Does he ever bring his wife?"

"No. Most of the men who come are married, but not many bring their wives. Oh, nothin' serious goes on. Everyone just comes to drink and have some fun."

"I'm interested in Baker. What is it you have to tell me about him?"

"Well, there was one girl in particular he seemed to always be with. She was one of the girls who worked for Danner."

"Do you know the girl's name?"

"Yeah, it was Mary Link."

The reporter froze and looked up from his notepad. "Do you mean the same Mary Link who some thought was the murdered girl?"

"Yes."

A look of astonishment could be seen on the reporter's face. His next words were spoken as if to himself. "Baker and Mary Link. So that's it." He looked at Walsh and asked in earnest, "What else can you tell me about their relationship?"

"Well, the reason I wanted to talk to you was because something happened at one of the picnics I thought you might be interested in." Walsh paused and had another sip of beer. "We were all sitting around enjoying ourselves when a commotion started several tables away. Baker and Mary were having a heated argument and before anyone got close enough to stop it, Mary threw her hands at Baker and began clawin' at his face. Baker tried to protect himself by slappin' and scratchin' at her face. Finally, they were pulled apart. Both were pretty cut up."

He might have had more to say, but he tensed up and became quiet when he noticed the manager of Danner's, Charles Schlundt, enter the room. Walsh sat back in his chair, finished his beer, and without another word, left the table, and exited the bar.

The news of a relationship between Baker and Mary Link was a major discovery and the reporter knew he couldn't leave without trying to approach the manager to find out what he might know. Since no one was in the bar, he might be more open to answering some questions. The reporter had to take a chance. He picked up his empty glass and went to the bar asking for another drink.

Schlundt filled the glass and put it down. It surprised the reporter when the manager started a conversation. "I saw you in here a few times last week. Somebody told me you worked for a newspaper and you were asking questions about Stu Baker."

"That's right, I work for the *World*."

"When I came in you were talkin' with Walsh. What did he tell you?"

"Nothing much. Just that a girl named Mary Link used to work here."

Schlundt said nothing.

The reporter pressed. "Did Mary Link work here?"

"She worked here for a while. It had to be two years ago. Danner let her go after the picnic season. He didn't need her any more."

"Have you seen the girl since she left?"

"No. I don't think anybody has."

"I'm sure you know about the reports naming Mary as the murdered girl. What do you think? Do you think the murdered girl was Mary Link?"

It was difficult to tell if Schlundt wanted to answer or not, but after looking around the bar to be certain they were alone, he moved closer to the reporter. "I can't say positively, but that girl in some ways did look like Mary."

"What about her clothes or any of her articles? Did they look familiar?"

"Can't say for sure. Remember it was some time ago that I saw her last. Some of the clothing was like the kind Mary wore. And the bag looked like the one Mary carried. That's what I think, but I wouldn't swear to it."

"Any truth to Baker knowing Mary Link and associating with her?"

"I don't want to say anything more one way or another. Baker might have known Mary. He probably did. He came to most of the parties we had here and knew everybody around the place."

"Do you know anything about a fight between Baker and Mary that took place at one of the picnics?"

"I can't say for sure. I mean I can't remember a picnic when we didn't have at least one or two fights. He might have had a fight with Mary, but I don't know about it."

The reporter had gotten all he wanted and more. He thanked the manager and walked outside blinded by the brightness of the midday sun. If he hurried, he could get the story in on time for the Thursday edition. There was excitement in his steps as he headed to the telegraph office, reveling in the knowledge that his story would help bring the mystery to a close.

~~~~~

Detective Keron arrived on the eleven o'clock train and went directly to the mayor's office. He had been notified to come as soon as he could to discuss the latest story printed in the *World*. When he got to the office, Daly was waiting for him. The mayor wasted no time and asked, "Looks like we've got another story on our hands. What do you think of this one?"

"First off, I really don't trust anything I read in that paper. They don't get their facts straight and sometimes they make up their own." Keron sat down behind the mayor's desk before continuing. "As for the story itself, there are some things that make sense and some things that don't. It is possible Baker could be involved. He probably did attend the picnics and after a few beers, I can see him getting friendly with the girls. This one girl may have wanted to get more serious with him, but because he was married, he couldn't. Who knows, maybe she threatened to tell his wife. That would be a reason to get rid of her. The Mary Link connection to Baker at the picnics might be true, but I think we're all in agreement that Mary Link wasn't the murdered girl. And if that's the case, we've got nothing."

The mayor agreed. If Mary Link wasn't the murdered girl, Baker was guilty of nothing more than socializing with a woman other than his wife. Still, the article demanded attention and Daly knew he had to pay Baker another visit and confront him with the allegations.

"You and I are going to Baker's. Maybe we can finally get to the bottom of this. I sent Tooker over to Danner's to find the plumber and the manager. He'll work on getting more out of them. I told him if he got back before we did, to come here and wait for us so we can sort everything out together. One way or another, this basket story has to come to an end."

~~~~~

Stewart Baker acted as though he was expecting the mayor and almost seemed relieved as Daly and Keron walked into his store.

"It's about time you came back, Mayor. The police and newspapers keep coming around here bothering me, but they don't give my side of the story. I offered to bring them dozens of reliable people who have lived in my house or have done trade with me who will say no such basket was ever in my place. I allowed officers full liberty in my house at all hours of the night to search it and question my family and friends. I don't know how many times they went through my chicken coop. My neighbors kept tellin' me I should'a bounced them out, but I figured that would just give people more reason to talk. I'm sick and tired of all this and I'm ready to answer any questions you still have for me."

Daly was surprised by how even-tempered Baker was, not at all the way he acted at their first meeting. "You say you have plenty of witnesses to support your story that the basket was never in your store. Yet three witnesses claim they saw it here. Why do you think Keefe and Osborne and Columbus Banks would lie about something like that?"

"I still haven't figured Keefe out. He was my friend. I don't know why he's doin' this. I can only imagine he dreamed up the yarn. It's a good story, but it ain't true. With Osborne, it's easy to tell what he's up to. He's just tryin' to get some of the reward money. He'd say anythin' to get a few hundred dollars. And Banks is a senile old man. No tellin' what he might say."

"Some serious accusations have been made against you and we're here to get to the truth once and for all. We have to ask you some questions that might offend you, but it's important we hear your answers. Where were you on the night of the murder?"

It was the first time Baker was asked a question by an official implying he was directly involved with the murder. This question from the mayor hit a nerve. His answer was firm but controlled. "It's a long stretch, Mr. Mayor, to accuse me of killin' that girl. I had nothin' to do with it and I can prove it. I was in my store until I closed for the night and then I went upstairs to get ready for bed. I never left the place."

"Was anyone around who could verify that?"

"My wife could. And so could Elmer Ferguson. You know Elmer. He's the brother of Mrs. Ackerman who lives out on New Dover Road. He was here at my house on the night of the murder. He slept in the room next to the one where my wife and me sleep. He was with me in the store until I closed up, and from there, we went directly upstairs. We sat and talked until my wife prepared the spare room for him. It was sometime after that we went to bed."

"What time would you say it was when you were finally in bed?"

"It had to be close to midnight. I closed the store at ten-thirty and we must'a talked for a good hour after that."

"When did you first hear about the murder?"

"The next mornin' my wife called to me and told me to look out the back window. There was a large crowd of people along Central. I woke Elmer up and we walked over to find out what was going on."

The next subject was more delicate. Keron brought it up. "Is there any truth to the story about you and Mary Link?"

"One of my customers showed me that story in the paper. It's all a lie. I don't know what people are tryin' to do to me, but they're lyin'."

"What can you tell us about Mary Link?"

"I can't tell you anything. The only time I ever saw that name was in the papers when somebody thought she was the girl that was killed. I never knew that girl or any other girl by that name."

"Are you telling us you didn't know Mary Link?"

"I have no idea who she is."

"Did you go to picnics at Danner's?"

"Maybe a couple. I went to some."

"I want to be sure on this. You're telling us you never knew Mary Link and so you never had an argument and fight with her as a witness claims you did."

"I saw that in the paper. I couldn't believe it. He musta' mixed me up with somebody else. I never had a fight with a girl. I wouldn't do that."

"There are witnesses who say almost everyone who goes to Danner's knows you. Is it likely you could be mistaken for someone else?"

"Most of the men who drink at Danner's know me from making deliveries and not so much from the picnics. I stop there almost every other day to drop off grocery orders. The person who said I was fightin' with a girl is mistaken. It had to be somebody else. It wasn't me."

Keron wasn't sure what to think and looked to the mayor. Daly decided there was nothing more to be learned from the interview. ""I don't have any more questions. If you're finished, Detective, I suggest we leave Mr. Baker to get back to his work."

Before going, Daly asked Baker if he would give his statement under oath. Baker assured him he would welcome signing an affidavit and added his mother would also like to make a statement and swear to its truthfulness.

~~~~~

Chief Tooker had completed his mission at Danner's and was waiting in the mayor's office when Daly and Keron returned. He had caught up with Walsh and Schlundt but came back with nothing to report to help settle the issue. If anything, his findings would only add more confusion to the already complicated riddle.

"You're not going to believe this, Mayor, but both Walsh and Schlundt deny almost everything that's in that newspaper story. When I got to Danner's, Schlundt was behind the bar and as soon as I walked in, he came runnin' to me to tell me how the reporter twisted his words around. He said he told him he didn't think the murdered girl was Mary Link, but the article made it seem like he was positive it was her. And, he said the same thing about the clothes. He said they looked like clothes she wore, but he didn't say they were the clothes he saw on display. He also said Mary Link was a much taller girl and had pierced ears so she couldn't be the murdered girl. 'Everybody knows that,' he said. He felt real bad and felt awful sorry he told the reporter anything. He didn't think he was going to twist his words.

"It took me a little longer to find Walsh. When I did track him down all he could say was, 'After thinkin' about it some more, I can't be totally sure it was Baker who had the fight. It was two years ago and I might be wrong.' That's all he would say, 'I might be wrong.'"

"That does it as far as I'm concerned." There was a sound of finality in the mayor's voice. "I say we drop Baker from the investigation. It's been three weeks and we can't prove a single thing. All that will happen if we continue is more people will get involved and more people will end up being embarrassed. Enough is enough! The hard feelings that have developed will take years to heal, if they'll ever heal. We can't put the town through any more of this."

Keron was only interested in solving the crime and wasn't concerned if reputations were damaged or neighborhoods upset, but he agreed with the mayor. "I never like giving up on an investigation, but I can't see anything coming out of this one. Keefe's story has too many detractors and I don't think many would believe the witnesses who maintain Baker is lying. Baker's got a good alibi for where he was on the night of the murder, so it would be difficult to connect him to that. Unless something comes up to definitely prove he had some knowledge of the basket, and I don't think that's going to happen, we have nothing. I think you're right, Mayor. We're chasing our tails going after Baker." Keron checked his pocket watch. "This is the damnedest case I've ever come across. I don't know what you gentlemen are going to do from here on, but I'm going back to Elizabeth. I've got other cases to work on."

~~~~~

Near the end of the summer, Detective Keron received a letter from Casper Strombach postmarked Salem, Illinois, August 11, 1887. Strombach was the crank zither player who gave himself up in a rural Midwestern town and confessed to the Rahway murder.

The letter was written in German. When translated, Strombach stated that his mind was now free of trouble, which Keron took to mean he no longer thought of himself as a murderer. Included in the letter was the address of a New York pawnshop. Strombach asked the detective if he would secure his zither from the pawnbroker and forward it to him in Salem. He was anxious to get it so he could start to earn money for passage back to New York. He ended the letter by thanking Keron for all his kindness and in a postscript noted he would pay all expenses incurred in shipping the instrument.

Keron, who couldn't help but see some humor in the whole affair, instructed one of his subordinates to look into fulfilling the request.

Thursday, October 20 – Tuesday, October 24, 1887

Detective John Gregory of New Brunswick had been a familiar face in Rahway during the early weeks of the murder investigation. The police regarded him as an amateur sleuth, and it was generally accepted his primary interest was collecting the reward money. Convinced the killer was either Clinton Froat or William Keech, he interrogated the residents of Milton to the point of harassment. Once the authorities determined Froat and Keech were no longer suspects, Gregory reluctantly left the city, less than satisfied their conclusion was correct. His fascination with the case, however, remained strong and he continued to actively investigate other possibilities.

On Thursday, October 20, Gregory returned. This time he brought two women with him. They came to notify Chief Tooker that they had discovered the name of the unknown woman and also had information that would shed light on the identity of her assailant.

Tooker was not happy to see the detective. He disliked the man and his tactics and his presence meant the case, which had been dormant for the last two months, would resurface, opening wounds that were still festering. Regardless of his personal feelings, Tooker knew he had to hear the man out. With the women present, he would try his best to be civil.

"So what brings you to Rahway, Detective? Or, let me guess. You've got a new lead on the murdered girl."

"I can do better than that. While everybody in this county was giving up on the case, I wasn't going to let it drop. I plan to keep working on it until it's solved. My latest investigation led me to these ladies. This is Mrs. Stevens of New Brunswick and Mrs. Wilson of Bound Brook. I think after you hear their accounts, you'll agree we have uncovered the true identity of the girl and are ready to close in on the killer."

There was no look of surprise or even interest on Tooker's face. He had heard so many of these stories before, he had no expectations this one would prove to be any different. He eyed the two women and asked, "Alright, ladies, why don't you tell me what you know about the murder and the victim."

Mrs. Stevens spoke first. "Your murdered girl's name was Annie Ingram, I can tell you that. Annie came to work for me in June of last year. I'm the proprietress of the United States Hotel in New Brunswick and I'm always looking for girls. I usually hire the ones that just arrive from Europe and have no job and no place to live. I give the girls work and find them lodging. From the brief interview I had with Annie before I hired her, I learned she arrived in February and found a position in Metuchen working as a domestic for a man named Martin. I don't know anything about the man or why she left his employ. I don't ask too many questions of my girls. It's better not to know too much. She wasn't a bad worker, but she drank a lot and when she had too much, she had an ugly temper and used vulgar language. I kept her on for a few months, but because of her drinking habit, I had to dismiss her. It was around the end of August. That's the last I saw of her.

"I followed the story of the murder in the newspapers, but never made a connection until Detective Gregory traced her to the hotel and showed me the pictures. I saw a strong resemblance to Annie. He asked me to come here and said you'd show me the girl's effects. Perhaps if I could see them, I'll recognize something."

Tooker gave no response to the woman's request but asked her to repeat the name to make sure he had it correct. Mrs. Stevens responded with confidence, "Her name was Annie Ingram." He wanted to hear what Mrs. Wilson could add. "What do you know about this Ingram girl?"

"Annie came to my home in early September of last year hoping to find work. I needed a girl and took her on. As Mrs. Stevens has already said, Annie did like to drink. During her stay with me, her drinking became a problem and my husband was especially annoyed by her coarse language. He grew weary of her bad manners and found employment for her at the Einstein Cloth Mills, thinking she might eventually move out of our house to be closer to the mills. She started the new job in December, but as it turned out, she worked there for less than a week. She met a man and after just four days, on December 8, she married him. The workers had a small party for the couple. I wasn't there, but I heard Annie got real drunk and walked out. She came back to my house that night and described the whole affair. She said she scarcely knew what she was doing when she married and was going to leave in the morning to escape her husband. When morning came she got up early, packed her things in a little black bag, and left for Philadelphia. Can you imagine? She married a man and left him an hour later. I guess when she drank she was liable to do anything."

"What was the husband's name?"

"I'm pretty sure she said it was Credeford, Frank Credeford."

"I take it he's the gentleman you presume to be the killer." The question was directed to Gregory.

"It makes sense. As we speak, I have men on his trail. We're close to finding him and when we do we'll piece this whole story together."

"Mrs. Wilson, what makes you think Ingram is the murdered girl?"

"Annie wrote me several times after she left. She said she found work in Philadelphia. She never mentioned anything about Credeford. The letters stopped coming sometime in January. I never heard from her after that. I knew about the Rahway murder, but didn't pay it much mind. Then I saw a picture of the girl and it reminded me of Annie. I began to think maybe that's the reason she stopped writing. I contacted the police in my town and they got word off to Detective Gregory. Oh, there's one more thing. Annie left a trunk behind."

"Did you open it? Do you know what's in it?"

"When I told Detective Gregory about it he advised me to open it. There wasn't much in it except some clothing, some photographs, and a large packet of letters from a sister who lives in England."

Tooker's interest was heightened and although he would wager this was going to be another waste of time, he had to go through the motions. "The girl's possessions have been brought here and placed upstairs. Let's go up and have a look."

In a corner of the second floor police courtroom, stood a coat rack and a glass display case. Articles of clothing hung from the four hooks on the rack. Inside the case were the same articles found by the body, which thousands had already seen. Tooker stood back and watched as the ladies examined the evidence.

Mrs. Stevens was clearly upset by the display and had a difficult time controlling her emotions. "I know that skirt. I remember seeing

Annie wear it. And that chased ring was Annie's. I have no doubt these things belonged to her." The woman turned away and started to sob.

Mrs. Wilson was better at keeping her composure and after looking over the items for several minutes exclaimed, "I've seen a number of these articles before. There can be no mistake. These are Annie's clothes. I'm sure this undergarment is hers because I made it for her. The two more expensive rings are the ones I loaned her on the night she ended up getting married. That's the black bag she carried when she left. And, I know that knife. I saw Annie in my own kitchen peeling potatoes with it. I'm sure of it."

"Well, Chief, what do you say now?" There was obvious ridicule in Gregory's question.

"I'll let the mayor know what's transpired and we'll contact Keron in Elizabeth. All I can say is this better not turn out to be another wild lead. If it does and we end up with nothing, I wouldn't show my face in this town for a long time if I were you."

~~~~~

By the end of the weekend, the history of Annie Ingram was beginning to reveal itself. Detective Gregory's reappearance and his conference with Chief Tooker awakened newspaper reporters and local officials who immediately went scurrying off in search of Mr. Martin of Metuchen and the jilted husband. The *New York Times* sent wires to England to get facts concerning Ingram's life before coming to America. It turned out to be a productive three days as the blanks in the story were starting to fill.

The reporters had no trouble finding the Metuchen farmer. Mr. Joseph Martin was an inoffensive, middle-aged bachelor who lived alone on the outskirts of the small community. He told them about a day in early February of the year before when he went to town to buy groceries. After he filled his order, he made a usual stop at a local saloon. A woman he had never seen before was at the bar asking if anyone knew where she might find a job. The bartender teased Martin saying he could use "a woman's touch" around his place and grinned as he added, "A woman might do you some good." Embarrassed, Martin eventually let himself be convinced that he did need someone to cook and clean, so by the time he finally left the woman went with him. Her name was Annie Ingram.

It wasn't long before Martin realized he had made a big mistake. The woman was addicted to alcohol and he couldn't remember many occasions when she was sober. She quarreled over everything and bullied the farmer without mercy. One evening she completely lost control, destroyed all his furniture, and beat him with a leg she had broken off a chair. Martin escaped serious injury by fleeing to town where he called on the police to arrest her. Ingram was brought to jail to spend the night and cool off. The next morning she was released with a warning not to return to the farm.

Martin told the reporters, "She got angry at me because I wouldn't marry her. Whenever she talked about marriage and I said, 'no', she'd fly into a terrible rage. It got so bad that one night, I had to get the police."

When Martin was told about the murdered girl and shown the photographs he responded, "I can see a resemblance. It looks a bit like her." He concluded by telling them, "If she's dead or not, I don't care. I just hope I never see her again."

~~~~~

The wires returning from the other side of the Atlantic gave several bits of interesting, if not useful information. The letters in Ingram's trunk were from a sister who lived in Birmingham, England. When correspondents went to her home, she produced a marriage certificate dated 1875 and made out to a Mr. George Harris at Alfreton, County Derby. The name of the woman he married was Ann Ingram whose age was recorded as twenty-five. It was also learned that Harris died shortly after the marriage, leaving his young widow a comfortable inheritance. Annie lived off the bequest for a number of years and according to the sister, the money would have lasted even longer had she not wasted it away on liquor. When it was depleted, she left the country.

~~~~~

The hunt for Frank Credeford began at the Einstein Cloth Mill in Bound Brook. Knowing the presence of police and reporters would disrupt the daily operations of the plant, the owners assigned a foreman named Ryan to answer their questions. Ryan had never liked Credeford and seemed to take pleasure in the disparaging comments he made about his worker. He told them Credeford had worked at the mill for seven years and was considered a hard worker, but added, "He had an ungovernable temper." The foreman went on to tell the group, "It wouldn't surprise me if he killed somebody. In the years I've known him, I always considered him a dangerous man. No one knew his background and no one dared ask him." When asked if he was aware of a relationship between Credeford and Ingram he said, "He seemed fascinated by the new girl. She hadn't been in the mill an hour before he was in conversation with her." In response to a question regarding what had become of the man, the foreman responded, "He was gone the same day the girl left. I remember it was a Saturday and he came to work, but only to demand his wages. He got his money and walked out the gate. He never came back to work. The story going around was he went to Philadelphia, but I can't tell you for sure what happened to him or where he is now."

Based on Ryan's less than objective comments, it was surmised that Credeford, angered by his bride's desertion, followed after her, found her by late March, and got his revenge on a lonely field in Rahway.

~~~~~

By Sunday afternoon as a manhunt was underway in and around Philadelphia, Detective Keron finished his investigation certain Ingram was not the murdered girl. Armed with all the details that had surfaced, he had enough reasons to support his deduction and presented them to the mayor and Tooker.

"The Ingram identification is bogus. I went to Bound Brook yesterday to question Mrs. Wilson and to inspect the trunk. When I asked her to describe Ingram she gave a description that wasn't even close to the victim. The height was different, the weight was different, even the hair color was wrong. As far as the clothes and rings are concerned, she really couldn't describe them with any accuracy. When she saw them on display, I think she simply saw what she wanted to see and not what was there. We can blame Gregory for that. By urging the woman on, they came to have total faith in their stories.

"I looked through the articles in the trunk and found dresses which were made for a large woman. I took measurements of several garments. The waist sizes were at least five and a half inches bigger than the waist of the victim. The clothes could not have belonged to the murdered girl."

"Every report we've gotten on Ingram alludes to her drinking habit. This is a woman who drank at every opportunity, yet the post mortem exam didn't reveal the slightest trace of alcohol.

"Finally, gentlemen, there's a document from 1875 that states Ingram was twenty-five years old. If that were true, our victim would have been thirty-seven or thirty-eight when she was killed. The autopsy shows the girl to be ten years younger. The murdered girl can't be Annie Ingram."

~~~~~

The mystery of Credeford's whereabouts was solved Sunday night, when he was arrested just before midnight by two Philadelphia police officers that had tracked him to his North Second Street boarding house. The officers found him asleep and when they stirred him, they quickly realized they had aroused a drunken man. After a brief scuffle, Credeford was fettered and brought to the station house.

The next morning, the Philadelphia papers ran a one-inch story titled, "Arrest of Supposed Rahway Murderer." Chief of Detectives Wood of the Sixth District Station was disappointed after leafing through the paper and finally spotting the small news item. He felt the capture deserved more ink and was only placated by reasoning the papers got the information too late to print a full story. He was confident his department would get more credit in the Tuesday morning editions.

The prisoner had yet to say much. When picked up, he was in such an inebriated condition he was unable to comprehend why he was being arrested and was oblivious to any references to a murder. Wood planned to question him more fully at eleven o'clock when he would be more sober.

The hour came and Credeford was brought to Wood's office loudly demanding to know why he was arrested. His defiant attitude ceased when Wood told him, "We have reason to believe you killed a girl in Jersey back in March."

The words shocked Credeford to his senses. "You're wrong. You got the wrong man. You've got me mixed up with somebody else. I never killed nobody. You've made a mistake."

"We'll see about that. Now if you'll cooperate and answer some questions, maybe we'll find out who's made a mistake. How long have you been in Philadelphia?"

Credeford looked away with a snort. For a brief moment, he thought he should be stubborn and not say anything, but realizing it might only make matters worse, he uttered an answer, "I got here in December."

"Why did you come to this city?"

"I was lookin' for work. I needed a job."

"Did you find one?"

"Yeah. I been workin' at a woolen mill. I been there about six months."

"Where were you before you came to Philadelphia?"

"I worked at a cloth mill in New Jersey. I worked there a pretty long time."

"Why did you leave?"

"I got tired of the job. I wanted to try somethin' new. I came here because I heard places were hirin'."

In the same even tone Wood asked, "Did you come to Philadelphia looking for Annie Ingram?"

"Why do you ask me that? What do you know about Annie?"

"Did you come here trying to find her?"

"No. I came lookin' for work. I told you that."

"Is it true you were married to Annie Ingram?"

"Yeah, but the whore ran off after we got married and I haven't seen her since."

"You sound angry. Were you angry at her after she walked out on you in front of your friends?"

"Yeah, I was angry. Wouldn't you be? Have a woman do that to you."

"Were you angry enough to kill her?"

"No. I told you I didn't kill nobody."

"It's suspected you were so angry you went after the girl and when you found her, you killed her."

"That ain't true. I don't know what you're talkin' about. I admit I got hooked up with a girl who was crazy and she ran off on me. But I wouldn't go out of my way to kill her."

"Why do you say she was crazy?"

"I knew her for one day and she started talkin' about gettin' married. She wouldn't leave me alone. Everybody thought she was odd."

"Why did you marry the girl if you hardly knew her and you thought her behavior was strange?"

"I don't know. She was pretty and seemed like a girl who liked to have a good time. We got drunk together and I guess I wasn't thinkin' right. I'm probably better off without her."

The detective was impressed by the honest answers. He called for an officer to take him back to his cell and told him as he was leaving, "It's necessary you remain in custody a little longer until we clear this up. You might be needed to answer more questions."

~~~~~

The Tuesday papers did run complete stories of the capture of the murder suspect printing all details including the name of the alleged victim. They also gave kudos to the men of the Sixth District Station for their fine work, much to the satisfaction of Detective Wood. As desk officers were passing the articles around and congratulating one another, a gentleman entered the station house asking to see the officer in charge.

"What business do you have with him?" inquired the desk sergeant.

"I just read this article in the *Inquirer* that says you arrested someone last night for murder. I have information that the police need to know about."

"Detective Wood is in charge of the case. He's the one you want to see." The visitor was led down a hallway to the detective's office.

The man introduced himself as Lester Metcham and said he lived with his wife on Wiley Avenue. He said he read the news about a woman named Annie Ingram who was murdered in New Jersey. "What I came to tell you is I married a woman two months ago whose name is Annie Ingram. I don't exactly know how to say this, but I think she's the woman you believe was killed."

Wood looked at Metcham with a start. "Is there any reason other than the name that makes you think it's the same woman?"

"Just about everything. When she arrived in this country, the places she worked in Jersey, when she came to Philadelphia. The whole history matches with what I know of my wife. And the part about her drinking a lot…I'm sorry to say, but that's true too."

Wood quickly realized this information could overturn the entire investigation and wanted to get it straightened out as fast as he could. "If I send an officer to your house, would your wife be home and would she come to the station?"

"She should be at home and I think she'd come, providing the man you send doesn't annoy her."

Wood gave orders to locate Mrs. Metcham and bring her to headquarters. He also wanted Credeford brought up.

By the time Mrs. Metcham arrived, the building was filled with reporters who had gotten wind of the unusual development. There was an air of arrogance about the woman as she made her way to Wood's office, giving the impression that if there was going to be trouble she was the one who would dish it out. As soon as she entered the room, she spotted Credeford and proceeded to deliver a stream of vulgar allusions making even the most hardened officers and reporters blush with embarrassment. Credeford cursed back with equal fury and had to be removed to restore order.

With Credeford gone, Wood turned his attention to the woman. "Alright Mrs. Metcham, settle down and watch your tongue. You make a poor spectacle of yourself using such language."

The woman heard his words, but was still in a humor to wrangle. "What was that bastard doing here? What did he say about me? What's the idea of bringing me here?"

"He said he was married to you. Is that true?"

"For just a couple of hours, that's all. Then I came to my senses and escaped from the louse."

Mr. Metcham, who had witnessed the scene with absolute surprise, was wide-eyed as he heard the words come from his wife.

Detective Wood recognized the investigation had exploded and his suspect was innocent, but he was now interested in this woman who had two husbands. He continued his questions not knowing what to expect. "How many husbands do you have, if I may ask?"

"I was married when I was living in England, but he died. Last December I married that no good, drunken bum who was just here. Then I came to Philadelphia and married Lester."

Wood found her story to be remarkable and was at a loss for words. All he could say was, "Don't you know it's a crime to have two husbands?"

"Look here," she replied with impertinence. "I'll have forty husbands if I want to."

Her impudence astounded the detective who told Metcham to take his wife home. As she was leaving, Wood cautioned her not to take on any more husbands, and if she did, it had better be because she was a widow. Wood wasn't certain, but he thought her reply was a short laugh.

Wednesday, February 29 – Friday, March 2, 1888

In the weeks and months following the Annie Ingram fiasco, only two identifications surfaced, which were given any attention. One report came out of Richmond, Virginia, and the second from Staten Island, New York. These new stories, however, did not excite the people of Rahway, who by this time had resigned themselves to believing the events surrounding the mystery of the unknown woman would never be unraveled. Little or no interest was given to any new clue and when approached for opinions, the locals would look at their questioners with a "What do you take me for?" sort of expression and laugh. The populace had reached a point where nothing but the capture of the murderer and an open confession of guilt would remove the shroud still hanging over the city.

In late February of 1888, a dispatch arrived from the authorities in Richmond, Virginia, with a report that they were holding a tramp who claimed to have been an accomplice in the murder at Rahway. The man, whose name was Frederick Grupy, alias John Thompson, alias John Smith, was arrested January 31 for vagrancy. According to his confession, he and a friend met a woman named Fannie Gunther in Baltimore in 1881. The three grew to be more than friends and both men eventually became romantically intimate with the woman. Being devotees of the Baltimore brothels, they introduced their lady friend to one of the houses of ill repute where she took up residency and joined the indelicate profession. In the meantime, Grupy's friend, whose name he gave as Carl Woolf, had fallen in love with another woman whom he wanted to marry. When Fannie learned of the impending union, she objected and threatened to interfere. Fearing she would cause him trouble, Woolf devised a plan to silence her for good.

In a statement to the police, Grupy outlined the details of the crime. "Prior to March 1887, Woolf had gotten a job near Rahway, New Jersey. He sent me word to bring Fannie to meet him at the railway station in Jersey City. Then Woolf, Fannie, and me took the train for Rahway. It was March 28.

"The train started about half past eight and the run was about an hour and a half to Rahway. Fannie was in the ladies' car while me and Woolf were in the 'smoker.' Woolf had a tin box containing her letters and trinkets. I had a valise containing his clothing and mine. When we reached Rahway, all three of us got off. Woolf and Fannie walked a short distance from the platform and he killed her just as the train was moving off. Both of us jumped back on the train. Woolf was very pale and excited. We got off at Red Bank, walked to Keyport, and stayed at a local hotel under the name of Wilson (Al and Harry).

"I buried the tin box on a farm near Deal Beach. I put Woolf's bloodstained cuff and the razor he used to do the deed in the box.

"The next day, we took a boat to New York where I stayed until April 1st. Woolf returned to Baltimore. As we parted he said, 'Thank God the affair is over and my mind is easy. Now I am a free man and can marry whom I please.'"

Neither Mayor Daly nor Chief Tooker needed to read very far into the communiqué before they were sure Grupy's account was a total fabrication. The episode begins on March 28, three days after the crime. The excursion from Jersey City to Rahway takes no more than half an hour, not one and a half hours as noted in the confession. According to the story, the crime was committed a short distance from the station when the actual distance to the Central Avenue site is about one mile. The train station is in the center of town and it would have been next to impossible for the murder to have taken place as described. No mention was made of the basket of eggs or any of the others items carried by the victim. The last scheduled train out of Rahway to Red Bank was an early evening local. Grupy and Woolf could not have jumped a train for that destination at the late hour given in the story. Finally, the name Carl Woolf was evidently plucked from newspaper accounts written during the days of the inquest. In the end, it was judged Mr. Grupy wanted free passage to New Jersey and concocted the absurd tale to achieve that end.

Wednesday, October 24 – Saturday, October 27, 1888

A story came out of Staten Island in the fall of 1888, when Mrs. Johanna Sandberg, a resident of that borough, brought several photographs of a pretty, blond-haired woman to the local police precinct with a claim they were images of the Rahway murder victim. Inspector Joseph Cobb was on duty to conduct the interview and although the crime was outside his jurisdiction, he would listen to the woman's story before contacting the proper authorities.

Mrs. Sandberg began by saying she had just returned from spending the summer in Sweden where she visited with relatives and friends. "During my visit, I went to the home of the Jansens who were close friends of my Swedish cousins. Mrs. Jansen was overjoyed to see me and anxiously asked me about the welfare of her daughter, Josephine, who had sailed to America in March of '87 to seek her fortune and to visit friends including myself. I surprised her when I replied that I had never seen or heard from Josephine and was not aware she came to the United States. Mrs. Jansen was stunned by my news. She nervously asked all manner of questions and gave particulars about her daughter that made me suspect that Josephine Jansen might be the murdered unknown woman. She was blond and twenty-five years old. She was well dressed and was carrying $3,000. She was scheduled to land in mid-March and had not written to her mother since that time. I left the distraught mother, but took with me photographs of Josephine and a patch of cloth that was left over from the dress she wore when she departed. I have a bad feeling she came here and fell in the hands of a villain who robbed and killed her."

Inspector Cobb asked to see the photographs and compared them to the ones he had on file. He thought there were striking similarities. He suggested that Mrs. Sandberg go to Rahway to view the effects and told her he would telegraph the chief of police to alert him of her coming. He also said he would notify a New York City detective who he knew had been working on the mystery from the beginning. He called for his sergeant and told him to contact Inspector Thomas Byrnes.

~~~~~

Inspector Byrnes got a bad taste in his mouth whenever anything came up regarding the Rahway murder case. For someone who was accustomed to "always getting his man," this case rankled him like no other. The Louis DeCamp arrest made him a figure of ridicule rendering his investigative work within the Rahway city limits ineffectual. His search for Casper Strombach not only cost him time and money, but also tarnished his reputation. In his opinion, the county's inquest botched up the entire investigation and actually aided the killer in his escape. With the victim buried and unknown and her assailant more than likely long gone and far away, he had come to regard the crime as one that might never be solved. Harboring these feelings, it was with mixed emotions that Byrnes read the telegram from Staten Island. More out of a sense of duty than with hopes something might develop, he sent three of his inspectors to Castle Garden.

The detectives spent a full day at the entry port returning with no more than the name of another "lost" woman. A check of lists of names from logbooks revealed a passenger named Josephine Jansen had arrived on March 20, 1887. With this fact in hand, Byrnes's men questioned immigration agents, employment officials, boardinghouse proprietors, and ferry line captains trying to discover a trail. Unfortunately, no one was able to supply the slightest bit of help. What became of the Jansen woman after she landed was anyone's guess. Byrnes saw this as another dead end and his interest in the lead, as well as in the murder case itself, was over.

~~~~~

In Rahway, Mrs. Sandberg carefully studied the clothing and effects but didn't recognize any of the items. The piece of cloth she carried didn't match any article of clothing on display. When she lined up the photographs she brought next to the many from the Rahway police file, she found images that were completely different. Apologizing for not being able to help solve the mystery, she went off quite certain her suspicions were unfounded and, at the same time relieved, her Swedish friend was not the murdered woman.

~~~~~

The Fannie Gunther and Josephine Jansen identifications were the last two to be investigated by County or City authorities. In the next dozen years, information concerning the crime, the victim, and the killer would occasionally come forth to rekindle the memories of the strange and troubling episode. These new clues, however, only served to keep the mystery alive and did nothing to bring closure to the matter. The answers to the basic questions, "Who was the woman, who killed her, and why?" never came to light and the enigmatic case of the unknown woman remained unsolved.

Epilogue

Of all the attempts to name the unknown woman, the Mary Dorman story was the most compelling. Dorman's two sisters, Mrs. Agnes Space and Mrs. Jane Harris, were both positive the murdered woman was their younger sister, Mary. Undertaker Ryno was struck by how much the two sisters looked like the body in his morgue. Coroner Terrill believed so strongly that the victim was Dorman he wrote her name on the burial certificate. Even though the autopsy report stated the victim had never given birth (Dorman had a child), Dr. Cladek, the physician who assisted in the post-mortem examination, questioned the point.

The identification took on new life several months after the burial when a letter was brought forth again implicating Andrew Kirkwood, brother-in-law of the two sisters. According to a letter written by Mrs. Harris, Kirkwood showed up at her door a day after the murder. His clothes, hands, and face were spotted with blood. When she questioned him, he told her he had gotten into a fight with a fellow worker over a game of pool. He asked her to wash his clothes, which she did. Mrs. Harris said she would have mentioned the episode when Mayor Daly and Detective Keron interviewed her in April, but feared Kirkwood would do her harm. She now regretted not having told all she knew.

News of the letter was ignored by officials, who felt Mrs. Harris held such a deep-seated dislike for her brother-in-law she would go to any extent to bring him down. The police had accepted Kirkwood's alibi that he was in Paterson on the night of the murder, but because the accusation caused concern, officers were sent back to the city where they found Thomas Murphy, an employee of the Roger's Locomotive

Works. Murphy backed up the alibi by emphatically stating he was with Kirkwood until late into the night on Friday, March 25. The County was satisfied with the verification and considered Kirkwood innocent.

~~~~~

In December 1887, Mrs. Space received a letter from Scotland penned by her aged mother. According to her mother, Mary was alive, well, and living in the north of Scotland. The mother had not actually seen Mary but had a letter confirming her health and whereabouts. Mrs. Space found it extremely peculiar, however, that Andrew Kirkwood sent the letter to her mother. Understandably troubled, Mrs. Space implored Mayor Daly to pursue the matter. With some reluctance, the County cabled the Scottish authorities requesting a search be conducted for Dorman and Kirkwood. A limited hunt was carried out with no results. No trace of either person was found. The investigators did secure a photograph of Dorman and shipped it to Elizabeth. When the image finally reached the County Seat, it was given to Detective Keron who had photographer James Stacy examine it and compare it to the many he had taken. He found the photograph to be of a Scottish lassie with darkish hair and freckled face without the features or form of the woman in his photographs. In his judgment, they were not images of the same person.

The publication of the story revived the name of Mary Dorman. A theory soon circulated that the investigation in Scotland was dropped when it was intimated that someone connected with the family, namely brother-in-law, Andrew Kirkwood, was suspected. County officials discounted the theory as rumor mongering and closed the file on the Dorman identification. For adherents of the story, however, there remained enough loose ends to keep them believing the murdered woman was in fact Mary Dorman.

~~~~~

The names Clinton Froat and William Keech were on the lips of almost everyone in the days following the murder. Their proximity to the murder site, the connection they had with young foreign women, and their disagreeable and reclusive behavior made them obvious suspects. The fact that nothing could be proven to connect them to the crime did not put an end to the suspicions. Even after they moved out of Rahway and after months and years passed, their names were brought up as new accusations were leveled against them.

In December of 1887, a story was reported that Froat's twelve-year-old daughter had made a confession accusing her father of the murder. According to the young girl, a party was given at her family's home on Friday, March 25. One of the guests was a pretty young woman who attracted the attention of both her father and her uncle, William Keech. After drinking beer together and flirting with the woman, her father became jealous and persuaded the woman to go out for some air. The daughter reportedly said later, "My father came back, but the woman didn't." The description she gave of the woman tallied with that of the murdered woman.

The authorities took little stock in the tale given by the twelve year old. Froat had a reputation of being a brutal man and witnesses were found who told of the harsh punishments he often laid upon his children. They reasoned the daughter was driven to confess due to her father's abusive nature.

Detective Keron arrested Froat, who by this time had altered the spelling and pronunciation of his name to Foront, in Elizabeth and held him for questioning. After a grilling by Keron and Chief Tooker, it was their assessment the daughter had made the allegation to protect a younger sibling from her mean-spirited father. No charges were brought against Froat and he was released.

~~~~~

Late in the year 1889, Detective John Gregory, against the advice given earlier by Chief Tooker, showed his face back in Rahway. Gregory had previously led several failed investigations, but he was undaunted in his passion to solve the case and intent on proving a connection between the Froat family and the crime.

This time, his investigation involved a nephew of Froat, twenty-year-old William Froat, who lived outside of New Brunswick about eight miles from Rahway. A story was given to Detective Gregory by sixteen-year-old Mamie Hughes of New Brunswick, who lodged a complaint that the Froats held her captive over a period of five weeks. The story she would tell Gregory contained enough circumstantial evidence implicating William Froat to the Rahway murder to make the detective feel he was on the verge of breaking the case.

According to the young girl, she left her home on Tuesday, October 29, with the intention of visiting an aunt in New York. She walked to

Stelten to catch a train, but got to the depot after the last eastbound train had gone through. Too late to return home, she decided to go to a friend's house to spend the night. Unfortunately, in the darkness she became confused and lost her way in a thickly wooded area. To make matters worse, it began to rain heavily. Cold, wet, and frightened, the young girl searched for shelter. She was relieved when she saw lights coming from the windows of a small shanty standing alone in a clearing. She hurried to the secluded dwelling. It turned out to be the home of John Froat who lived there with his wife and son, William.

Mamie went on to say she was taken in by the family, but to her dismay, she was held against her will for the next five weeks. From the day she arrived, the son paid her constant attention and assured her she had no cause to worry saying he and his father had detained other girls before and nothing very terrible happened to them. In the time she was with them, no harm was done to her, but she found it strange that they treated her almost as a member of the family. Perhaps that was their design, for one afternoon, William caught her completely by surprise when he offered to marry her. Of course, she refused and when she did, he became angry and told her she was not the first girl who jilted him. He then proceeded to tell her a story about an incident that occurred in the springtime more than two years before. He said he met a young German woman traveling alone towards Amboy and took her to his parents' home where she stayed for two weeks. He described her as a nice-looking girl with dark brown hair and black piercing eyes. On Friday evening, March 25, he and the woman started out for Rahway to attend a party at his uncle's house. The woman was dressed fairly well and carried a large satchel. As they walked, they got into a quarrel and the woman ran off. At this point in his story, Mamie asked if he knew what became of the woman after she left him or if he ever saw her again. His response frightened her. He grew furious and threatened to shoot her if she asked any more questions or if she spoke to anyone about what he had told her. Mamie couldn't remember if he mentioned the woman's name, or if he did, she didn't remember it.

The Froats were an odd bunch and for no apparent reason on a morning in early December, John Froat put Mamie in a wagon and drove her to a road that would lead her back to New Brunswick. He was quiet the entire way and when they got to the road, he simply told her she could get out. The next day, the police led by Detective Gregory, arrived at the Froat house and arrested all three family members. They were jailed to await examination. Their bail was set at $1,500.

When pieced together, the story did contain some fascinating possibilities. The woman found murdered could possibly have been of German descent and in a number of ways answered the description William gave the girl. The murder was committed at approximately 9:00 p.m.. William and his companion would have reached the spot of the murder around that exact time if they left the house in the early evening. They walked through the woods, which would explain why no one on the main roads saw them. William certainly would have been invited to his uncle's party, but no one mentioned his being there. Most intriguing of all, however, is the fact that the Froats of New Brunswick raised chickens and sold eggs to help eke out their living. It would be quite natural for them to send a basket of eggs to the party of a relative.

In the end, however, the authorities judged there was not enough hard evidence secured by detectives to warrant a formal charge of murder against William Froat. They concluded the entire theory was based on nothing more than supposition. After a week in jail, the Froats were allowed to go home.

~~~~~

In February 1894, an old woman named Margaret Grace was battling with a troubled conscience. In an effort to unburden herself, she contacted Detective Gregory and related a strange, but not impossible story.

Mrs. Grace said that on the Friday afternoon before the body was found, she went to Clinton Froat's house to deliver milk. William Keech and a young woman were seated in the kitchen. Mrs. Grace was always uncomfortable when the surly, one-eyed man was around and was relieved when he got up and left the room. She had never seen the young woman before, but her friendly mien was calming, and the two had a brief and pleasant conversation. She told Mrs. Grace her name was Ellen Maher and that she had recently arrived from Coleraine, County Donegal, Ireland. Her plans were to go west and start a new life.

On Easter Sunday, Mrs. Grace visited Ryno's to view the body and was shocked to see the Irish girl she had met in Froat's kitchen lying in the coffin. Too distraught to utter a sound, she left the funeral parlor and rushed home to gather herself. Over the next several days, she considered alerting the authorities, but was afraid to tell her story for fear Keech would make her his next victim. As time went on, she became more and more convinced Keech would kill her if she told what she knew. Frightening herself beyond reason, she vowed not to say a word to anyone. Finally, after seven years, she called on Gregory to release her secret.

The authorities had no interest in Mrs. Grace's story or in reviving the mystery. Years had passed, the unknown woman was buried, and William Keech had moved away some years before, his whereabouts no longer known.

~~~~~

Besides Detective Gregory, another person who never gave up hope of solving the mystery was John Ross, the fish dealer, who just days after the murder had overheard an old woman's story in Klien's Tavern in Roselle. In the fall of 1889, after two years of amateur detective work, Ross claimed to have found the identification of the unknown woman and her killer. It was his belief the woman's name was Annie Miller, a German immigrant who had worked as a domestic for a farmer named Benedict in Roselle, and later for a Mr. Shindler in Linden.

Ross maintained that Miller left Shindler's sometime in mid-March 1887, and on the night of March 24, stopped by the home of Mrs. Sarah Ann Jackson to ask for a night's lodging. Mrs. Jackson obliged and let her stay. The next morning, she was gone without a word to her hostess. Since that time, Ross had not been able to find Miller and believes she was the woman who went into Rahway where she was murdered.

In his search for clues, Ross learned that while on the Benedict farm, Miller had become acquainted with a farmhand named Thomas Bannister, who he interviewed a few months after the crime. Bannister informed Ross that he and Miller planned to get married and he couldn't understand why she would run off without talking things over. He said he had absolutely no idea what caused her to leave and could offer no clue as to where she might have gone. She never mentioned having friends or relatives in the area, so he concluded she could be anywhere. Before Ross left, Bannister gave him a miniature photograph of Miller.

Ross didn't know exactly why, but there was something about Bannister's answers and the way he answered the questions that made him suspicious. The amateur sleuth set out to find out as much as he could about the farmhand and after two years of detective work, he was ready to call for an arrest. He came to the authorities claiming to have two items in his possession to tie Bannister to the crime. He said he had a photograph of Miller given to him by Bannister, which had a great likeness to the images on the official photographs. He also had a letter written by Bannister to a man in New York telling him, "Annie Miller would not be at Shindler's long." Ross would not divulge how he obtained the letter.

He also told of another potential witness. He discovered that Miller had a friend who worked in a bakery in Elizabeth by the name of Annie O'Brien. Unfortunately, when interviewed, O'Brien refused to give any pertinent information unless there was money in it for her. Ross did find out that she made frequent visits to Linden while Miller was working at Shindler's. Not long after Ross spoke with her, she moved to New York City. He had not been able to locate her since her departure, but had a feeling she was hiding something important concerning what happened to her friend.

Ross saved what he felt was the most incriminating bit of evidence for last. He said Bannister had recently left the Roselle farm and moved to Connecticut. As he saw it, Bannister had been warned by friends that his arrest was imminent so he fled from the state to avoid capture. Ross strongly encouraged the police to help him find both O'Brien and Bannister before they had a chance to flee too far off and be lost for good.

The police were not about to accommodate Ross' requests. His interpretation of what happened and who was involved wasn't taken seriously in the days following the murder and his new clues did nothing to change opinions. Ross left Rahway dejected, but still determined. Rumors had it he was planning a trip into Connecticut.

~~~~~

The Stewart Baker/Billy Burns connection to the murder resurfaced as a topic of discussion late in the year 1900, as a result of a tragic house fire. Early in the morning of Friday, November 30, a fire broke out in a cabin situated two miles outside of Rahway. Due to its remote location, the structure was completely destroyed before fire companies could even be alerted. When police and firefighters arrived, they sifted through the ashes and made a shocking discovery. Pinned under blackened ceiling beams, they found the charred remains of Billy Burns.

Burns was the helper at Baker's grocery store who was arrested and questioned regarding the willow basket found at the murder site. Although no sufficient evidence was ever gathered to convict him, there were those who continued to believe Burns and Baker were somehow involved. Burns's horrific death renewed and added to their suspicions.

Stories intimated that Baker and Burns killed the woman and made a pact to keep the bloody deed a secret between them. It was further conjectured that for some reason after thirteen years of silence, Burns decided to come clean and expose his former employer. Baker, of course, couldn't let that happen so on a night when Burns was drunk he followed him home, waited until he was unconscious, and set the fire.

The official investigation came up with a different finding. A man by the name of Smith was also in the house that night and was able to escape the blaze and run for help. When questioned, he said he went to bed at eleven-thirty leaving Burns asleep at the kitchen table. He made a point to say there was a lighted lamp on the table. It was his guess the lamp was accidentally knocked over and Burns being in a deep sleep was helpless and perished in the flames. When asked if Burns had been drinking, Smith said he wasn't sure. Witnesses were later found who stated they had seen Burns walking away from Milton in a drunken condition.

The true origin of the fire was never found. The officials saw no reason to question Stewart Baker and concluded there was no foul play in the death of Billy Burns.

~~~~~

In the annals of murder investigations, no name is more infamous than "Jack the Ripper." Between the years 1888 and 1891, the ruthless killer (or killers) went on a murder spree killing at least eleven women in London's East End. The murders were so savage, the name "Jack the Ripper" became known throughout most of the world. Yet, as notorious as he was, it has never been established who the assassin was or if more than one person was responsible for the killings.

Over the years, crime experts have concluded that "the Ripper" is possibly one of four suspects. Of the four, one was an American "quack doctor" by the name of Francis J. Tumblety, who in 1887 was practicing in New York City. As the name "Jack the Ripper" made its way to America, there were whispers in Rahway that the unknown woman might have been one more victim to add to his list.

The facts are remote, but possible. Tumblety grew up in Rochester, New York, a poor, uncared for, uneducated boy. In his teens, he worked in a drugstore with a druggist whose reputation was less than respectable. The entire scope of the young teen's medical knowledge came while working in the disreputable establishment.

Around 1850, he moved to Detroit and actually began his own medical practice. His name soon became associated with several dubious medical prescriptions and procedures, and he eventually had to run off to Canada to avoid being arrested for an attempted abortion on a prostitute.

His history in Canada was no better. In 1860, after a patient of his died from a prescription he had written, he again went on the lam and sailed for London. In the years that followed, he traveled back and forth across the Atlantic, usually leaving each time because of brushes with the law. The authorities in both countries became familiar with his background and often had him under surveillance, learning a number of things about the doctor as they shadowed him. In speaking with acquaintances, they found he fit many of the traits of a serial killer, including a deep hatred toward women, especially prostitutes.

In 1887, Dr. Tumblety was living in New York City, just twenty miles from the Rahway murder site. It would have been easy for the doctor to gain the confidence of a newly arrived immigrant, take her to Jersey, and commit his foul deed. One of the early theories concerning the motive for the Rahway crime suggested it was committed by a human monster.

In the fall of 1887, Tumblety escaped from New York and went back to London just ahead of the police who were about to arrest him on a malpractice charge. The "Jack the Ripper" murders began on April 3, 1888. Like Rahway's murdered woman, seven of the eleven women had their throats cut from ear to ear.

~~~~~

The murdered woman was laid to rest on May 3, 1887, and because her name was unknown, no headstone was placed on her plot to mark her final resting place. A number of citizens were troubled by this and started a campaign to solicit money for the purpose of erecting a suitable memorial. Unfortunately, as interest in the story dropped, so did the number and amount of contributions and before long the idea for a monument died out.

It was not until more than three years later, that a stone was placed on the woman's grave. In late December 1890, Mayor Daly received a letter from Mrs. Space concerning the headstone for the woman who she still maintained was her sister. Her letter read as follows:

Dear Sir:

Will you give me a permit to erect a small tombstone at the head of the grave of the girl who was murdered at Rahway on the 25th of March 1887, who I still believe to be my sister, Mary Dorman? An early reply will oblige.

Very respectfully,
Agnes Space

Daly had no personal objections to her request and communicated her wishes to the cemetery officials for their sanction. Once he was given their approval, the mayor sent an affirmative reply to Mrs. Space. There was one condition, however. Because a number of officials were concerned with the wording Mrs. Space might elect to use, the approval was granted with the understanding that no name could be inscribed on the stone.

Within a week, Mayor Daly received the following note:

Dear Sir:

I return many thanks to you for your kind letter and also thank you for granting my request about the tombstone; and I assure you I will not do anything but what the people of Rahway will be pleased with and also the cemetery authorities—because the people of Rahway were exceedingly kind to the body of the murdered girl and I will never forget them—especially Mr. and Mrs. Ryno, Reverend Wm. Alfred Gay, and the little ones who gave the pillow of roses that was on the casket. May God grant that none of them will ever have to tread the thorny path that the poor dead girl had to tread. When I think about everything, I am very sad. Everything is just as fresh in my mind today as it was when I looked for the last time on that poor bruised face.

I will contact a stonecutter. It will take a little time before we can put the tombstone up.

Again respectfully,
Agnes Space

Whether it was Mrs. Space who finally placed the headstone or if it was someone else, it is uncertain. Devoid of any "soft" words or delicate designs, it might be argued the stone was quickly cut and put in place by local authorities who thought it prudent to order the wording themselves rather than allow Mrs. Space to write the epitaph. Mrs. Space was certainly an emotional woman and honestly believed the unnamed victim was her sister. It's hard to imagine she would write the cold, stark words that were chiseled on the inconspicuous, white, sandstone slab that was eventually placed over the grave.

An
Unknown Woman
Found Dead
March 25, 1887

~~~~~

On March 26, 1907, on the anniversary of the discovery of the woman's body, a woman dressed in black and whose face was covered with a veil was seen visiting the lonely grave. She stood in silence for many minutes, obviously deep in prayer. In her arms, she cradled a bouquet of flowers, which she placed at the base of the headstone. After she gently touched the marker, she turned, and left, never raising the veil and without speaking a word to anyone.

Over the years, flowers have been left at the gravesite by any number of sympathetic visitors, a practice that has continued to the present.

~~~~~

At 8:00 a.m. on Friday, December 29, 1887, a fire started in a faulty heater in the hose house of Protection Hose Company #3, a building that abutted the police station. By the time firefighters arrived, smoke and flames were pouring out of both buildings.

The fire was discovered by a neighbor who heard screams coming from inmates who were locked in a jail cell. Mr. John Roland, who was walking along Main Street, also heard the cries and using an ax, broke through a wall to free the men. When Roland found the five tramps who were occupying the cells, he said they were on their knees praying loudly, thinking they had seen their last.

Strong winds and the excessive cold made fighting the blaze difficult and dangerous. Water froze on ladders and windowsills, attributing to the injuries to four firemen. Under the harsh conditions, it took over an hour to get the fire under control. The loss was estimated at more than four thousand dollars, but because both buildings were brick, the damage by fire and water was mainly to the interiors.

Although the contents and furniture in the second floor police courtroom was generally destroyed, the clothing and effects of the murdered girl were somehow fortunately saved. In need of a place to store them, the articles were given to Chief Tooker who brought them to his home for safekeeping. For the next three decades, his wife would "air them out" once each year on the anniversary of the woman's death.

The clothes continued to embody a mysterious aura. The annual cleaning always brought crowds of curious citizens to her front porch, where the story would be rehashed for children and grandchildren. Every theatrical troupe that came through Rahway wanted to see them and occasionally a sum would be offered if by chance they might be for sale. A famous New York museum sent a representative to the city and offered one thousand dollars for their use in an exhibit they were considering that would depict the now famous murder.

The city never sold the items nor did they lend them out, and in 1920, placed them in a closet in the new police station. What became of them since is as mysterious as the crime itself. Over the years, each piece of clothing, every article found at the crime scene, and every photograph, has been lost, taken, or discarded.

~~~~~

Sergeant George Conger died on January 7, 1930, at the age of eighty-two. His thirty-five years of honorable service in the Rahway Police Department were marked with distinction and he earned a statewide reputation in the field of criminal detection. Stories of his prowess as a detective became legendary in the police force. As good as he was, however, there was one case he couldn't crack. A reference is made to the crime in his obituary and in an unusual way, he is given credit as being a better detective than his peers.

> Probably the only great crime that baffled the great policeman was that of the murdered girl in 1887, when the entire state puzzled over the strange circumstances of the girl found murdered along a road in the outskirts of the city. It is testimony to his ability that since he could not afford a solution, nobody else could either.

To give Conger further credit using the same rational, no one to this day has been able to solve the uncanny mystery of the unknown woman.